WESTMAR COLLEGE LIBRARY

W9-BYT-573

CHINESE THEATER

CHINESE THEATER
From Its Origins to the Present Day

Edited by
Colin Mackerras

University of Hawaii Press • Honolulu

PN
2871
.C534
1983

© 1983 University of Hawaii Press
All Rights Reserved
Manufactured in the United States of America

Library of Congress Cataloging in Publication Data
Main entry under title:

Chinese theater.

Includes bibliographies and index.
Contents: Early Chinese plays and theater /
William Dolby—Yuan drama / William Dolby—
Ming Dynasty drama / John Hu—[etc.]
    1. Theater—China. 2. Chinese drama—History
and criticism. I. Mackerras, Colin.
PN2871.C534   1983   792'.0951   83–6687
ISBN 0–8248–0813–4

102856

CONTENTS

Illustrations follow page 126

PREFACE

THIS BOOK OUTLINES the major aspects of Chinese theater from its beginnings to the present. Although it is in no way intended to be difficult and will most certainly have failed if its readers find it esoteric, it does assume some knowledge of China's history and civilization. The chapters provide a historical survey of theater in traditional China as well as a topical discussion of developments in the twentieth century. The range of coverage varies enormously, in that the first chapter scans thousands of years from the dawn of Chinese history down to the thirteenth century, while the seventh focuses on a mere thirty-three years from the establishment of the People's Republic to 1982. The periods considered are not necessarily a unity in theatrical terms. The Han and Song dynasties are both treated in the first chapter and yet are vastly different from one another in many respects. The chapters on the Yuan, Ming, and Qing dynasties specifically draw attention to differing schools or subperiods. Chapter VI, even more strikingly, charts a distinct movement, the Cultural Revolution, and the inevitable reaction to it.

Since theater is produced and maintained in popularity by the society it reflects, the chapters in this text try to identify both the artistic values intrinsic to a theatrical tradition and the social values or forces related to this tradition. Analysis of aesthetic qualities is thus usually combined with observation of social and political factors that have decisively influenced the development of Chinese theater. Chapter VI, for example, deals with the masses' relationship to the theater, linking the period of the Republic (1912–1949) and the war against Japan (1937–1945) with that of the People's Republic. Revolutionary theory on the arts, and revolutionary theater itself, were born in the Republican years. Marx's concept that the new society is produced in the womb of the old makes good sense in this case, especially since the great significance of amateur theater in post-1949 China is based upon the institutionalization of practices that proved extremely effective during the war against Japan and the later civil war.

Two other topical chapters describe the performance techniques and training methods of the Beijing opera (chap. V) and the aesthetic principles and values of traditional theater performance in contemporary China (chap. VII). The author of the former deals with the Beijing opera "as it was staged before 1949," yet most of what he says about performance and the categories and skills of actors would in fact also hold true for traditional operas of the postliberation period. The latter describes the characteristic aesthetic patterns of traditional theater forms and addresses the difficulties posed by these patterns as practitioners attempt to adapt traditional artistry to the requirements of contemporary politics and audience preferences.

Some technical matters require comment. The first is that this book uses the *pinyin* system of romanization consistently throughout. Since the Chinese themselves began using this system in their foreign-language publications at the beginning of 1979, most books and journals in the West have adopted it, and there seems no point in adhering any longer to the Wade-Giles system.

All drama titles are given in English translation, but the romanized Chinese title is included also, the first time each is mentioned. Chinese terms are normally rendered into English, but some of them are untranslatable. A term such as *zaju* means literally "mixed dramas," which gives little idea of the word's true meaning. Good sense suggested it be left in the original.

It is my pleasure to thank all who have helped prepare this book, especially my fellow contributors.

CHINESE THEATER

INTRODUCTION

Colin Mackerras
Elizabeth Wichmann

PERHAPS THE SINGLE MOST striking feature of the Chinese theatrical tradition is its variety. The many regional cultures within China, and each social class within those cultures, have for centuries nourished both regional and certain national forms, several hundred of which are still performed today. Theater may combine any of a variety of arts, including literature, music, acting, singing, costume and make-up, and dance or acrobatics. The varied forms of Chinese theater combine most if not always all of these elements; the Chinese theatrical tradition has excelled in each. Indeed, Chinese audiences do not think of these arts as separate elements. The skill of traditional theater practitioners is considered by the spectator to lie in their synthesis of the several arts. This emphasis upon synthesis is perhaps the most obvious distinguishing characteristic of Chinese stage aesthetics, as well as perhaps the one most puzzling or alien to the untutored Western spectator.

Until relatively recently, a Chinese audience would not have considered a piece to be theater without music or singing of some kind. In this sense, all traditional theater can be called "opera." The spoken drama *(huaju)* as a nonmusical genre is new to the twentieth century, when Western-educated or Western-oriented urban intellectuals of the Republican era imported European stage plays and staging practices to China. Music is not only the dominant feature of all traditional theater; it is the characteristic music of each regional form that most distinguishes it from others and provides most of the wide variation between the regional styles.

Two other important characteristics of the traditional stage are well known in the West; these are the intricate costumes and makeup and the elaborate acrobatic routines. From as early as the Yuan dynasty, the particular styles of costume and makeup were indicative of the nature of the character wearing them. At least in terms of refinement and elaboration, the Beijing opera *(jingju)* and other allied styles of Qing dynasty regional theater probably represent the high point of Chinese stage costume, and their styles of "painted face" makeup are more numerous and complex than the stage makeups of any other culture or period. Acrobatics were to be found on the Chinese stage as early as the Han dynasty, before the birth of Christ, and have retained their popularity all the way to the present. Even during the Cultural Revolution, when there was marked official hostility to many elements of traditional stage practice, acrobatics retained their usual place and were featured in the battle scenes of the "model" operas. Ancient heroes struggling with their enemies, rebels trying to overwhelm the forces of authority, or any violent struggle between good and evil are depicted through acrobatic feats, especially in those traditional plays called military.

The "military" versus "civil" dichotomy came to be applied to the dramatic repertoire after the Yuan dynasty, when reticence in the drama toward military affairs gave way to a fascination with such topics and their inherent theatricality. These two categories are by no means exclusive but are used to indicate whether a given play primarily features acrobatics and martial scenes or civilian affairs and singing. Civil plays often involve love stories, domestic intrigues, and judicial proceedings and may have their share of acrobatics as well, while a military play usually includes a fair amount of singing. During the Cultural Revolution, the model repertoire essentially eliminated this ancient dichotomy, as well as the time-honored theme of love so common in the traditional dramas. Retained, however, was another dominant element of Chinese theater—humor. The Chinese audience has little patience with unrelieved solemnity, and there is no genre of tragedy as in the West. The most serious plays contain some humor, as well as the inevitable happy ending demanded by the audience. Even if the Communist hero of a revolutionary model opera dies in the course of his struggles, the happy ending betokens the eventual success of the revolution.

The range of social classes portrayed on the Chinese stage is great and was often the object of imperial or governmental edict. Confucius approved of a major character being an ancient king, the founder of a dynasty. During the Ming period, rulers and members of their households were not to be given dramatic treatment. Throughout the

Cultural Revolution, plays portraying the former aristocracy were proscribed; Mao Zedong insisted that only the Chinese masses be heroically depicted on stage. Overall, however, characters in Chinese traditional theater tend to be of the upper strata of society, with the major exception of some clown figures.

Whence came the dramatists? This question is complicated by the fact that, especially in the numerous forms of regional theater, many plays have had no written script. Troupes would take a rough scenario and improvise the production so as to enhance opportunities for leading actors to demonstrate their skills in performance; the latter, along with their musical accompanists, would have to be considered the "authors." Others might then learn by rote, and pass on, the production as it was given on stage by the originator or inheritor of the piece. The dramas of the more elite forms did have authors in the conventional sense. The writing societies of the Yuan and Ming dynasties, and the literati of the Ming and Qing, were succeeded by progressive intellectuals of the Republican period who wrote most of the spoken dramas that achieved success in urban centers. While many of the dramas of the People's Republic are composed in advance of production, they are often the work of collective dramatists—scripts-by-committee—and have been repeatedly revised on the basis of production experiences and audience comments.

In China, as in most Asian cultures, there have always coexisted a popular theater and a theater for the elite. Prior to the People's Republic period, certain theater forms were patronized more by the wealthy, the court, or other privileged persons. The most famous drama patron in Chinese history was the Tang emperor Xuanzong (r. 712–756). But popular, often amateur theater thrived among the populace from earliest times and, especially from the Qing dynasty on, surpassed the elite theater in terms of vitality and even artistry.

As every region of a largely rural China has its favorite musical tunes and its distinctive vernacular, the omnipresence of theatrical activity gave rise to an astonishingly large number of viable, distinct regional forms. The number of forms reached its peak during the period of the Ming dynasty, while during the Qing period there appeared a number of especially successful forms compounded of influences from a number of regional genres—notably, Beijing opera. The manner and implications of the spread of various styles of drama from one region to another and the changes that occurred in the process are a particularly fascinating aspect of Chinese theater history. Indeed, as all traditional theater forms can be said to embody certain fundamental aesthetic patterns and values despite the many variations by region, the ubiquity of these patterns may have been due in part to the extraregional influence exerted by touring performers.

Prior to the modern era, the Chinese actor, whether rural amateur or urban professional, rarely enjoyed the respect that society pays him or her today. Until recently, in fact, a theater practitioner could hardly earn his living with one stationary troupe and often became an itinerant performer, travelling among small towns and rural villages to perform during festivals or to celebrate important occasions in the lives of the local gentry. Most individual actors were at least part-time itinerants, contributing to the image of the vagabond good-for-nothing that afflicted his profession for centuries. In the imperial period, entire urban troupes might tour the countryside at harvest, New Year, and other festival times. In the twentieth century, actors have gone in search of audiences, not simply as a means of ensuring an uncertain livelihood, but out of patriotism and social activism. Small troupes, often amateur, demonstrated the powerful impact of agitprop performance in mobilizing the masses to combat the Japanese and Guomindang during the 1930s and 1940s. After 1949, local-level amateur theater became an important part of each new political or economic campaign, and of the daily life of most communities. Government policy and ideology require theatrical troupes to deliberately make their art available to workers at their work places, as well as to suburban or rural audiences who have no opportunity to travel to the city theaters. The professional actor, however, enjoying a much higher status than was afforded the performer of earlier Chinese societies, has tended to resist these pressures to tour the countryside like his footloose predecessors. While some amateur troupes have drawn criticism in the press for touring so much as to neglect their own work, the professional performers have been accused of unwillingness to leave the comfortable work conditions and style of life afforded by their state-supported, permanent troupes.

While today's conscious attempts to use theater for socialist propaganda is astonishingly extensive and organized, the theater in China has always been the medium most suited to the creation and building up of ethical imagery in the popular mind. China has always had a largely rural and, until recently, illiterate population, and the theater, requiring no literacy of the spectator, has been universally popular among all social classes. Virtually anyone can become influenced by the value system of the characters on stage without realizing it. In earliest times, religious themes commonly found their way into the dramas, and not merely because religious festivals were occasions for performance in rural towns and villages. People enjoy the spectacle of good triumphing over evil, and the necessity of providing theatrical conflict inevitably made theater a powerful, if inadvertent, didactic medium. In the Yuan dynasty a disenfranchised elite, forbidden to publish except in the "vulgar" genre of dramatic poetry, began to explore how theater might be used to promote particular political views and social ideology. Some dramas were more focused on the conscious depiction of social problems and others expressed passive reflection upon society.

By the Ming dynasty, it was evident to government officials that the stage was an effective forum for airing political and moral issues, and steps were taken to make theater less a public forum than a channel for the propagation of conventional morality and official ideology. Certainly, drama in the Ming dynasty evinced opposition views far less frequently than in the Yuan. In the Qing, theater became noticeably more politicized, as both government and opponents of prevailing order made more intensive efforts to use the theater for their own ends. In the twentieth century, there has been an almost constant struggle between various groups or parties played out in the nation's theaters. The unabashedly partisan and moralistic spoken dramas of the Republic and the model operas of the Cultural Revolution are only extreme examples of a centuries-old battle to promote, oppose, or maintain systems of social values through theater.

All Chinese governments have exercised censorship and control over the theater. Form and extent have varied, but no regime has felt able to relax restraints altogether. Specific titles have been prohibited, and bans or punishments have been meted out to authors who overstepped a boundary and made themselves offensive to ever-sensitive officials. Today, government control and supervision over theater is not only a right but a duty, notwithstanding the periodic resurgence of the slogan "let a hundred flowers bloom."

In terms of effect produced on the people, negative censorship is much less important than positive. That is, a government, actors, rebel groups, or any commercial or other enterprise can achieve much more influence much more effectively by arranging for particular types of drama to be shown than by barring or preventing the performance of plays they consider harmful or immoral.

Ming and Qing governments sought to keep their Confucian value system strong by encouraging dramas enshrining the appropriate Confucian virtues and excoriating evil according to the same canon.

The Communists before liberation used theater as a medium to persuade the people to their social program by actively promoting performances which led the audiences to identify themselves with the Communist heroes or positive characters, and to reject as bad those among the Communists' opponents whom the drama was portraying as negative. All three authorities—Ming, Qing, and Communist—also practiced censorship, but that was secondary. Through dramatic performance all three tried to create ethical images for popular edification. Some authors no doubt intended to entertain or amuse rather than to instruct, but a theatrical work can be a political document without mentioning any actual political event. Indirect comment on the structures of a social system, and implicit support of certain values against others, can be readily communicated by an apparently apolitical stage attraction. Mao Zedong affirmed this potential for indirect or unconscious propaganda when he stated that a literary or artistic work could not be evaluated according to the author's intent, and that the work's effect upon audiences and society should be the primary criterion of judgment. During the Cultural Revolution, Mao's dictum achieved its most extreme application when the entire traditional repertoire was banned, and it was propounded that class struggle should form the core of all dramatic experience. If a drama did not explicitly teach socialist revolutionary virtues and remind the spectator of the unending battle against the forces of reaction, then it was a counterrevolutionary play and could not be shown. Policies furthering mass amateur theater and the touring of socialist plays to the rural masses, whose contact with political organizations was more attenuated, grew step by step with this radical program for dramatic content.

Although many of the cultural policies of the Cultural Revolution period have been considerably modified, the Chinese people remain today as much purveyors as consumers of theater, and thus of the value systems communicated through this medium. The challenge today seems to be not so much a question of how to make theater an effective political and social instrument, but how to keep it artistically and commercially viable so that it can continue to contribute dynamically to the development of China's ancient culture. Many traditional forms are in crisis, their audiences dwindling or their continued value to a modernizing society called into question. It remains unclear how best to preserve a unique and diverse cultural legacy while providing for the theater's joint purposes of education, entertainment, commercial viability, and aesthetic vitality.

CHAPTER I

EARLY CHINESE PLAYS
AND THEATER

William Dolby

THE EARLIEST full-fledged Chinese drama arose in the thirteenth century A.D. Like so many popular entertainments, its origins are sparsely chronicled, and discussion is bound to be fraught with doubts. Modern research is steadily filling out the picture, while archaeology has unearthed valuable clues and will no doubt bring yet more to light. On the other hand, many vital aspects may well remain hidden, perhaps never having been recorded in writing or depicted or reflected in enduring objects of art or craft. It is quite likely that the present common body of written materials may continue to be the major source of information.

A key point is whether the Chinese theater is considered to have one chronologically antecedent or structurally most important source; or whether, as seems more plausible, it was the synthesis of various elements that was crucial. Certainly some elements of Chinese drama were more basic to it than others, but no one element seems to claim absolute precedence. Acting, for instance, is a central aspect of drama, but it does not automatically evolve into drama. The existence in any society of a number of the component arts of and facilities for drama makes it more likely that drama will evolve, and certainly must ease the advent or introduction of drama.

This chapter will discuss the antecedents of Chinese drama in four chronological sections:

1. Shamanism and early dances
2. Jesters, acting, and horn butting
3. Tang dances, plays, and other contributions
4. Song *zaju* and Jin *yuanben*

SHAMANISM AND EARLY DANCES

In the dense mists of the earliest Chinese history is found evidence of
the combination of singing with dance, gesture, posture, and costume, in a way that gave considerable scope for mimetic art. This was
in performances associated with shamanism. As far back as can be
traced, shamans were important in Chinese religion and society. A
shaman may loosely be defined as a priest or intermediary recognized
as possessing special powers to invoke and communicate with spirits
and gods. The rituals performed by Chinese shamans often, possibly
generally, involved dancing and singing for the invocation of spirits.
This invocation was sometimes intended to please or entertain. A
modern authority on world shamanism points out the "dramatic
structure of shamanic seance":

> We refer not only to the sometimes highly elaborate "staging" that
> obviously exercises a beneficial influence on the patient. But every gen-
> uinely shamanic seance ends as a *spectacle* unequaled in the world of
> daily experience. The fire-tricks, the "miracles" of the rope-trick or
> mango-trick type, the exhibition of magical feats, reveal another world
> —the fabulous world of the gods and magicians, the world in which
> *everything seems possible,* where the dead return to life and the living
> die only to live again, where one can disappear and reappear instanta-
> neously, where the "laws of nature" are abolished, and a certain super-
> human "freedom" is exemplified and made dazzlingly *present.*[1]

Chinese shamans similarly impressed their audiences in a dramatic
manner.

According to the ancient *Book of Documents (Shujing),* said to
have been edited by Confucius, shamans were practicing in China as
early as the third millenium B.C. Although such early dating extends
into the realms of mythology, Chinese shamanism could easily date
back that far. Parts of the same work that deal with the Shang dynasty
(traditionally 1766–1122 B.C.) mention dancing and singing in connection with shamans. The Shang period was indeed marked by the
omnipresence of religion, much of it apparently shamanistic in tendency, and even the royal courts were deeply influenced. For the
Zhou dynasty (1027–256 B.C.) evidence is more extensive and explicit. The anthology of poetry known as *Elegies of Chu (Chuci)* shows
strong connections with shamanism, especially the part referred to as
"Nine Songs" ("Jiuge"). The anthology in its present form was ed-

ited by Wang Yi (d. A.D. 158) and said by him to have been compiled by Liu Xiang (77–6 B.C.); its earliest poems, probably including the "Nine Songs," date from about the period 329–265 B.C. They include incantations of male and female shamans or compositions deriving from or cast as such.

The shamans, purified, perfumed, and clad in gorgeous or elaborate costumes, sing their songs to draw the spirits down to them, using terms of wooing and courtship, almost as a sensual liturgy. Sometimes the songs distinctly mirror a performance and imply some form of acting, with gestures, musical accompaniment, and special costume. It is probable, however, that, while containing shamanistic elements, these songs derive from heterogeneous sources, not originally existing together as a cycle, and were later edited and adapted as material for a Chu court that enjoyed the performance of religious masques, much as European courts once took pleasure in religious music composed by talented laymen.

This theory reinforces the notion of dramatic tendencies in the songs and also provides a conceptual link to the court dances of the Zhou period, which likewise sometimes combined singing, dancing, and costume. From the *Zhou Rites (Zhouli)*, late Zhou or early Han periods, and elsewhere, we see these dances as far removed from mere ritual. Some were claimed to be of great antiquity, going back to the Shang and Xia periods or even earlier, and, at least early in the Zhou period, were apparently very unrestrained, even licentious. Poems in the classical *Book of Odes (Shijing)*, an anthology mainly of early and mid-Zhou songs, have been explained recently as the lyrics of the songs accompanying the dances, their wording frequently revealing a controlled progression of action akin to that of drama.

Some of the dances also may have had popular currency, in somewhat different form. The following is a description by Sima Qian (145–86 B.C.) of a version of the "Great Warrior Dance," which concerns King Mu's overthrow of the Shang dynasty to found the Zhou, and the establishment of good government by his ministers Duke Zhou and Duke Zhao;

> Bin Mougu was in attendance upon Confucius. . . . "Sit down," said the Master, "and I'll tell you. This musical entertainment is made up of symbolic movements. When they grasp their shields and stand stock-still, it concerns King Wu's enterprise [waiting for the other princes to help him overthrow Shang]. And when ranks break and intermingle and they all kneel down, that is the establishment by

Duke Zhou and Duke Zhao of order and good government. Now this is how the Great Warrior Dance goes: First of all King Wu comes forth from the north. In the second movement he destroys Shang. In the third movement he "faces south" as monarch. In the fourth movement he settles his frontiers with the southern countries. In the fifth movement he partitions Shan, with Duke Zhou on the left and Duke Zhao on the right. And in the sixth movement all the dancers rejoin their positions to venerate him as Son of Heaven. When they dance in two rows and lunge in all directions with their weapons, they are spreading the awe of his military might throughout the Central States. When they divide up and advance in twos, it indicates that the enterprise has now been successfully accomplished. When they stand for a long time in their dancing positions, they are waiting for the arrival of the rulers of the various states."[2]

The Great Warrior Dance shows chronological progression, depicts and symbolizes a fairly full story, and uses dancing, singing, gestures, actions, stage properties and, surely, costume. Recalling how Zeami (1363–1443), the "father" of Japanese *noh* drama, traced the origins of drama to dances associated with gods, and how often dance has been intimately connected with drama, it is easy to imagine how similar to plays these early Chinese dances often must have been.

JESTERS, ACTING, AND HORN BUTTING

As dances became more solemn and formal, professional court establishments were developed to provide for their performance. As central political power crumbled in the latter half of the Zhou period, the regional princes, striving in various ways to imitate the central court, may also have formed their own troupes of musicians and entertainers. Certainly they had officials with musical duties and court musicians. Music and entertainment were inextricably linked, and the term for music man, *yueren,* had very wide connotations, sometimes meaning court entertainer in general. Court entertainers were also called *you, chang,* and *pai,* or names combining or including these syllables. *Pai* and *you,* strictly speaking, may have meant those who entertained with witty language and satire—the jesters—while *chang* and *ling* referred to the musical entertainers. Their uses overlapped, however, and all seem to have served as generic terms for "entertainer," one who was master both of song and wit.

Remarkably similar to the court jesters of Europe, Africa, and elsewhere, the Chinese jesters had a dual function: to amuse by music, song, mime, and wit, and—by means of humor and subtlety, often by satire—to give advice, instruction, or warning. Generally they were either dwarfs or exceptionally tall, their physical apartness securing for them a measure of special tolerance from rulers who were otherwise sometimes arbitrary tyrants. Most famous of the Zhou jesters is Jester Meng, a *yueren* of Chu, and very tall. Among the tales told of him by Sima Qian is one in which he impersonates the prime minister Sun Shuao: "Then he dressed himself up in a hat and robes such as Sun Shuao had been wont to wear, and set about learning to imitate his gestures and speech."[3] His performance involved singing, gestures, actions, and dressing up, but nothing that could really be termed a play, let alone a drama. Yet the wit of his acting so attracted later ages that even in the twentieth century Chinese drama as a whole has been referred to as "the hat and robes of Jester Meng."

Theories concerning the origins of other kinds of drama in the world often trace evidence back to primitive imitations of animals and hunting episodes. Indeed, for hunters of animals such imitation has frequently been a necessary skill, but religion, entertainment, sport, and social cohesion also have been among its purposes. There is something seemingly eternal about these performances. A twentieth-century description of a show in Nagar in the Himalayas is a vivid reminder of the widespread appeal of animal portrayals:

> At Nagar . . . a polo match was arranged for our entertainment, and a tournament, and fireworks at night; also in the courtyard of the Prince's house, there was a kind of theatrical performance which was full of humour. The players disguised themselves as hunters, or as dogs with movable tails, or as eagles; or put on ibex skins with horns, or skins of markhors with flat horns growing backwards, or of orials with horns descending in spirals; and each one mimed the adventures of the most improbable hunting expeditions amidst shouts of laughter from everyone.[4]

The combats of horned beasts must always have excited human curiosity and imagination, and often people donned horns to simulate such combats, for sport, religion, or both, or for one evolving into the other.

In China in the Han dynasty (206 B.C.–A.D. 220), the "horn butting game" flourished. Originally a way of fighting, under Emperor Wudi (r. 140–87 B.C.) it became one of the "hundred games," which involved enacting simple combat plays on subjects such as the following:

> There was a certain man in the Eastern Lands named Mr. Huang, who when young practiced magic and was versed in the arts of taming snakes and tigers. He wore a red gold sword at his waist and tied a red silk turban round his hair. He was able in a trice to conjure up clouds and fogs and effortlessly to create mountains and rivers. But when he grew old, he used to drink far too much wine, with the result that he lost his magic powers. Towards the end of the Qin dynasty, a white tiger appeared in the Eastern Lands, and Mr. Huang sallied forth with red sword to deal with it. Since his magic had lost its potency, however, he was killed by the tiger. The ordinary people made a game round this theme, and the Han emperors also utilized it as one of the horn butting games.[5]

In performance this game was probably a comic sketch with some combat between magician and tiger. It easily could have grown into more elaborate plays or dramas. The widespread currency of such simple shows, circuslike spectacles, and acting in the broad sense suggests a fertile ground in which theater could sprout.

Archaeology has made an important contribution to knowledge of the performing arts of the Han period. A particularly interesting illustrative example is a tomb in Mixian, Henan province, dating probably from the second century A.D., which was excavated in 1960–1961. One picture in the central chamber shows a "horn butting game" (see plate 1). Two large men stand in wrestling pose and costume. Their hair is tied in a single braid that points upward.

Another wall in the central chamber depicts presumably the main occupant of the tomb as host at an aristocratic banquet (see plates 2–5). The guests sit on either side while a considerable variety of entertainment takes place in the center. Indeed, each group of guests seems to have its own show. This mural is not only extraordinarily large among those found in Han dynasty tombs, it is also unusual in the richness of the pictorial images it provides of the musical and dancing performances of the time. In addition, it is strong archaeological evidence that high-ranking families of the Han dynasty could provide such entertainment for guests at their banquets.

Through the Three Kingdoms (220–265) and Six Dynasties (222–589) periods there are hints of court acting establishments, and proof survives of the continued employment of court jesters. Puppets, originating from the Han dynasty, may have been used in comic shows in the sixth century or earlier. Considering the contacts with India through the importation of Buddhism, Sanskrit drama, mature in the first few centuries of the common era, must have been known of in China in the Tang dynasty (618–907) or earlier. There is no solid evidence, however, of any influence from it.

TANG DANCES AND PLAYS AND OTHER CONTRIBUTIONS

During the Tang period, thriving commerce and more settled times were perhaps conducive to the growth of theater, and we see the first indubitable signs of widespread playacting, some of which may have been a direct part-ancestor of the drama. Dance was in some cases intimately connected with Tang playacting. A number of dances in the nature of musical sketches, using flute, clappers, and drums for their musical instruments, flourished during the dynasty. One of them, *Mask (Daimian)*, concerning a prince of Lanling, may survive in part in extant traditions of Japanese court music ultimately derived from Tang China. Most interesting is one that developed into a play called *Stepping and Singing Woman (Tayao niang)*. One description, by Cui Lingqin (fl. c. 749), is as follows:

> *Stepping and Singing Woman.* In the Northern Qi there was a man surnamed Su who had a red swollen nose, and who, although actually holding no official post, dubbed himself "government secretary." He was overfond of boozing, and would become ill-tempered in his cups and was always getting drunk and beating his wife. His wife would lament and complain to the neighbors. People at that time made a play on this. A man would dress up as a woman, who would come on stage with slow steps, singing as she went. After every verse of her song, bystanders would respond by singing in unison, "Come join in the stepping and singing, come join the griefs of the stepping and singing woman!" It is because she sang as she stepped that it is called "stepping and singing," and because she voiced her grievances that it says "griefs." When her husband came on, they portrayed him beating and fighting with her, this being taken as the occasion for laughter and merriment.[6]

This typically slapstick show has similarities to the Tang "adjutant plays" *(canjun xi)*. These flourished from the eighth century or earlier and continued to be performed into the early part of the Song dynasty (960–1279) or later. From sparse and scattered references we know that both men and women performed in adjutant plays, actresses being, if anything, more usual. Women sometimes played a male part, and there were, sometimes, at least three roles. String and woodwind instruments and perhaps drums were used with the plays. Of their origin, Duan Anjie (fl. c. 894) says:

> During the Kaiyuan period [713–741] Huang Fanchuo and Zhang Yehu played the *Adjutant*. This originated with Shi Dan, magistrate of Guantao during the Later Han. Dan committed the crime of embezzlement, but Emperor Hedi [r. 85–105], cherishing his talents, excused him from formal punishment. But whenever there were feasts or parties, he had him put on a white linen smock and commanded the actors to make sport of and humiliate him; this went on for years before it was dropped.[7]

The adjutant plays constitute the first definite link between a play type and the drama. The link lay chiefly in the use of role categories, which became a salient characteristic of the drama. Two set role categories developed in these plays, the "adjutant" *(canjun)* and the "grey hawk" *(canggu)*. A much later commentary by Yu Shenxing (1545–1607) describes these roles:

> When jester-actors performed their jester-plays, it was with one man in an officer's cap and green robe, called "adjutant," and another wearing his hair loose and tufted with hemp-straw like women in mourning, and clad in worn-out clothes, in the appearance of a menial, he being called "grey hawk." It was so with the adjutant even in the Song, but we do not know the pattern of his performance.[8]

The adjutant plays were indeed closely associated with those of the jesters. Many full accounts survive of Tang plays of the court jester duo kind. If these seem nowadays far from theater, in the history of Chinese drama they were very close to it. A duo in which the comedian verbally lambastes or lords it over his stooge is perhaps not very different from an act in which he deals physical, although harmless, blows.

More than the obviously playlike shows, however, three things during the Tang period may have helped pave the way for drama:

1. the general flourishing of urban life and all manner of entertainment
2. the particular flourishing of the type of balladry known as *bianwen* ("texts of the unusual"?)

3. the vogue for writing the kind of short stories known as "marvel tales" *(chuanqi)*

The sheer volume of entertainment must have favored the development of new varieties of spectacle.

Entertainment skills seem especially to have been fostered under Emperor Xuanzong (also called Minghuang, r. 712–756). Although the theater's eventual deification of him as its patron god and the tradition that his Liyuan (Pear Orchard) conservatory was a drama academy are both due to misapprehensions, there is some justice in its acknowledging the part that his reign played in the history of entertainment and probably of theater. One of the standard histories of the Tang period says:

> Minghuang was both versed in music and passionately fond of dharma songs, . . . so he selected three hundred youngsters from his entertainers in close attendance and taught them in the Pear Orchard, . . . calling them "the emperor's Pear Orchard pupils," . . . and several hundred of his palace ladies also became "Pear Orchard pupils," dwelling in the Yichun court.[9]

The Yichun court was an establishment housing female entertainers. Other entertainers were organized under the Imperial Academy of Music (Jiaofang) into which the Pear Orchard pupils were eventually drawn. Dating from the period 618–626, the Imperial Academy was for centuries the main organ concerned with the cultivation, control, and supply of entertainers. In 714 Minghuang expanded its powers and organization, and thousands of performers were assigned to it. A very small proportion of these may have been actors. As the above quotation shows, the Pear Orchard was mainly concerned with dharma melodies, a kind of song of Buddhist origin accompanied by a wide range of instruments. These songs may well have had their own influence on the development of drama, and probably Buddhism even more so.

Bianwen

Buddhists conducted missionary work at a popular level more vigorously than did either Confucianists or Taoists. The techniques of proselytizing and doctrinal dissemination were to some extent imported from India and Central Asia, but were developed in China, partly in natural response to the need for conveying information in as lively and striking a manner as possible. A basic problem was how to present the often obscure scriptures to the ordinary, illiterate or partly literate public. Orally, this was done in various ways: by hymns, with music, by straightforward spoken exegeses, and by freer dramatized renderings known as popular expositions. The following passage concerns Wenshu, described by Duan Anjie as a "popular exposition bonze," and comes from Zhao Lin (fl. c. 855):

> There is a certain bonze Wenshu who publicly assembles crowds and discourses to them, falsely attributing his words to the sutras and abhidharmas, but speaking of nothing but lewd, filthy matters of vile smut. Criminal malcontents, transformed in appearance, wave fans and lean against trees; foolish fellows and wanton women delight in hearing his talk and listen filling, blocking the monastery buildings with their crowds, gazing up to him with veneration, worshipping him, adoring him, calling him "bonze imperial entertainer." They imitate his intonations, taking them for songs. These rustic masses are truly easy to seduce. Any Buddhists with even a rough knowledge of the true principles and even slightly versed in the meaning of the texts would laugh in scorn at him.[10]

This and other accounts of Wenshu indicate the importance of his activities. His sensuous and sonorous chanting of sutras, or his versions of them, was stirring crowds during the period 821–824. In July 826 Emperor Jingzong (r. 825–827) visited the Xingfu Monastery to "observe" his performance. Emperor Wenzong (r. 827–840) employed him in the palace. After he was deported for some offense, his disciples collected his instruments and writings from court and continued to perform in his style of musical exposition.

Some fifty works surviving from the Tang period and termed *bianwen* probably are representative of the kind of material and approach used by Wenshu and other preachers and storytellers of that time. A number have Buddhist themes, others secular. The *bianwen* were new in Chinese tradition in their manner of mixing speech and song, and their origins perhaps may be sought in India, where they were used very early. The verse parts generally use lines of seven syllables, but sometimes only three, or more rarely, five or six. The prose parts generally use rough and simple vernacular, but occasionally parallelistic prose of high refinement. The *bianwen* probably arose no earlier than the early eighth century A.D. The latest extant example is dated 921. Government attitudes may have been responsible partly or fully for the demise of the genre. Emperor Shizong (r. 954–959) of the later Zhou period destroyed thousands of monasteries, and Emperor Zhen-zong (r. 998–1022) of the Song was a fervent Taoist under whom Buddhism suffered. It is possible, though debated, that when the *bianwen* left the temples, and they had already done so to some extent during the Tang, the influence of monkish performers may have continued in the amusement parks, playhouses, and other secular milieus during the Song period.

The *bianwen* may have assisted the advent of drama in various ways. Some have argued that the narrative ballads and forms and habits of oral storytelling were derived from or partly fostered by them. Much of their structure and language resembles the drama, especially their alternation of prose and song, the use of broad colloquial, the direct speech and dialogues. Some *bianwen* themes were also famous as drama topics, such as how the saintly Mulian saved his mother from hell. A play about him may have been the first Chinese drama of great length, and is a key one in the history of popular Chinese drama. Several among the first Chinese dramas were also about Buddhistic conversions.

"Marvel Tale" Novellas

It is difficult to see how Chinese drama could have become anything like the powerful and varied genre it is without the wealth of lively, ready-made stories that awaited its advent. In several ways the most important single body of narratives used in early Chinese drama was the Tang marvel tales. In the early Tang period, or even somewhat before, there was a trend away from the stories called "records of weird things" generically typical of the Six Dynasties period. Increasingly people wrote lengthier, more complex, more tightly structured and fully plotted stories, using a lively and densely concise classical Chinese. These stories were known as marvel tales. The maturing of the genre came during the first half of the eighth century, possibly under the influence of the *bianwen,* or with some mutual influence between the two. Some of the stories, like many *bianwen,* have alternate passages of verse and prose. There was also some impact from the general Tang movement for the promotion of plain, unadorned classical Chinese that produced such masters of prose as Han Yu (768–824) and Liu Zongyuan (773–819).

The marvel tales have a wide range of subject matter, and many of them have been used as the basic material for other forms of literature and entertainment, including plays and dramas. *The Story of Little Oriole (Yingying zhuan)* by Yuan Zhen (779–831) was the ultimate source of the most famous of all Chinese dramas, *West Wing (Xixiang Ji)* by Wang Shifu (fl. late thirteenth century). *The Story of Eternal Bitter Regrets (Changhen zhuan)* by Chen Hong (fl. c. 813) and the earlier poem on the same topic by his friend Bai Juyi (772–846) were the prime inspirations of the famous drama *Rain on the Paulownia Tree (Wutong yu)* by Bai Pu (1226–post-1306) and of *The Palace of Eternal Youth (Changsheng dian)*, the celebrated play of the Qing dynasty by Hong Sheng (1645–1704), discussed in chapter IV. *The Story of Li Wa (Li Wa zhuan)* by Bai Xingjian (d. 826) was also an outstanding source of plays and of frequent dramatic allusion, and indeed a considerable proportion of the marvel tales of the Tang dynasty was directly or indirectly used by the drama.

Locales and Structures

Where were early entertainments performed? Generally, it seems they were performed everywhere and anywhere. In the palace, they might be held at the foot of steps at the lower end of the imperial or royal hall, at the upper end before the emperor, or within the space formed or contained by the bell and gong stands in the hall. They might be held at the foot of some building of more than one story or in an upper story, and wherever feasts, parties, and festivals were celebrated. Places of performance were sometimes referred to as "playing places" or as "singing places." People mounted stages to sing, and the following description, by Duan Anjie, seems to be of a stage used for a particular kind of palace musical concert that was termed "bear section":

> There are twelve stands, all ten or so feet high and made of carved wood, being shaped like benches, on top of which are placed four boards, with railings made at the sides. Access is by ascent in the middle. Emperor Wudi [r. 502–549] of the Liang was the first to establish the "twelve stands of drum and wind music."[11]

The awnings or mat-sheds so often used for Chinese theater, even in the twentieth century, were in fact used as early as 606—for a huge imperial reception—as the standard history of the Sui dynasty written early in the seventh century records:

> In the second year of the Daye reign period the Turkic Ran'gan [Khan] came to pay homage at court, and Emperor Yang, wanting to show off to him, sought common entertainers from all over China and assembled them in great numbers in the Eastern Capital. Thenceforth in the

first month every year, when representatives of other countries came to court, they were kept till the fifteenth day; playhouses were lined for eight *li* from beyond Upright Gate to inside State Establishing Gate, winding on nonstop. The mandarins and gentry all set up mat-shed stands on both sides of the road. From these they watched their fill without let from dust till dawn, ceasing only at the end of the month. The entertainers all wore splendid brocade and embroidered silks and colored satins, the singers and dancers among them mostly wearing women's dress, and there were probably 30,000 of them tinkling their jade girdle pendants and adorned to dazzle the eye.[12]

So often the records talk chiefly of the palace or of imperial sprees that included theatrical performances, but we know that places of entertainment were erected also by the commercial or ordinary populace of the Tang capital, Chang'an. During the period 785–805, a certain Kang Kunlun, from his name probably a non-Chinese southwesterner, who was a fine player of the Chinese lute *(pipa),* was engaged for a competition between the east and west quarters of Heavenly Gate Street. Representing the east, he was asked to mount a "multicolored tower" and play. Then the west constructed a similar tower onto which stepped a bonze disguised as a girl, whose playing so astonished Kunlun that he asked the bonze to become his teacher.[13] The "multicolored tower" was a high-standing raised temporary rostrum, estrade, or stage lashed together with poles and mats or cloths. It can be seen that the concept of a stage was familiar in Tang times.

SONG *ZAJU* AND JIN *YUANBEN*

From 960 to 1127 the Song dynasty ruled both north and south China, and from 1127 to 1279, the south only. In 1115 the Jin dynasty arose and ousted the Song from the north, but it was itself destroyed in 1234 by the Mongols. It is during the Song and Jin dynasties that we can be sure there was an abundance of varied plays, of the kinds known as Song *zaju* and Jin *yuanben.* It is then also that we first can be sure of the existence of a thriving, enduring theater as part of a booming entertainment world supported by urban commerce and affected by palace interest and institutions.

About 1235, an author with the pen name Naideweng wrote of the amusement parks in the Northern Song capital Bianliang (presently Kaifeng in Henan province), which were "places where gentry and commoners lived it up, and also the sites of young men's abandonment to debauchery and ruination." He lists thirteen categories of entertainment, each supervised by a "category chief" and officials. Those of the *zaju* section "wore 'jest turbans,' while the others merely had ordinary hats or officers' square headgear." Picking out the *zaju* for special attention, Naideweng continues:

> In *zaju* the actor-director *(moni)* is senior, and there are always four or five people to one performance, first performing a section of the usual, familiar things, called "charm section," then performing the "*zaju* proper," also known as "the two sections." The *moni* role directs the general settings, the playleader *(yinxi)* role gives the specific directions, the clown *(fujing)* role does the fooling, the jester *(fumo)* role the quipping, and sometimes another actor is added to play the "mandarin role." The one who plays the "melody break" and "send-off" with the flute is called *base*. In general their performances are nothing but farcical comedy about matters old and new, using such things as the creative basis for admonitory examples, and sometimes they cryptically convey corrective advice. . . .
>
> . . . When the court was in Bianliang, village people were largely strangers to the city, so these incident sketches were worked up, mostly involving dressing up as Shandong or Hebei villagers to provide mirth.[14]

Xia Tingzhi (c. 1300–post-1368), writing in 1335, more than a century after Naideweng, by which time both the Song and the Jin dynasties had succumbed to the Mongols and their Yuan dynasty, tells us:

> In the Tang period there were the marvel tales, which were all written by literary men, and which were like the "unofficial histories," merely providing amusement. In the play-text plays of the Song there were singing and recitation and jesting. In the Jin period *yuanben* and *zaju* were a unity, one and the same thing, but in our own dynasty [Yuan] they divided into two: *yuanben* and *zaju*. When *yuanben* were first created there were in all five performers in them: the clown *(fujing)*, anciently termed "adjutant"; the jester *(fumo)*, anciently termed "grey hawk" . . . ; the playleader *(yinxi)*; the actor-director *(moni)*; and the "mandarin role." They were also known as five-flower Cuan plays. It is said that in the Song dynasty Emperor Huizong (r. 1101–1126) received at court some people of the Cuan nation,[15] come to pay homage, and they wore ornaments [costume? wrappings?], leather sandals, and turbans, making up their faces with powder and black ink,

and such was their deportment that the actors were set to making plays in imitation of them, hence the name "Cuan plays." At the beginning of this dynasty there were the three Imperial Academy of Music category chiefs Wei, Wu, and Liu. Wei excelled in recitation, Wu in tumbling, and Liu in expressions and gestures, and their arts are still performed nowadays.[16]

Very similar remarks were made by Tao Zongyi in 1366, with the more explicit comment that Wei, Wu, and Liu had "made a radically new compilation and assembly" of *yuanben,* and they were acknowledged up to his day by entertainers as the source mentors of their arts.[17]

In the history of drama, obviously there was some inheritance from the adjutant plays, but also some new development under Cuan stimulus during the period 1101–1126. Whatever the Cuan plays were, they surely cannot have constituted the whole of the Song *zaju* and *yuanben.* They must have been one aspect of the genre, apparently one in which the costume and physical appearance of the characters were most marked. It may be possible to argue that the Cuan actually performed at the Tang court, the southwestern peoples being still celebrated for their dance plays, and that the Cuan plays were a particular kind of dance play stressing costume or tableaux.

In the two statements quoted above, Naideweng and Xia both point out the centrality of role categories. Throughout the centuries their use has been one of the main characteristics of Chinese drama. The system began with the slapstick pair "adjutant" and "grey hawk" as early as the Tang dynasty, but developed during the Song and Jin periods. Both Naideweng and Xia point out the primacy of farcical comedy in Song *zaju* and *yuanben,* and the *fujing* clown was in general the main role category in both. His partner in comedy, the *fumo* jester, quipped and buffeted him with a soft, leather-cushioned cudgel. The "mandarin role," the *moni* actor-director, and the *yinxi* playleader were also common in these plays or the bill within which the plays appeared, the latter two as stage functionaries. The *base* seems to have been a flute player with a key introductory and rounding-off musical functions.

Banquets and Multiple Bills

Song *zaju* and Jin *yuanben* may have been mostly too short to constitute an independent program of entertainment. This must have been so whether they were performed in the popular entertainment parks or in the palace. Usually, one imagines, they were a central part, but only a part, of a composite or multiple bill. Certainly, in the thirteenth century, *yuanben,* along with other shows, were performed as curtain raisers to dramas, and in the fourteenth century or earlier, as interludes within dramas. *Zaju* were also items in the programs of entertainment for imperial banquets and grand occasions from the early Song period onwards.

Zhou Mi (1232–1298), for instance, records a sequence of seventy-three or so items in a program for palace celebrations of the birthday of Emperor Lizong (r. 1225–1264).[18] These were mainly instrumental pieces—on the Kucha double-reeded wind shawm, drum, xylophone, flute, *pipa*—performed solo, in groups, and orchestrally, but also included were dancing, conjuring, singing, a song suite with dance and orchestras, three puppet shows, and four *zaju.*

Other records of imperial occasions in both Bianliang, capital of the Northern Song (960–1126), and Hangzhou, capital of the Southern Song (1127–1279), show the importance of the *zaju* in palace programs, and multiple bills were no doubt performed also in socially less exalted milieus.

There is a tendency to treat the terms *zaju* and *yuanben* as referring to the playlet or unified single sketch, but in the writings of Naideweng, Xia, and others the terms may sometimes have meant the whole complex of entertainments including such playlets or sketches as their center. A common formula for such a complex would seem to have been:

1. musical prelude and dancing
2. brief sketch, or some other brief item of acrobatics or dancing
3. core show: the *zaju* proper, a *yuanben,* or a *yuanben* plus the more dramalike *yuanyao* play
4. the afterpiece: comic patter, dancing, and so on
5. the musical round-off

This formula was not always used in full. In the palace programs, for instance, the accompanying items were allied rather to the general program.

Contents

What were the Song *zaju* and *yuanben* about? The general notion of the subject matter derives principally from two rather late lists of play titles: Zhou Mi's list around 1280 of 280 Song "official text miscellany plays," and a 1366 list by Tao Zongyi of 691 Jin and Yuan *yuanben*. [19] Both lists indicate several subtypes of plays. The range is very wide, including laudatory pieces, sketches based on dance, song, acrobatics, clever verse exchanges, nimble patter, wordplay, riddles, caricatures, comic duos, and so forth, all perhaps with very slight story content. What may have been the *zaju* and *yuanben* proper apparently had a wide range of themes: love affairs, ghosts, gods, demons, doctors, maidservants, and so on, being mainly slapstick playlets. A number of plays called *yuanyao* in Tao's list may have been more like drama, that is, a halfway stage between *yuanben* and drama; and a small number in Zhou's list may have been "southern plays" *(nanxi)*. The overall impression is that Zhou's list contains an earlier or more conservative body of diversions, giving greater weight to musical, dance, and structurally more limited, less playlike pieces.

No listing of play titles can indicate their contents and treatment. Accounts of some Song jester plays survive; they were sometimes performed in the palace by actors of the Imperial Academy of Music and sometimes termed *zaju*. Some involved a green-robed "adjutant." Hong Mai (1123–1202) describes a *zaju* performed around 1102 in which an "adjutant" played a prime minister, received in audience a bonze, a Taoist, and a scholar, and was in the end cudgelled about the shoulders by his private steward. [20] This was a satire, said to have made even the emperor smile, and perhaps represents some midway stage between adjutant plays and the Song *zaju*.

Some Song *zaju* and *yuanben* were assuredly more than such accounts suggest. A number survive in Yuan and Ming (1368–1644) dramas and a Ming novel. They are late and otherwise suspect as examples but support the likelihood that the Song and Jin had plays with more elaborate humor and slapstick, more intricate plot, and some with more song than any of the known jester plays.

Song Suites, Dances, and Ballads

The first full-fledged drama used as its structural frame four suites of the type of song known as *qu*. The four suites largely coincided with the unfolding of the plot and created four acts. We know that Song *zaju* and *yuanben* used individual tunes. We do not know to what extent they used suites of tunes in mode groupings like the drama, or in other groupings. Some clearly did use such suites of tunes because of influence from what are now termed "the song-and-dance play songs" and the ballads of the Song and Jin, including the *daqu*, the "drum lyrics" *(guzi ci),* and the "various modes" *(zhugong diao),* some of which derived from the Tang dynasty or earlier, some of which arose during the Song period. Many examples of these song forms tell or closely reflect an elaborate story, and all consisted of a number of songs or sometimes suites of songs in the same mode. The dance songs were in some cases dance plays with complex interplay or recitation, song, dancing, music, movement, and gestures, performed on mats and sometimes either using props or miming the use of them.

The *daqu* may have been the most vital single influence on the Song *zaju,* as the "various modes" may have been on the drama. The *daqu* could contain as many as twenty-four stanzas. It was much cultivated in the palace and Imperial Academy of Music, and no fewer than 103 of Zhou's list of 280 plays of the Song period seem to have used the *daqu* tunes as their main or prominent feature of performance.

The *daqu* changed much during the Song period, it seems, attaining its zenith of popularity during the Southern Song. The "various modes" form likewise reached its height under the Jin dynasty. It promoted the use of song suites, the telling of long, full tales in dramatic fashion, the alternation of prose and verse and speech and song, and the extensive use of direct speech. The most famous, the *West Wing zhugong diao* by Dong Jieyuan (fl. c. 1200), was the chief inspiration of the drama *West Wing.*

Milieus of Song and Jin Performance

Many entertainments flourished during the Song and Jin and many no doubt affected and were influenced by playacting. For instance, storytelling and puppetry were both highly developed. The very concentration of varied entertainments together must have encouraged innovation, and the milieus of performance were a powerful element in the growth of protodrama. Roughly speaking, there were three: the palace, the amusement parks, and any convenient busking spot. Zhou Nan (1159–1213) gives a vivid account of unregulated busking in Hangzhou's crowded places, although there is no reason to conclude that the level of the subject matter was in any way typical:

> South of the city there were three down-and-outs and their two female companions, of whom nobody could tell whether they were brothers and sisters or husbands and wives, and who cadged money by jesting. The townspeople referred to them as "those *zaju* players" and also termed them "of the actors' ilk." Whenever there was a hub of con-

course or a packed shopping area, beside government offices and courts, or in spots where religious processions took place, they drew out a performing area and provided bystanders with amusement. They would accept anything from a copper upwards, but you could not watch for nothing[?]. The subjects of their mimicries and mockery were people with speech oddities, people with bizarre hats, the legless and the lame; and everybody knew the places where they would be playing and found them diverting.[21]

More crucial or obviously important were the amusement parks. The taste of townsfolk and tradesmen is amply reflected in the themes of the various entertainments, and in the ways in which they grew. The amusement parks were major melting pots of the skills and fashions of performance. One twelfth-century author, Meng Yuanlao, writes of the size, form, and variety of entertainment available in three of the amusement parks in Bianliang. Together they contained some fifty stages or theaters. The largest held several thousand people and had been the venue of performances by truly great and famous actors. Other purveyors of amusement included "vendors of herbal medicines, fortunetellers, criers of old clothes, stalls displaying food and drink for sale, trimmers of papercuts." "If you spent the whole day there," Meng continues, "it would slip away before you even realized."[22] He also lists entertainments performed in the amusement parks. They involved *zaju,* "various modes," a kind of football, storytelling, shadow shows, performing insects, riddle-guessing duos, dancing, little boys' wrestling, sword juggling, sword fighting with wooden swords, joke telling, and many others; "be it windy or rainy, winter or summer, every day the stages entertain people thus."[23]

Palace entertainments were greatly influenced by those of the amusement parks and ordinary outside world, and in turn exercised their own influence over popular diversions. Zhao Sheng (fl. c. 1231) gives a broad view of the palace organization controlling and fostering entertainments:

Ever since the Han obtained the *pipa* lute and Kucha shawm, China has used western and eastern barbarian music mixed in with its own. In the Tang era, such kinds of music were all assigned to the charge of the Grand Constancy Office. Then Emperor Minghuang provided the Imperial Academy of Music as a separate establishment for them, female entertainers becoming pupils of the Pear Orchard. *The Record of the Imperial Music Academy (Jiaofang ji)* of course gives an account of that. In the present dynasty it was increased to two Academies, eastern and western. . . . But at the end of the Shaoxing period the censor

Wang Shipeng (1112–1171) memorialized the throne, and the court abolished them. Thereafter some famous actors and excellent entertainers were retained in the capacity of messengers of the Virtue Longevity Palace, and the rest mostly put under the Entertainers of the Front Palace of Lin'an Prefecture. Nowadays, . . . when such things as great feasts occur, the Entertainers of the Front Palace are always sent for temporarily to fulfill the requirements. If they prove insufficient, then townsfolk are employed as supernumeraries. In recent years the Entertainers of the Front Palace have ceased to exist and the former members of the Imperial Academy of Music have mostly become "bywaymen" [i.e., unregistered or itinerant entertainers] of the low town quarters, so I think there is little need to criticize these performers' musicology and grasp of the entertainment arts![24]

It may well be that the abolition of the Imperial Academy and other court establishments of entertainers in 1161 in some way reflects the excellence and prosperity of the external entertainment world which might have rendered them somewhat superfluous. The palace had extensive provisions for the performance of *zaju* and related skills. Similar ranges of entertainments were used at the Jin court, and we know that the Liao Court (947–1125) entertained ambassadors with plays. How far the amusement parks survived under Jin rule is not clear. The skills that they fostered continued to be in demand, and there is no obvious reason why the Jin rulers should have abolished them.

Evidently entertainments flourished at all levels of society. Extant records speak mainly of court and city with little mention of rural conditions. As far as *zaju* and *yuanben* are concerned, this bias may reflect reality. There may have been a significant difference between the Song and Jin periods: the *yuanben* may have advanced further in theatricality. One key to the difference between the Song dynasty on the one hand and the Jin and Yuan on the other, may have been a more open and unrestrained encouragement of acting on the part of the non-Chinese rulers. More important perhaps was the vigorous variety of different kinds of music flourishing in the north.

Costume, Makeup, and Masks During the Song and Jin

While usage was dependent on the level and type of performance, there is ample evidence for the use of costume, makeup, and masks during the Song and Jin periods. The dress of townspeople would seem to have been much more diverse, specific, and colorful than in later China, as Meng Yuanlao testifies:

The sellers of herbal medicines and vendors of divination lots are all equipped with hats and belts, and all people, even to the beggars, have their rules and regulations, society permitting no slightest slackness or neglect of them. Scholars, farmers, artisans, merchants, all the trades, and every type of profession, all have their own categories of costume which they dare not transgress. For instance, the packagers of perfumes in the scent shops are hatted and cloaked, and the managers of pawn-shops wear black smocks and horn belts but no hats. Thus people passing through the markets and shopping areas can at once recognize what social category they belong to. [25]

Palace costumes were likewise very varied. Given such a variety, one would expect it to be echoed in the entertainments (see examples in plate 7). Puppeteers often used rich costume, and written stories and other writings make elaborate mention of attire. From puppets, writings, oral storytellers, plays, and other shows the populace developed conventional pictures of famous historical characters and types. Hong Mai records: "I once entered the theater to watch the actors, and as I was going home saw a craftsman making buckets, who took one and put it on his head, saying: 'Do I look like Liu Bei?' "[26]

Clearly, Liu Bei (r. 221–223), the famous Emperor of Shu, was depicted in the theater as wearing a peculiar bucket-shaped hat. But it is also certain that costumes were often generalized, no doubt for reasons of economy or of ignorance, but also by choice. One kind of choice involved the conflict between the generalization desirable for the role categories and the specific character to be portrayed. Yue Ke (1173–1240) mentions a play in which "a green-robed adjutant announced himself as a court professor."[27] Did the traditional adjutant role category costume then prevail over the actual costume of a professor? Examples are numerous of the use of costume in Song plays, and also of props such as a chair, a flag, a fan, fresh water-chestnuts, a crane, a wine bottle, and a bowl of hot pig's trotters.

Meng Yuanlao affords a glimpse of the wealth of guise usable in shows in a description of items on a lengthy bill:

Some mounted the stage with masks and wild flowing hair, their mouths spurting wolf's teeth [arrows?] and fireworks, looking like demons and spirits. They wore blue, short-backed robes plastered with golden patterns, and black pants with gold stuck over them, were bare-foot and carried big brass gongs. . . . There were some with their faces daubed blue and green and wearing masks, with golden eyes, adorned with such things as leopard skins and brocade and embroidered belts, being called hard ghosts. . . . There was one wearing a mask, long whiskers, a loose cloth hat, green robe and boots, and carrying a mandarin's writing tablet, like Zhong Kui the demon-catcher. . . . There were a hundred or so gaily costumed men all with flowery, patterned square cloth hats with the horns curling backwards, half of them clad in brocade padded coats of red, and half of blue, and wearing "honor aprons," belts, and silk shoes.[28]

Meng tells of many other costumes and props, some with "gorgeous colors flashing in the sunlight." From his and other Song descriptions we see that demon and spirit guises were highly developed and very specialized, no doubt in intimate connection with aspects of age-old religion, such as exorcism. Meng Jingchu once donned a whole suit of gold-plated bronze armor to play a general. He was a *zaju* actor, and the likelihood is that *zaju* and *yuanben* often did use specific costumes. Pictoral evidence supports this supposition. But in the usual, slapstick plays, the role categories may well have prevailed and costume been generalized. There is much detailed information about the costuming of palace dance troupes during the Song dynasty, and no doubt some of the plays were influenced by dance in this as more certainly in other things.

Masks and makeup were both common in the Song period, but it was makeup that largely prevailed in later Chinese theater. The use of both seems to be very ancient. Masks are most solidly connected with exorcism, possibly as early as the Zhou period, but very early also with merrymaking diversions. In the Han period and before, they seem chiefly to have been of spirits and animals, fish, lions, bears, leopards, or tigers.

During the Song dynasty the southwestern region of Guilin, in Guangxi, seems to have been a vital center of mask production. Lu You (1125–1210) records that during the Zhenghe period (1111–1118) Guilin sent masks to the Song capital for the Grand Exorcism; on arrival they were termed "one set," which people felt to be remarkably small a quantity for so big an occasion. It turned out, however, that one set meant eight hundred masks—of young, old, pretty, and ugly faces, not one, to everyone's astonishment, similar to another.[29] Zhou Chufei (fl. c. 1163–1180) confirms the importance of Guilin mask making:

The exorcism troupes of Guilin are famous in the capital . . . but in the town wards, alley quarters, villages, and hamlets there are also popular exorcisms besides. Their objects of attire for making themselves look fiercer are much ornamented, and as they advance and withdraw uttering their words, they looked admirable indeed, and their ceremonial implements seem superior to those of the Central Region costumed troupes. One deduces that this is so because the people of Guilin excel in the manufacture of play masks, the finest of them being worth as much as ten thousand copper coins, which are highly prized in other regions. This being so, their fame is only right![30]

Yet even in the Song and Jin periods it is likely that the *zaju* and *yuanben* generally preferred makeup to masks, which may have been restricted more or less to supernatural roles. Even in the early Tang dynasty the players of Su, the husband of the "stepping and singing woman," had reddened noses or wore crimson garb, with hat, and had bright faces to depict his drunkenness. A Tang adjutant in an adjutant play remarked: "I can, before the governor's court, daub my face with ink and don jade green smock to act the god."[31] Emperor Zhuangzong (r. 923–926) put on the comic actor's powder and black ink when he acted. And Wang Fu (d. 1126) and Cai You (d. 1126), powerful ministers of Emperor Huizong, would perform slapstick comedies with him in the palace, making themselves up with powder and ink as clowns. Cai You also made himself up with blue and red. Meng Yuanlao, as quoted above, shows the variety of makeup known to entertainers. And there is no reason to doubt that experiments were made with all kinds of colors.

A small amount of evidence confirms that makeup was used in Song *zaju* and *yuanben*. For instance, Xu Mengxin (1126–1207) mentions soldiers "rubbing ink beneath their eyes, like the players in the actors' *zaju*."[32] Xia Tingzhi, in his comments on Cuan plays, mentions the use of colored makeup by the Cuan, and the actors' imitating them. This seems to suggest that the use of makeup was widely imitated in plays. In general, two prime uses of makeup may be discerned: to render the player more comic or to render him more awe-inspiring. In demon roles, the masks may have taken much of the latter duty, and, it can be surmised from knowledge of Yuan and later period makeup that it was chiefly clown roles which used makeup in Song *zaju* and *yuanben*.

By the early and mid-thirteenth century, there is a wide range of scattered information available about dramas, acting, and other antecedents of the drama. Yet full, direct descriptions of performances and contents of dramas are lacking, so that any general conclusions must inevitably be very tentative. If we could be certain why there is such a lack, then much more could be assumed, but the possible answers are many—prejudice, over-familiarity, literary habits, and lost writings among them. Indeed, similar neglect continues in the records of later centuries, after the advent of the drama. The result is that, to a large extent, we are restricted to the sifting of terms and technicalities in the quest to achieve a fuller picture by attaining clearer definition of the minutiae. Nonetheless, already by the late Song dynasty, we can confidently perceive a situation that seemingly called for the advent of the drama.

NOTES

1. M. Eliade, *Shamanism* (Routledge and Kegan Paul, London, 1970), p. 511.

2. *Shiji* (Zhongua shuju, Beijing, 1959), vol. 4, pp. 1226–1229.

3. Ibid., vol. 10, p. 3201.

4. E. K. Maillart, *Forbidden Journey* (William Heinemann, London, 1949), pp. 292–293.

5. Ge Hong, *Xijing zaji,* in *Biji xiaoshuo daguan xubian* (Xinxing shuju, Taibei, 1966), p. 5.

6. *Jiaofang ji,* in *Zhongguo gudian xiqu lunzhu jicheng* (Zhongguo xiju chubanshe, Beijing, 1959), vol. 1, p. 18.

7. *Yuefu zalu,* in *Zhongguo gudian xiqu lunzhu jicheng,* vol. 1, p. 49.

8. *Gucheng shanfang bichen,* quoted in Jiao Xun, *Jushuo,* in *Zhongguo gudian xiqu linzhu jicheng* (Zhongguo xiju chubanshe, Beijing, 1960), vol. 8, p. 84.

9. *Xin Tangshu* (Zhonghua shuju, Beijing, 1975), vol. 4, p. 476.

10. *Yinhua lu,* in *Congshu jicheng jianbian* (Commercial Press, Taibei, 1966), vol. 134, chap. 4, p. 25.

11. *Yuefu zalu,* p. 44.

12. *Suishu* (Zhonghua shuju, Beijing, 1973), p. 380.

13. *Yuefu zalu,* pp. 50–51.

14. *Ducheng jisheng,* in *Dongjing menghua lu: wai sizhong* (Gudian wenxue chubanshe, Shanghai, 1957), pp. 95–96.

15. The Cuan were a non-Chinese people of Yunnan, identical with the White Lolos and Black Lolos, two prominent branches of the Lolo people. The Lolos are nowadays scattered through Yunnan, Guizhou, Sichuan, and northern Vietnam.

16. *Qinglou ji,* in *Zhongguo gudian xiqu lunzhu jicheng* (Zhongguo xiju chubanshe, Beijing, 1959), vol. 2, pp. 7–8.

17. *Chuogeng lu,* in *Congshu jicheng jianbian,* vol. 13, chap. 25, pp. 366–367.

18. *Wulin jiushi,* in *Dongjing menghua lu: wai sizhong,* pp. 348–354.

19. *Chuogeng lu,* pp. 367–385.

20. *Yijian zhi,* quoted in Wang Guowei, *Wang Guowei xiqu lunwen ji* (Zhongguo xiju chanbanshe, Beijing, 1957), pp. 256–257.

21. *Shanfang ji,* quoted in Hu Ji, *Song Jin zaju kao* (Gudian wenxue chubanshe, Shanghai, 1957), pp. 46–47.

22. *Dongjing menghua lu* (Hong Kong, 1961) pp. 67–68.

23. Ibid., p. 138.

24. *Chaoye leiyao,* quoted in Hu Ji, p. 57.

25. *Dongjing menghua lu,* p. 136.

26. *Rongzhi sanbi,* quoted in Hu Ji, p. 280.

27. *Tingshi,* in *Biji xiaoshuo daguan xubian,* p. 2162.

28. *Dongjing menghua lu,* pp. 202–204.

29. *Laoxue an biji,* quoted in Wang Guowei, p. 244.

30. *Lingwai daida,* quoted in Hu Ji, p. 284.

31. Wen Tingyun (fl. c. 859), *Gan sunzi,* quoted in Wang Guowei, p. 244.

32. See Hu Ji, pp. 285–286.

SELECTED READINGS

Crump, J. I. "Yüan-pen, Yüan Drama's Rowdy Ancestor." *Literature East and West* (Texas) vol. 14, no. 4 (1970):473–490. A bold, lively exposition of the *yuanben.*

Dolby, W. *A History of Chinese Drama.* Paul Elek, London, 1976.

Hu Ji. *Song Jin zaju kao* [Examination of the *zaju* of the Song and Jin]. Gudian wenxue chubanshe, Shanghai, 1957. The major modern study of Song and Jin plays, sifting the material with painstaking minuteness. Many secondary aspects that have already been treated extensively in other modern monographs are taken for granted, which poses some problems of reference, but most of the central, theatrical matters are fully presented.

Wang Guowei. *Wang Guowei xiqu lunwen ji* [A collection of theatrical theses by Wang Guowei]. Zhongguo xiju chubanshe, Beijing, 1957. A collection of studies by the modern pioneer of thoroughgoing research on ancient Chinese drama. A number of these studies are classics in this field, and much of the later Chinese investigation has built upon rather than radically restructured them. In many ways they have yet to be superseded.

West, S. H. *Vaudeville and Narrative: Aspects of Chin Theater.* Franz Steiner Verlag GMBH, Wiesbaden, 1977. Three studies, on plays, on the origin and structure of the *zhugong diao,* and on its thematic sources and formal devices. A wide-ranging and searching appraisal, rightly stressing the importance of the *zhugong diao* for theater.

Zhou Yibai. *Zhongguo xiju shi jiangzuo* [Lectures on the history of Chinese theater]. Zhongguo xiju chubanshe, Beijing, 1958. Zhou Yibai was the author of the most ample twentieth-century history of Chinese theater, and this book represents his more condensed, but still abundant, observations of decades later. He deals with the whole range, into the twentieth century, with lengthy chapters on the earliest periods.

CHAPTER II

YUAN DRAMA

William Dolby

IT WAS DURING the Yuan dynasty that the various theatrical elements developed in the preceding centuries definitely joined to create the first full-fledged Chinese dramas. While the available evidence is by no means as comprehensive as that for later periods of theatrical history, it is possible to deal with certain aspects of the Yuan theatrical tradition in some detail. This chapter begins with a brief treatment of the southern drama of the Yuan dynasty, and then, in keeping with the greater proportion of information available, it concentrates on the development of Yuan *zaju*.

SOUTHERN PLAYS

Because of the bulk of material that has survived about Yuan *zaju*, which arose in and around Dadu, present-day Beijing, in the north, it is easy to think of it as the totality of Yuan drama and as the earliest Chinese drama. There was, however, another form of drama which apparently arose earlier than the Yuan *zaju* and was of southern origin. It was known as Wenzhou *zaju* or Yongjia *zaju* after its place of origin in southern Zhejiang. "Southern plays" *(nanxi)* is the term now usually used for this genre.

The classic work on southern plays was written by the playwright Xu Wei (1521–1593). He gives an expansive account:

> Southern plays began in the reign of Emperor Guangzong [r. 1190–
> 1194] of the Song, with the two plays *Zhao Chaste Maid* and *Wang*

Kui, composed by people from Yongjia, actually leading the way for it; this is why Liu Kezhuang [1187–1269] has the lines:

Who cares about moral appraisal after death?
All the village listens to Cai Zhonglang singing.

. . . As for its songs, they were the *ci* poetry of the Song people with the addition of common folk songs, and they were not harmonized into mode suites, this being the reason gentlemen literati have rarely paid any attention to it. At the beginning of the Yuan, the *zaju* drama of the north spread to the southern regions, and for a while everyone fell in with the fashion, the Song *ci* poetry ceased, and the southern plays declined as well. In the reign of Emperor Shundi [r. 1333–1368] the south suddenly became popular again, as the north became unpopular, playwrights shooting up everywhere like a hedgehog's bristles. Their language was mostly vulgar and inferior, not like that of the north which had celebrated poets composing for it. The documents official Gao Ming [c. 1301–1370] of Yongjia . . . regretted that Boxie [i.e., Cai Zhonglang] had been slandered, so he composed his *Lute (Pipa)* to wipe out the injustice, and, using refined and graceful lyrics, at one go swept aside the playwrights' uncouthness.[1]

From these and a few other early comments it appears likely that the southern plays had their birth in the late Northern Song but attained full popularity only with the advent of the Southern Song dynasty, with the transfer of the court to Hangzhou. There they entered a new phase of sophistication, initiated by the two innovative plays *Zhao Chaste Maid* and *Wang Kui.* The southern plays were distinguished by their extensive use of song and by their greater length or ability to treat full stories; they were nearly all love comedies. After the Mongol conquest of the Southern Song dynasty, completed in 1280, southern plays were still performed, but the northern Yuan *zaju* prevailed then even in the south. Because of shifts in fashion, and probably through competitive adjustment to Yuan *zaju,* the southern plays revived in the last decades of the Yuan period. Few of their playwrights are known, and only three plays survive that definitely belong to its earlier stages, one of them perhaps from the late Southern Song period. Part of the reason for the anonymity of the southern plays is that many of them were written by "writing societies" *(shuhui).* These societies existed also in the north during the Yuan period, but how early and whether under southern influence, is not known. Many songs from Song, Yuan, or early Ming southern plays survive.

THE ADVENT OF YUAN *ZAJU*

The Mongol conquest of the Jin in 1234 and the Song by 1280 was vital to the birth and early growth of Yuan *zaju*. Chinese scholars of the Ming and later periods often stressed the negative side of this influence, namely the Mongol suppression of scholars, said to have driven highly literate men into popular entertainment for careers or to vent their indignation in their writings. Yet many people of considerable literary ability seem to have been involved more or less closely in the entertainment of the Song and Jin periods. Indeed, the Mongols and their other non-Chinese allies in China appear to have looked favorably upon playacting for their amusement even before their conquest of China. The *History of the Yuan* of 1370 records that when the Jin regions surrendered to the Mongol general Muqali (d. 1223), he gave this order: "These are rebel brigands, and if we spare them we shall deprive ourselves of a warning example to others for the future; apart from the artisans and actors, butcher them all."[2] It seems apparent that dramas provided not only more palatable diversion for the lusty, rough conquerors than the traditional formal court entertainment, but also more immediate and enjoyable instruction in Chinese culture than did formal education or written materials.

The Mongol Yuan court patronized drama and the composition of *zaju* extensively. In 1406 Zhu Youdun, an imperial prince and himself a knowledgeable playwright, wrote a poem making this quite clear:

> *Warning Duke Ling by a Corpse* was acted as a play,
> And in one morn forthwith sped to the emperor's knowledge;
> His decree was delivered to the central secretariat,
> Causing its lyrics to be sung in all the provinces.

The playwright Zheng Guangzu (fl. c. 1300) was famed in the palace for his plays, as were earlier Yuan *zaju* authors who similarly wrote plays stressing loyalty to the throne. Early playwrights like Zhao Jingfu and Zhang Guobao were members of the Imperial Academy of Music, and a prohibition which the Academy received on October 8, 1281, forbidding the enacting of deities known as the Four Heavenly Kings, among other things, confirms that it had continued to concern itself with *zaju*.[3]

If a positive contribution by the Mongols and their allies be admitted, it should not, however, be exaggerated, nor would it by any means exclude their negative contribution and the consequent protests noted by later writers. Indeed, some of the plays of the Yuan reveal a rollicking irreverence towards pompous power, a wealth of skeptical sentiment, and fierce indignation at the injustices of the world. Very occasionally this is identifiable still as a protest against something specific and contemporary. It is also highly likely that many fine and noble minds among the playwrights suffered considerably from or bitterly loathed the massacres and destruction of the conquests. Surely any scholar-playwrights must have been at least somewhat dubious about the regime's attitudes to scholars. Their access to government posts of importance was severely curtailed, and the accepted route thither of the civil service examinations was not reestablished until 1314. It was said, though reportedly in jest, that the Yuan statutes classified society into ten grades in order of honor, with mandarins and others officers first and second, and artisans, singing-girls, scholars, and beggars seventh, eighth, ninth, and tenth, respectively.[4]

The structural and spiritual core of the Yuan *zaju* was its *qu* songs. As nondramatic poetry *qu* songs seem to have been widely adopted earlier than the flourishing of Yuan *zaju*. The *qu* genre arose under the Jin and was used in entertainment then. Poets of the *qu* genre include Yuan Haowen (1190–1257), Shang Dao (1185–1231), Du Renjie (c. 1190?–c. 1270), Shi Junbao (1192?–1276?), and Yang Guo (1197–1269). The early *zaju* dramatists seem to have been writing at a somewhat later date than the *qu* poets; for example, Liang Jinzhi, Guan Hanqing, and Bai Pu were all born around 1220. We might suppose, then, that the change into a form of drama began in the late Jin period, with possibly the *yuanyao* (see chap. I) as an intermediary stage, culminating in the first plays of Guan Hanqing (see plate 8), the supposed "father" of Yuan *zaju* drama. A high point in its development was probably reached with the reign of Khublai Khan (r. 1260–1294), who set himself up as a Chinese-style emperor with his capital at Dadu and provided the first extended period of peace for a century. *Zaju* drama then continued in Dadu for a while under his successors, perhaps tailing off about 1310 or 1320 as a shift to the south was consolidated. After the Mongol conquest of the Southern Song, completed in 1280, a number of northern playwrights and *qu* poets seem to have visited or stayed in the south, around Hangzhou, and the center of Yuan *zaju* production gradually shifted there. This latter impression may owe something of its strength to the bias of surviving records.

HOW THE PLAYS HAVE COME DOWN TO US

We must ask how the records have come down to the present and how "Yuan" is what has reached us.

There is a marked contrast between the sparse Yuan printed editions of the plays and the full Ming manuscripts and editions. Sixteen plays have both Yuan and Ming versions surviving, the latter much fuller, principally in the speech parts. Does the fullness come from later editing? Or are the surviving Yuan editions not representative of the written or printed versions originally produced in the Yuan period and preserved in the private and published Ming collections? No definite answer can yet be provided.

Perhaps the first scripts of Yuan *zaju* only gave the essentials for the main role, this being what was printed. Later in the Yuan, it may have become the custom to provide at least a modicum of the essential speech for all characters in the scripts. Or this may have been demanded then in the printed versions. Such may have been an influence from the south, where the speech of southern plays, being more heavily versified, was more likely to be included in toto in a script. Still later, the full plays more or less as performed, sometimes minus the *yuanben* or other interludes, may have been scripted and/ or printed. Probably more and more fairly full printed texts of southern dramas and Yuan *zaju* came into circulation from 1310 or 1320 onwards, with an accompanying, steady sophistication of the art of creating and writing speech dialogues.

A large proportion of the scripts and editions of Yuan plays existing in the Yuan period must have found their way into the various huge libraries of Yuan *zaju* known to have existed in the Ming. Li Kaixian (1501–1568), for instance, possibly had some 1,750, although the figure may well include other genres; and, according to Li, the imperial collection must have been as big or bigger. The imperial collection seems to have played a major part in the transmission of Yuan *zaju* to later ages, and many of the surviving collections derive from it.

The imperial collection served the repertoire of the entertainers of the Imperial Academy of Music. If late Yuan texts were fairly full, they would not have needed much to make them actable. But with the sparser texts produced in the early phase, additions to the speech, either orally in performance or through editing, would have been required. Wang Jide (d. 1623–1624) remarks:

The songs of the various Yuan dramas are all excellent, but the speech is lewd and vulgar, and unlike the tone of language of literary men. This is because in those times all the speech was first written as a framework by the entertainer-artisans of the Imperial Academy, and then the court dramatists and gentlemen song composers were commissioned to compose the songs, which was called "filling in the lyrics." The scholars would feel it degrading to adapt themselves to what the entertainer-artisans had written, and so there are often contradictions, and the expressions often do not fit together in sense. They did not all derive from one hand as in the composition of southern songs [i.e., plays] nowadays, and one should not fault the gentlemen for it.[5]

This is a simplistic and in some ways inaccurate view, but valuable for its impressions and attempt to rationalize some of the evident inconsistencies in surviving texts. More probably it was the other way round, that early Ming court entertainers filled in around early Yuan and mid-Yuan songs, some by scholars and some not. There was considerable cooperation, indeed, intimate relationships, between early Yuan playwrights and entertainers, so the inconsistencies probably did not arise then.

Perhaps it was the example of early Ming Imperial Academy editing that partly spurred mid and late Ming scholars to edit and reedit available Yuan *zaju*, many of which had by then come into private hands from the imperial collection or as copies from it. The most famous and influential collection of Yuan *zaju* published has always been the *Selection of Yuan Songs (Yuanqu xuan)* produced by Zang Maoxun in 1615 and 1616. His preface of March 31, 1615 says:

I have many rare editions of *zaju* in my private collection, and when recently I passed through Hangzhou, I borrowed two hundred from Liu Yanbo, who said they were copied from the Imperial Play Institute. They were different from the present bookmart editions. So I mixed and collated them, selected a number of the most excellent among them, and organized them into ten groups numbered in sequence.[6]

In a letter Zang amplifies some of these points, stating that most of the manuscripts were inferior to the printed editions available in the bookshops. Only about twenty were really good. He continues:

Recently, becoming daily idle and senile, I took out the *zaju* for amusement and expunged and erased the rambling and untidy parts of them, altering what was inconsistent with the genre as I myself thought fit. And I consider myself to have quite mastered the knacks and techniques of the Yuan men.[7]

Zang's preface elsewhere shows him at loggerheads with Wang Shizhen (1526–1590), and there seems to have been a lot of bickering between editors and experts in those times. Ye Tang of the early Qing was decidedly critical of Zang's work in the *Selection of Yuan Songs.* He describes Zang's deletions and alterations as "simply ham-fisted," and bemoans his ignorance of music and literature. "I wonder how many splendid songs by Yuan playwrights he consigned to oblivion," he asks.[8]

The modern expert on textual transmission, Sun Kaidi, believes that, apart from Zang's highly edited work, most of the versions of Yuan *zaju* are based very closely on the Ming palace editions.[9] With the zeal of the early imperial quest for Yuan *zaju,* it would not be surprising if most Yuan versions then surviving came at some time into imperial collections, where the sparse ones were filled out by palace entertainers and officials. The late Ming compilers of collections may thus have used versions already edited in the palace. To these they may have added their own alterations of varying degree. Zang seems to stand out for the extent or obviousness of his editing. Yet we do not need to be as harsh as some of his critics. He performed a major service in reviving interest in and recirculating the Yuan plays in readable and actable form. Moreover, given the complexity of the *qu* song prosody, it seems likely that his alterations of the core poetry of the plays cannot have been so extensive as to deny posterity a fairly accurate insight into original Yuan compositions, which in any case might not have survived but for him.

PLAYWRIGHTS

Most of what we know about the Yuan *zaju* playwrights comes from Zhong Sicheng's *Register Recording Ghosts (Lugui bu)*. It lists, sometimes with a brief biography, seventy-two *qu* poets, seventy-seven Yuan *zaju* playwrights, one author of *yuanben,* and two editors of *qu* anthologies. Many of the playwrights were also nondramatic *qu* poets. Zhong also gives the titles of the playwrights' plays. Basically Zhong's lists of authors divide into two broad periods: those of the early Yuan, about 1220–1300, and those of his own, mid-Yuan time, about 1260–1340.

Jia Zhongming wrote a *Sequel to the Register Recording Ghosts (Lugui bu xubian)* in 1422, our main source of information about late Yuan dramatists. This lists seventy-one people, twenty as playwrights, thirty as *qu* poets, thirteen for reasons unknown but probably because they were playwrights or *qu* poets, and the remainder for other connections with poetry or art. Most seem to have been born in the late Yuan, approximately from 1300 to 1350, and worked in the period from about 1300 to 1420 or so.

We thus have three overlapping phases: early Yuan, mid-Yuan, and late Yuan. A number of general features emerge. First, the *qu* poets overall held much higher posts than did the playwrights. The latter included minor clerks, recluses, Taoists, medical men, entertainers, fortune-tellers, traders, a gold panner, and so forth, lowly vocations in the main. Yet a few were wealthy, socially elevated persons though unemployed, including Shi Zhang, Yang Zi, and Chen Bojiang. Shi was an early playwright, and a hereditary commander of ten thousand households. Yang, a middle period playwright, was a general who led a key advance contingent of five hundred men in a campaign against Java in 1293. He was later a grand minister of splendid counsel and military governor of Hangzhou province, and was posthumously made a marquis. Chen Bojiang, one of the very highest ministers in late Yuan government, was appointed in 1351 to high military command, dying in battle "bewailed by his officers and men without exception." There is in fact some contrast in the middle phase, where the playwrights mentioned by Zhong—he does not include Yang Zi— are more uniformly of low calling or suffered career disappointments. This may reflect the fact that they were by and large from the range of Zhong's personal acquaintances, perhaps a much narrower selection of playwrights. The records for the early and late phases may give a wider compass, of more mixed walks of life.

Second, the geographical distribution is interesting. The first phase, with only one or two exceptions, includes nothing but northerners. Of the fifty-three playwrights with stated domiciles, eighteen come from Dadu, eleven from four nearby places, and all but five of the remainder from the administrative region centered on Dadu. A number visited the south. In the middle phase, some twenty-three can be associated with places. No fewer than nine were Hangzhou people. The others were three from Yangzhou in Jiangsu, one from Raozhou in Jiangxi, one from Qingyuan in Zhejiang, one from Jiande in Zhejiang, two from Taiyuan in Shanxi, one from Dadu, one from

Daxing in Hebei, one from Pingyang in Shanxi, one from Dongping in Shandong, one from Daming in Hebei, and one from Bianliang in Henan. Thus only eight or so could be termed northerners, even by their domicile of origin. In fact all the latter fourteen were born in the south, lived, worked, or died there, nine in Hangzhou and the rest fairly nearby. So, for the second phase Hangzhou seems to emerge, overwhelmingly, as the center of Yuan *zaju* creation, while the minority of northern domiciles seems to show a transition from north to south. Yet we must again beware of the possible bias of Zhong's personal acquaintanceships. The change in the records could mean simply that during this phase Hangzhou became yet another major center of Yuan *zaju* production, while Dadu, and possibly other places, still throve unrecorded.

The nineteen or so playwrights of the third phase include eleven southerners (Jiangsu, five; Zhejiang, four; Jiangsi, one; Fujian, one), five northerners (Hebei, two; Shandong, one; Shanxi, one; and one "northerner"), one Gansu man, one Mongol, and one Uygur. This and more detailed considerations suggest a fairly even balance between north and south, between the Dadu and Hangzhou areas, and the emergence of Jinling, present-day Nanjing in Jiangsu, as an important center of Yuan *zaju* drama. Maybe this third phase saw the increased merging of northern and southern dramas into a more unified theater during the last decades of the Yuan.

A salient feature of Zhong's, Jia's, and other information on *zaju* dramatists and *qu* poets is the significance of non-Chinese—Jurchens, Mongols, Uygurs, and Kharizmians. In the early phase the two most outstanding playwrights were Jin loyalists. One playwright, at least, was a Jurchen, a number of plays used Jurchen topics, and there are many other signs of non-Chinese influence. The music of the *qu* songs and the instruments included much of foreign origin. In the middle phase, again perhaps because of the narrowness of Zhong's sources, this aspect is not seen so clearly, but the continued influence of non-Chinese is proclaimed by mention of the celebrated *qu* poets Guan Yunshi, a Uygur, and Aluwei, a Mongol. Guan (1286–1324) was a grandson of Ali Haiya, an important minister of Khublai. He lived in Hangzhou. Aluwei also lived in the south, in Fujian during 1321–1323, and elsewhere. Guan and his friend Yang Zi had a great effect on the music of later Chinese drama. Jia Zhongming's list for the third phase mentions three Uygurs and a Mongol who was the second most prolific, known *zaju* dramatist of the late Yuan and early

Ming. Throughout the Yuan, many non-Chinese names may have been hidden from us by the adoption of a Chinese surname, and countless connections with non-Chinese persons and cultures were doubtless never recorded. This blending of Chinese and other cultures and peoples was undoubtedly facilitated by the Mongol invasion.

Another feature often highlighted by our records is the virtuosity of the playwrights and *qu* poets. Some were, in addition, painters, calligraphers, expert riddlers, performers of the style called "various modes" (see chap. I), accomplished musicologists, and so on. As an illustration of this point, and also of how various men of the middle phase were masters both of northern and southern song and drama, witness Zhong Sicheng's comments on the *zaju* dramatist Shen He (d. c. 1330):

> A Hangzhou man, a skilled writer and masterly talker and joker, he was by nature a sparkling gallant fellow, and was versed in musical theory into the bargain. The use of northern and southern tunes in one and the same sung composition began with him, for example his *qu* songs *Eight Scenes of Xiao and Xiang (Xiao Xiang bajing)* and *Delightful Bitterly Beloved (Huanxi yuanjia),* which are most ingenious. Later he dwelt in Jiangzhou, and lived until recent years. It is he whom in Jiangxi they dub "the southern Guan Hanqing."[10]

Some editions list his *Delightful Bitterly Beloved* as a play, but that is open to doubt. Of another Yuan *zaju* playwright, Xiao Dexiang (fl. c. 1345?), Zhong says: "A Hangzhou man, his vocation was medicine, and he bore the cognomen Fuzhai. He would bevel just any ancient text into southern songs, and they were very popular in the ordinary market quarters. He also has some southern song play texts [i.e., southern plays]."[11]

THE TOPICS, THEIR SOURCES AND TREATMENT

The subject matter of Yuan *zaju* in surviving editions can be interpreted with confidence. For much of the rest we can reasonably infer their content by considering their probable source material or later pieces of literature on the same or similar themes.

A large number were about love or romance, either as central theme, side issue, or atmosphere. Among those primarily about love, various divisions may be discerned. Some were prominently about courtesans, socially ordinary or flighty women, while others were about polite or "respectable" young ladies. The most famous case in point of the latter type is Wang Shifu's *West Wing*. A minor but important division of the former were those which concerned saucy or resourceful maidservants, or nuns. On the other hand, an important subdivision of the young lady plays were those about love at the royal or imperial level, involving emperors, princes, and so forth. A fair number of plays involved love, with a romantic or seamy background, but were centrally concerned with other matters, such as the wiles, admirable courage and resourceful wit of wives or courtesans. Women indeed were very often depicted as vigorous in positive action or stoic in passive valor or fiercely chaste. Love or marriage also came into some plays that were more in the nature of sketches on the topic of domestic morality, in which broadly Confucianist virtues were seen to prevail. Confucianism being often paternalistic in its political principles, these domestic dramas bore some similarity to the body of dramas on the theme of noble ministers or loyalty to the state or monarch.

Regarding more general social themes, some plays dwelt on sterling friendship between men, on the scholar-paragon, on the examinations, on other educational matters, on the drunkard. An outstanding social theme was that of the law court or criminal case. The law court, or a judge—wise, foolish, or rascally—was often an element of other plays, but some dramas were principally cases of detection, or concerned with the unravelling of some case or the legal removal of injustice. The mandarin, the prefect or governor, sometimes with supernatural help, usually found the solution. The most frequent wise judge was Bao Zheng (999–1062), in real life a most eminent, stern, and indeed harsh official, Prefect of Kaifeng. His smile was said to have been as rare as clear waters in the Yellow River, and Bianliang people referred to him as "Old Bao King of Hell." The dramas showed him more benevolent, and he was the hero of many later Chinese tales of detection, the archetype of a judicial Sherlock Holmes.

A number of the plays dealt with the enemies of orderly society: the oppressors within, such as the tyrant noble or bullying bureaucrat, and, on its outer fringes, the robbers and brigands. The latter were principally those from the *Water Margin (Shuihu)* cycle of brigand tales, such as the rampageous, bibulous Buddhist monk Lu Zhishen and the "black whirlwind," Li Kui. Some of these plays no doubt gave scope for stage acrobatics.

Characters of a different kind, also outside society, were the hermits and recluses who were so much a part of Yuan fact and fiction. With age-old scriptural and traditional sanction they would opt out of a government career and into more universal, more philosophical, and perhaps more honest ways of life. Whereas in some plays they stoutly maintained their detachment, in others their bystander's clarity of vision enabled them to come to the rescue of the political world. Sometimes again, by contrast, famous politicians or other celebrities found themselves forced to become recluses through exile, and the plays dealt with their trials and triumphs in banishment. Disillusionment with power mongering in the short-lived and often troubled Yuan is reflected in the "Taoist" slant of many of these plays, but there is also a delight in the merry or ingenious eccentric and a recognition of his value to society.

More specifically Taoist were a number of dramas about famous Taoists or on theses of Taoist philosophy. There were a number of similar ones on Buddhist topics. Some took the form of the conversion or reconversion of a person, sometimes a banished immortal, to a state of Buddhist or Taoist enlightenment or morality. Some clearly sought to propagate the philosophical or religious belief involved, but not to the exclusion of general dramatic worth.

Supernatural beings appeared in these and other plays, but in only relatively few were ghosts, spirits, demons, or magic central to the theme. This paucity may be explained by the Chinese custom of regarding supernatural worlds and beings as much nearer to the normal human world in nature.

A large proportion of the dramas concerned high politics or war, mostly of fairly distant history. A famous example is Ma Zhiyuan's *Autumn in Han Palace (Hangong qiu),* about the Princess Wang Zhaojun forced to marry a foreign ruler and her subsequent suicide. A number dealt with the warrior-heroes of the Three Kingdoms period, Guan Yu, Zhang Fei, and Liu Bei. In some the historical personalities predominated, in others the general historical situation. The material for Yuan *zaju* dramas may occasionally have come solely from the dramatists' imagination. In a number of cases contemporary affairs were used; witness Xia Tingzhi's comment:

Fan Shizhen was a celebrated singing-girl of the capital. The counsellor Zhou Zhonghong took her as his mistress. When Zhou was going home to Jiangnan, Fan drank a goodbye cup with him to see him off outside Qihua Gate. "Look after yourself when I'm gone," said Zhou, "and don't give others any grounds for ridicule." Fan poured her wine on the ground as a libation. "If ever I prove untrue to you, my lord," she vowed, "I shall make amends to you by gouging out one of my eyes."

Very shortly afterwards, a man of powerful position and influence came to her. Her mother was pressed by awkward circumstances and also profited financially from him, and although Fan at first resolutely resisted his advances, in the end she was unable to retain command of herself.

Later, when Zhou came to the capital, Fan spoke with him. "It wasn't that I didn't try to hold out after you left," she said, "but in the end I was forced to it by the pressure of power. Don't imagine, though, that the vow I once made was sworn for empty show!" Then she pulled out her gold comb and stabbed her left eye with it. The blood ran all over the ground. Zhou was greatly shaken by this, and so they remained lovers as before. An enterprising gentleman wrote it up into a *zaju* called *Fan Shizhen Stabs Her Eye with a Gold Comb (Fan Shizhen jinbi cimu),* which has had a currency among the general public.[12]

Real life tragedies were also possible themes for dramas. A legal work compiled in 1322 records a case from the sacred Mt. Tai in Shandong province that occurred in 1313, where "recently a certain Liu Xin, in fulfillment of vows, threw his two-year-old doltish son into a sacrificial paper money brazier."[13] A perverse, anonymous playwright seems to have tried to make this incident acceptable in his play *Burning a Son to Save a Mother (Fener jiumu),* in which a butcher sacrifices his son to the gods in order that they may be induced to save his ill and dying mother. Impressed, the gods restore his son to him alive, substituting the son of another, less "worthy" person, and his mother recovers.

Some Yuan *zaju* derived material from oral legend, and others without doubt from other oral entertainments and storytelling. There is clear inheritance of subject matter down to the Yuan from the Song *zaju* and *yuanben,* but we are largely in the dark about the Song origins, for we know little for certain about tales that were current orally, or how they were treated in other entertainments. More securely, we can state that a large proportion of the Yuan *zaju* obtained inspiration from earlier works of history and literature—outstandingly, Sima Qian's *Records of a Historian (Shiji)*—the various official histories, and the Tang and Song novellas, but including all manner of written sources. Here, too, our ignorance of oral legend and oral entertainments sometimes leaves doubt as to whether the written sources were used directly, or indirectly through other oral genres. It seems that dramatists often used their written sources with great freedom and fantasy.

Songs were the structural basis and spiritual core of Yuan *zaju,* but this did not dilute the strength of the plot and action. In fact the songs very closely followed, and sometimes even carried, the action. Usually they made no excursions into lengthy poetic elaborations at key points in the action except for good theatrical reasons, to intensify atmosphere or to heighten dramatic tension. The very manner in which they were arranged, musically and prosodically, tended to contribute to the tightness and movement of the plot. They were by and large the thoughts of the protagonist, his confiding in the audience or in other characters on stage, his provision of scenic, historic, or other background, or his moral or philosophical interpretation of the action. Generally they intensified the play's immediate sense. Their wording was fairly immediately comprehensible, and this directness of language was fortified by the vigorous, clear style of singing, contrasted to the sinuous, mellifluous southern fashion. Actions and gestures played a large part in reinforcing communication with the audience, as did statements of the story at various points of a play. An interesting device to vivify the drama, or to avoid stage depiction of violent death, was the use of whole acts or passages to report scenes by an eyewitness.

Although few if any Yuan *zaju* can be identified as tragedies in the classical Western sense, a fair number involved the lamentable death of leading characters. They were surely classifiable as tearjerkers, but usually such plays seem to have ended with some resounding vindication, or some prospect to mitigate the hopelessness of the irretrievable loss.

Much less can be said for certain about the southern plays, but the few surviving pieces, the many extant fragments, and a consideration of probable sources and literature on the same or similar themes do suggest a number of points. The great majority of them were about romance between a man and a woman. At a rough estimate, some eighty-five plays were principally concerned with romance, and a further thirty or so had it as an aspect of the plot. Of the former, some forty were about love between a scholar and a lady, in one case a princess. Sixteen were about love between a scholar and a courtesan, female entertainer, or lady turned harlot. Two concerned love between a monarch and a lady, and one or two love between a monarch and a courtesan. Three or four were about love between a man and an immortal. The men here included a scholar, a woodcutter, and perhaps a warrior. The women included a dragon princess, a spider fairy, another fairy, and a plum tree sprite. Other plays on love included one between two immortals; one about a dyer and a poor girl turned harlot; one about a triangle affair between scholar, maidservant, and young lady; another about a rice-shop keeper's son and a wealthy man's daughter; and another about a young gentleman trader and one or two young ladies. The scholar-lady romances greatly predominated, with the scholar-courtesan romance an important second category, perhaps half as common.

Closely related was a group of eight plays in which the prominent theme was that of a scholar's infidelity in love, in two cases with a courtesan. Some of the most famous southern plays were in this group, and their popularity mirrored the social problem that may often have been so crucially real when a scholar of lowly or poor background was suddenly shot to power and celebrity by imperial examinations or patronage. In one or two cases the plays showed the infidelity as forced upon the scholar. Often there was an astonishing "happy ending," with the scholar and wronged girl finally reunited.

Some twelve plays were mainly on a topic involving the supernatural, the range being quite broad, for example, the theft of a wife by a gibbon sprite, a birthday feast in heaven, Buddha's quelling of the Demon Mother, and Taoist conversions to immortality. Sixteen or so plays included a supernatural element as a secondary or minor feature: ghosts acting as matchmakers; a magical Malay slave; a punishment in hell; a girl's supernatural entry into her lover's tomb and their transformation into a pair of butterflies; the action of Buddhist *karma* and a god's intervention to restore the balance of fortune; and other kinds of magic and miracle. A further three plays had as a secondary but important theme, that of ghostly vengeance. Two others involved dreams, one principally so.

Some twenty-four plays were mainly on the theme of some person's virtue, and four others had it as a side issue. Of the former, eleven concerned women, who were picked out for the fidelity, sagacity, filial piety, chastity or self-sacrifice. The men included the loyal minister, the filial son, the selfless brother, the steadfast patriot, and the noble warrior. Another play depicted the comic debauchment of a prudish literatus. Some eight other plays were chiefly, and three others incidentally, in the nature of domestic dramas, often involving questions of virtue. These were on such topics as a Taoist's proof of his wife's infidelity; how a daughter-in-law is reconciled to her mother-in-law by her husband's device; how an old mandarin marries his young cousin; how an oppressive stepmother is thwarted; how a filial son repays his stepmother's ill with good; how a bonze abducts a wife.

Eight or so plays were primarily legal cases, four about murder, and three about murder and adultery. Two of these were solved by Bao Zheng and two with supernatural help. A further eight or nine plays seem to have been mainly about famous historical situations, including one about the assassination of Jia Sidao, the prime minister blamed for Song defeats at the hands of the Mongols, and another about a traitor's murder of a Song national hero, Yue Fei.

These groping statistics serve at least to indicate the rarity of vigorous and military plays, and the overwhelming dominance of plays suitable for *sheng* (male role) and *dan* (female role) paired as the characters. A large proportion no doubt were comedies or contained some comedy, and only one or two may have been tragedies—of love. In addition, however, a score or two plays have left us little or no hint as to their possible contents. The sources of the southern plays seem similar to those of the Yuan *zaju,* with more bias toward novellas and less toward histories. Many indeed were assuredly composed in imitation of popular Yuan *zaju.*

LANGUAGE AND MUSIC

The dramatic effect of Yuan *zaju* derives not only from the content but also from the types of sounds heard on the stage.

There were usually four acts in Yuan *zaju,* but any of them might be preceded by a "wedge," an introduction to the main action or a brief extension of it. The prose section could be one character's extended monologue, or dialogue; humor played a significant part, puns or vulgar language being common. On the other hand, the lyric sections were sung, not spoken, by one main character per act. It was indeed a special feature of the *zaju* that in each act only one character, whether male or female, should sing. Certainly this was not the case in the southern plays, in which the singing was not restricted to main roles, but was shared and often alternated.

Another difference was in the rhyming system. In the *zaju* only one rhyme was used throughout a complete act. There could be over a hundred words in the same act all rhyming with one another. The great majority fell at the end of the line, but internal rhymes also occurred.

At the same time, as this additional rigidity came into use in the rules of *qu* poetry, extra freedom was allowed in another area: that of rhyme tones. Whereas in earlier poetry the rules laid down most carefully which groupings of tones actually constituted rhymes, the system now changed so that there was greater flexibility within the same rhyme group as to which tones could be used.[14] As a result, any risk of monotony due to the single rhyme throughout the act would have been reduced.

A further device which fulfilled the function of promoting variety was that the meter of the lyrics looked comparatively free. It is true that there were prescribed syllables, but it was possible to add nonmetric words. Sometimes the nonmetric outnumbered the prescribed syllables. The addition of nonmetric words may not have affected the basic rhythm, but it did suspend it and made the poetic lines and songs much more fluid and brisk. One contemporary authority argues that "the irregularity of line length and rhythm effected through the use of non-metric words enhances the naturalness,"[15] which she sees as the hallmark of the *qu* as a poetic genre. Southern plays appear to have included some nonmetric words. However, according to Wang Jide, the differing musical instruments accompanying the southern plays and *zaju* made the former far less susceptible to nonmetric words. He states that because the dominant accompaniment in the northern *qu* was stringed, the nonmetric words were appropriate; but that in the southern it was percussion, so the beat was clear and definite, militating against the use of nonmetric words.[16]

The stringed instruments which were so fundamental to the *zaju* included the Chinese lute *(pipa)*. There were several varieties, some wih four strings, others with five. But common to all was that the strings were plucked, not bowed. Another stringed instrument was the zither *(qin)*, which was sometimes played as part of the plot.

A mural found in a temple in Shanxi province and dated 1324 has something to tell us about the musical instruments of the *zaju* (see plate 9). Curiously enough there are no stringed instruments there. But in the back row there is a player of the side-blown flute *(dizi)*, a person in female attire playing the clappers, and one in male garb near a drum of which he or the person peeping from behind the curtain is perhaps the player. It is thus clear that not only string and wind instruments, but also percussion, were used in the *zaju*. Wang Jide's statement that they dominated the southern plays is not to be interpreted as meaning that they were totally absent in the *zaju*.

There were nine main modes in Yuan *zaju* and a definite modal structure, about which not much is yet known. What is clear is that generally only one mode was used in any one act. In almost all extant plays it is the same one of the nine modes that occurs in the first act, and a high degree of consistency applies also for the fourth acts.

Music was thus important in Yuan *zaju* drama, but perhaps overall less so than in some more southern and esoteric later forms of Chinese drama where the sound of song had greater dominance over word meanings. In Yuan *zaju* it was almost certainly word sense that held sway, with music ideally as its willing vassal and helper. Music's chief dramatic contribution may have been to the structure of the plays, the organization of the songs into one mode suite per act no doubt conveying to the audience a sense of the divisions and progression of the story, while the sequence of songs within each mode may have done something similar. It was clearly subordinated to song and the human voice, there being no proof that purely instrumental passages of any length were a marked feature of the *zaju*. Probably the musical instruments accompanied, introduced, and rounded off, providing rhythmic backing and possibly bridge passages. Alternation of mode and tune surely also helped to alter and create atmosphere and to signify such generalities as tension or joy.

Vagueness about Yuan drama music is partly excusable by the absence of surviving musical scores. Learning from master to pupil, the theater musicians no doubt felt no need for the wobbly crutch of musical notation. A small amount of written music does survive from the thirteenth century—including the oldest example of tablature for a stringed instrument in any musical culture—for the zither and from a printing done in 1202. None of this music is for the theater. Xu Dachun (1693–1771) studies the matter freshly and openly and remarks:

Northern *qu* songs such as Dong's [Dong Jieyuan's] *West Wing* [*zhu-gong diao*] could only be put to strings, being unamenable to harmonizing with wind instruments. Their melodies excelled in their rise and fall and rhythm, the words coming quickly and the beat being compressed. It was not until Wang Shifu's *West Wing* and the Yuan *zaju* that they could be harmonized with wind instruments. . . . In mid-Ming, Kun music [i.e., *kunqu*]became popular, and this popularity is maintained unfailingly to this day. Its singing occasionally includes one or two tunes of northern *qu*, but these too have been changed to Kun music northern songs, and are not the northern *qu* of former times. This was a spontaneous change of fashions.[17]

Others, too, have alluded to the dying out of the traditions of Yuan *qu* music during the Ming. A number of Qing anthologies of musical scores give many pieces purporting to be of Yuan origin. Unreliable as these are, it may well be that future painstaking studies of them and other Ming and Yuan material will provide much more precise hints as to the nature of Yuan *zaju* music.

PERFORMANCE AND PERFORMERS

Just as our knowledge of *zaju* music is incomplete, so we have no thorough Yuan description of the physical theater and performance conditions. Information may be gleaned from a very few writings. Xia Tingzhi tells us in 1355:

> As for *zaju* they just have *dan* and *mo*. The *dan* was originally played by a woman, . . . the *mo* originally played by a man. . . . The other characters presented to the audience are all performed by secondary role categories. . . . At the center in the capital, and also outside in all the provincial capitals, there are what are called theaters, where crowds of actors are assembled and entertainments practiced, the spectators strewing gifts of money to them. *Yuanben* are by and large merely ribald jesting and joking, but not so the *zaju*.[18]

A much earlier description of Yuan theater is a poem by Du Renjie. In it a farmer takes his first trip to a playhouse. This is clearly a novel experience for him, and that fact in itself suggests that Yuan northern drama was principally urban, at least during its early days. This is how he comes into the theater:

> Cross street-top—hey, what's up?
> Gaudy poster over on that wall,
> Crowd milling round, all bustle and flap!
> What next meets my eye?
> Chap propping open roofplank door.
> "Roll up," he bellows,
> "Come late," he jabbers, "and we'll be full, standing only."
> "First half," he says, "is a *yuanben* called *Fixing Romance*,

Second half's a *yaomo* featuring Liu Shuahe himself!"
"Can see market hams any day," he shouts, "rarely get real acting like
    this!"
Cadges half a nickel, lets me past,
Through a door, up a wooden slope.
See folks sit round, layer on layer, bank on bank.
Glance up, like a belfry there,
Look down, human whirlpool there.
Couple of dames sitting on the stage . . .
What are they at? Thumping drums, bashing gongs non-stop![19]

This seems to describe a mat-shed theater, the spectator mat-sheds
reached by a gangplank and the area they enclose being the standing
pit. He notes with surprise the female musicians occupying the "music bench" actually on stage.

Another early poem, by Gao Andao (thirteenth or early fourteenth
century), gives a fuller picture of a less respectable theater, including
descriptions of each of the role categories, the *dan* for example:

Her oafish body's like a water buffalo's . . .
She bears headdress and coiffure on thick and stuckout neck,
Pincering her book of words, vainly stabbing with murky finger.
The poster painter's been pulling our legs:
Writing she's got "dancing grace and sings like honey!"[20]

The poem later adds that the troupe has:

Nothing but filthy props,
And wretched hotchpotch costumes . . .
Their lime-smeared mud-daubed clowning is sloppy and dismal . . .
Only fit to knock up shows in brothel yards or traipse their acts round
    villages and hamlets.

A southern play entitled *The Wrong Career of an Official's Son
(Huanmen zidi cuo lishen)*, probably plagiarized from a lost Yuan
zaju, is largely about a troupe of northern itinerant actors. It gives us
insights into conditions often typical of northern performance. The
troupe hails from Dongping, a key center of Yuan *zaju*. As actors they
have lowly social status, and are liable to be summarily summoned to
entertain mandarins and severely punished for offending them. Yet it
is seen as possible for one of their number to marry into a high
mandarin family. The troupe initially consists of three, a mother
and father and their star celebrity daughter. Rather puzzlingly, the
mother refers to herself as an ex-actress, and the father seems to be

stage-managing rather than acting. Possibly they both acted minor parts too.

Standard roles are the main woman *(dan)*, the mandarin, and the young man *(sheng)*. And which of them plays the young male lead? Or do they limit themselves to plays that require only one hero or one heroine, the girl acting either? Perhaps they hire extras at places they tour to. The troupe also acts *yuanben,* which involve a clown who capers, grimaces, wears makeup, whistles, and utters meaningless sounds, and their bills include music on flute, drum, and strings and acrobatics with flags and ropedancing.

They use playbooks, mostly it seems of Yuan *zaju* but possibly of southern plays or other forms as well. Sometimes, at least, playbooks are obtained from professional writers:

> I can add and insert at great speed,
> My writing brush ever flying;
> I can write playbooks in fine clear model script,
> The writing clubs of the imperial capital surpassing.[21]

Performances seem to be principally in towns, and the journeys along long country roads in between, humping props and baggage, are arduous, with stops at lonely inns on the way. Sometimes the troupe performs in teahouses, perhaps as after-dinner shows, and customers able to pay for it have the right to request particular items. The girl performs out-of-theater by rendering the songs only.

The prominence of actresses in the Yuan is witnessed by many pieces of evidence. There seems to be little general distinction made between the career of actress and that of harlot. That Xia Tingzhi wrote enthusiastic biographies of female entertainers, including actresses, but seemingly never got round to a work on "male actors," may hint that the ladies even predominated in Yuan theaters. Many of his biographies show their great versatility, for instance the following:

> Zhu Jinxiu was the wife of Hou Yaoqiao. She was accomplished in both the *dan* and *mo* role categories of *zaju,* and her voice when she sang "brought dust down from the rafters." Although in figure she was not superior to the average, in her high quality artistry she truly excelled her fellows. And Hou excelled at *yuanben,* being acclaimed in his time as the paragon of his arts.[22]

Xia describes some actresses closely connected with the Imperial Academy of Music and court, one married to a vice-director of the

Imperial Academy and Tianran Xiu, who was "especially loved and admired" by the playwright Bai Pu and the celebrated orthodox literary man, imperial academician, and eminent mandarin Li Jiong (1274–1332). The passages quoted above confirm beyond all doubt that women commonly acted male roles. Xia's preface, quoted at the beginning of this section, seems to suggest that men also sometimes acted female parts in the Yuan period, but evidence for that is not strong otherwise.

What emerges from the sources and the surviving plays is that the use of role categories in Yuan *zaju,* although largely deriving from the Song *zaju* and *yuanben,* differed very significantly from them. The greater variety of themes, and the move away from slapstick, required this difference. The main man *(mo)* and main woman *(dan)* role categories had the virtual monopoly of singing, and only one of them sang in any one act, or throughout the play. Secondary role categories were termed "old," "young," or "extra," mixedly depending on the character played. The clown, cut down in size, had much in common with the clown of the *yuanben,* but may have added more villainy and general complexity to his range of portrayals. The southern plays had four prominent role categories: the "young man" *(sheng),* the *dan,* and the two virtually identical clowns *chou* and *jing.* The *mo* was among the secondary role categories.

COSTUMES

Discussion of the performers raises the question of what they wore. Unfortunately Yuan and early Ming records say very little of Yuan play costumes. Did they deem the matter too obvious or unimportant? Did costuming depend on too complex permutations of economic and other circumstances? Was it too derivative from other types of costuming? Or have fuller records been lost? Some of these possibilities may be dismissed, but others remain. Wang Jide mused over the matter in 1610:

> I once saw Yuan play texts, some of which had set out at the head of each folio a list of role categories used, with, moreover, the names of their hats, clothes, and implements set forth, saying that such and such a person wore such a hat, was clad in such a garment, and held such an implement, all in the greatest detail. But what was meant by the terms for hats, clothes, and implements is nowadays no longer to be recognized.[23]

Perhaps what he was recalling were the many surviving Ming versions of Yuan plays which bear indications of the "vital items of attire" of the characters, act by act. These indications perhaps reflect Ming palace custom, but also possibly derive directly from the Yuan. For instance, *Presenting Shoes at Yi Bridge (Yiqiao jinlü)* by Li Wenwei (thirteenth century) is given with all the costuming for its characters. The items are described in enormous detail—whether they be headwear, shoes, beard, or walking staffs—and the descriptions sometimes include the color.[24]

What the "vital items of attire" seem to show as a whole is that the following were differentiated by costume:

1. Chinese and non-Chinese
2. military and civil
3. noble and mean
4. young and old
5. rich and poor
6. good and evil[25]

Historicity is clearly not strong in costumes stipulated. For instance, characters of the Eastern Jin (317–420) could in some cases be costumed exactly as some from the Song. There are, however, distinct costumes given for famous individual characters. The renowned strategist Zhuge Liang (181–234), for example, holds a feather fan, part of his stage portrayal in later ages, too. The hats listed give us an idea of the wide variety of attire recommended: flower-stuck square cap, rabbit horns square cap, extended horns square cap, hairpin and tassel lord's headpiece, phoenix wing helmet, leather helmet, strewn hair helmet, tiger knocked brain helmet, red bowl helmet, Uygur hat, fox hat, bonze's hat, and many others. The lists also give props, including baby dolls, bamboo nodule maces, rosaries, and demon mask heads. Another item is Uygur noses, for Uygur soldiers!

The likelihood that Ming imperial theater costumes either reflected or continued the practices of Yuan drama seems strengthened by a consideration of the costumes stipulated for Yuan court dancers.[26] These sometimes coincide with the items of the *zaju* costumes. Since *zaju* were performed at, and well known to, the Yuan court, there must surely have been some influence or interinfluence. Interestingly, the dance costumes included various held items, such as axes and writing tablets, gold armor, and various masks for deities. It is thus probable that masks were often used in Yuan *zaju* to imitate the faces of supernatural beings.

More definite information is obtained from the Yuan mural of 1324 (plate 9) and some Yuan pottery models of actors (plates 10, 11), and from scattered Yuan plays and poems. The Yuan mural depicts a troupe of actors and actresses on stage. From the picture on the back-cloth, they could be acting the play *Zhou Chu and the Two Pests (Zhou Chu sanhai)* by Yu Tianxi (thirteenth century) or the anonymous Yuan or Ming *zaju Slaying the Flood Dragon (Zhan jianjiao)*, but these and other suggestions are uncertain. There are ten people on stage and one peeping out from the back curtain, at the stage entrance. In the back row are the three musicians discussed earlier and a person in female attire holding a fan, who is probably a minor female character. The remaining six people seem by their grouping to be more central to the play. Right to the fore is a main male character dressed as a lofty minister in scarlet robe and holding a writing tablet. To his left is an old man, probably a secondary role, with a three-strand artificial beard seemingly tied round his ears and held in his mouth (in the manner of later times) and wearing a light blue coat that has black borders, cuffs, and shoulders that are outlined in white and decorated with red and green leaves. To his left is a male character in a fawn colored robe richly embroidered with bird insignia, carrying a long-handled sword. To the right of the main male is surely a clown in an ochre coat with shoulders, cuffs, and borders lavishly decorated with bird and flower patterns. To his right is a male character bearing a fan and clad in a long blue robe decorated with bird or other insignia. Behind the clown and main male is another male character with a light blue jacket and mauve pleated kilt. Many more details of costume may be seen, which convey some notion of the richness and variety of attire.

From the mural, from Du Renjie's and Gao Andao's poems, and from the dramas and other literature, enough material emerges to assure us of the widespread use of costume in the Yuan, including the southern plays. Gao, who mentioned "wretched hotchpotch costumes," says of the lady musicians on stage:

> My eager stare reports them one hundred percent ugly.
> Every one with a green calico skirt tight-lapped round her paunch,
> And a black silk strip wrapped low round her forehead.[27]

Du Renjie describes an actor, probably a clown, wearing a black bonnet with a "writing brush" stuck on the top of it, face all chalked and daubed with black stripes, and wearing a long robe like "a Taoist's cassock of flowery cloth."[28] The Persian Juvaini, writing in 1260, tells of a Chinese play consisting of tableaux of various people, including a Muslim depicted wearing a turban and long white beard.[29] This was in the period 1229–1241, and such a play must have required a fairly precise differentiation of costumes.

A different question is that of the players' offstage attire. Given that dress distinguished the wearer's rank sharply in the Song, were entertainers also clad in a special manner, or even subject to sumptuary laws? Apparently they were so at least at the beginning of the Ming. Xu Fuzha (1560–1630 or after) writes:

> The regular system at the beginning of this dynasty was that actors always wore green headwraps, and round their waists red stomachers were tied; and on their feet they wore hair-spread pigskin boots which did not allow them to walk in the middle of the street, so they went along only to the left and right sides of the road. Female entertainers wore black headgear and were not permitted any jewelry of gold or silver. They clad themselves in black sleeveless surcoats, not being allowed any brocade, embroidered garments.[30]

The black sleeveless surcoat was indeed the stipulated garment for entertainers during the Yuan and Ming, subsequently the normal dress for singing girls and maidservants and only worn by "polite" noblewomen in private. But how true the rest was of the Yuan we do not know for sure.

In many ways, what we know so far of Yuan drama is as elusively incomplete as our knowledge of Song and Jin playacting. The path towards greater clarity may well lie in two main areas: the reaching of a more complex and finely graded exposition of early Yuan society, in all its multinational and postconquest implications, and the closer investigation of the extent of Ming editing and transmission. In the latter area, computer studies may some day bring considerable light to bear. Archaeology remains another hope.

Many major elements of drama were already present in the Song *zaju* and *yuanben*: costume, makeup, even large theaters. The major addition of the southern plays and the Yuan *zaju* was the extended plot. Earlier, a playlet might form the centerpiece of a complex of entertainment that also included acrobatics, dancing, comic patter, and other items. But in the forms that this chapter discusses, the whole focus was on portraying a story through the agency of actors who enter into the characters of those they play. The variety of the plots is not only quantitatively different from anything that had come before, but qualitatively so. For the first time in China we can unquestionably see that combination of acting, costume, stagecraft, and the complex interrelation of characters in a detailed story that makes real drama. In contrast to our understanding of earlier theater, the information available leaves no doubt whatsoever as to the existence during the Yuan of a rich drama, current in the main northern and Yangzi basin heartlands and at all levels of society. Chinese drama had laid powerful foundations for the theater of later ages.

NOTES

1. *Nanci xulu,* in *Zhongguo gudian xiqu lunzhu jicheng* (Zhongguo xiju chubanshe, Beijing, 1959), vol. 3, p. 239.

2. *Yuanshi* (Zhonghua shuju, Beijing, 1976), p. 2932.

3. *Yuan dianzhang,* quoted in *Yuan Ming Qing xiqu yanjiu lunwen ji* (Zuojia chubanshe, Beijing, 1957), p. 4.

4. Xie Fangde (1226–1289), quoted in Luo Jintang, *Xiancun Yuanren zaju benshi kao* (Zhongguo wenhua shiye gongsi, Taibei, 1960), p. 426.

5. *Qulü,* in *Zhongguo gudian xiqu lunzhu jicheng* (Zhongguo xiju chubanshe, Beijing, 1959), vol. 4, p. 148.

6. *Yuanqu xuan* (Zhonghua shuju, Beijing, 1958), p. 3.

7. *Fubao tang ji* (Shanghai, 1958), pp. 91–92.

8. *Ciyu conghua,* in *Zhongguo gudian xiqu lunzhu jicheng* (Zhongguo xiju chubanshe, Beijing, 1959), vol. 9, p. 271.

9. *Yeshiyuan gujin zaju kao* (Shangza chubanshe, Shanghai, 1953), p. 150.

10. *Lugui bu,* in *Zhongguo gudian xiqu lunzhu jicheng* (Zhongguo xiju chubanshe, Beijing, 1959), vol. 2, p. 121.

11. Ibid., pp. 134–135.

12. *Qinglou ji, Zhongguo gudian xiqu lunzhu jicheng,* vol. 2, p. 25.

13. *Yuan dianzhang,* quoted in Zheng Qian, *Jiaoding yuankan zaju sanshizhong* (Shijie shuju, Taibei, 1953), preface, p. 6.

14. Shih, Chung-wen, *The Golden Age of Chinese Drama: Yüan Tsa-chü* (Princeton University Press, Princeton, 1976), p. 120.

15. Ibid., p. 123.

16. *Qulü,* p. 125.

17. *Yuefu chuansheng,* in *Zhongguo gudian xiqu lunzhu jicheng* (Zhongguo xiju chubanshe, Beijing, 1959), vol. 7, p. 157.

18. *Qinglou ji,* p. 7.

19. Sui Shusen, *Quan Yuan sanqu* (Zhonghua shuju, Beijing, 1964), vol. 1, pp. 31–32.

20. Ibid., vol. 2, pp. 1109–1111.

21. *Huanmen zidi cuo lishen (Yongle dadian)* (Zhonghua shuju, Beijing, 1960, ed.), p. 59a.

22. *Qinglou ji,* pp. 29–30.

23. *Qulü*, p. 143.

24. See *Guben Yuan Ming zaju* (Zhongguo xiju chubanshe, Beijing, 1958), pp. 19b–20a.

25. See Feng Yuanjun, *Guju shuohui* (Zuojia chubanshe, Beijing, 1956), pp. 340–385.

26. Cf. Li Xin, "Lun xiqu fuzhuang di yanbian yu fazhan," *Xiqu yanjiu*, no. 3 (1958):69–82.

27. Sui Shusen, vol. 2, p. 1109.

28. Ibid., vol. 1, p. 31.

29. J. A. Boyle, trans., *The History of the World-Conqueror* (Manchester University Press, Manchester, 1958), Vol. 1, p. 207.

30. *Qulun, Zhongguo gudian xiqu lunzhu jicheng*, vol. 4, p. 243.

SELECTED READINGS

Aoki Masaru. *Gen zatsugeki kenkyū [Research on Yuan zaju]*. Kōbundō, Tokyo, 1950. A refreshingly unprejudiced and vigorous study of all major aspects of Yuan *zaju* drama. Many of this work's novel conclusions have yet to be brought into the generality of Yuan drama research.

Crump., J. I. *Chinese Theater in the Days of Kublai Khan*. University of Arizona Press, Tucson, 1980. Includes chapters on social and historical background, as well as stages, theaters and actors, and complete translations of three Yuan dramas.

Dolby. W. *A History of Chinese Drama*. Paul Elek, London, 1976.

Dolby, William, trans. *Eight Chinese Plays from the Thirteenth Century to the Present*. Columbia University Press, New York, 1978. The eight plays include three from the Yuan, two from the Ming, one from the Qing, and two traditional pieces arranged in the twentieth century.

Liu Jung-en, trans. *Six Yuan Plays*. Penguin Harmondsworth, 1972. A translation of six *zaju*, including *Autumn in Han Palace (Hangong qiu)* by Ma Zhiyuan, one of the best known of all Yuan dramas, together with a long explanatory introduction.

Luo Jintang. *Xiancun Yuanren zaju benshi kao [Studies on the source material of extant Yuan zaju]*. Zhongguo wenhua shiye gongsi, Taibei, 1960. A copious consideration of the editions, sources, and subject matter of the extant Yuan *zaju*. It includes plot synopses of each play and analyzes the various kinds of theme.

Perng, Ching-hsi. *Double Jeopardy! A Critique of Seven Yuan Courtroom Dramas*. The University of Michigan Center for Chinese Studies, Ann Arbor, 1978. No. 35 of the Michigan Papers in Chinese Studies, this book attempts to evaluate seven "judgement reversal" *zaju* dramas.

Qian Nanyang. *Song Yuan xiwen jiyi [Fragments of Song and Yuan southern plays]*. Gudian wenxue chubanshe, Shanghai, 1956. An anthology of the most reliable fragments of Song, Yuan, and early Ming southern plays.

Schlepp, Wayne. *San-ch'ü*. University of Wisconsin Press, Madison, 1970. A major study of the *qu* poetry, which was the spiritual and structural heart of the Yuan *zaju*.

Selected Plays of Kuan Han-ching. Translated from Chinese to English by Yang Hsien-yi and Gladys Yang. New Art and Literature Publishing House, Shanghai, 1958. Pioneer translations of several of Guan Hanqing's dramas, together with a foreword by Wang Chi-ssu.

Shih Chung-wen. *The Golden Age of Chinese Drama: Yuan Tsa-chü.* Princeton University Press, Princeton, 1976. The most extensive survey in English of Yuan *zaju*, with a good bibliography, lists of Chinese characters, and a deeper than usual delving into matters of language and literature. It also has some mention of the southern plays and the beginnings of Chinese drama.

The Romance of the Western Chamber. Translated and adapted by T. C. Lai and Ed Gamarekian. Heinemann, Hong Kong. 1973. A rendering of the *Xixiang ji.* "This is not a word-for-word translation. It was written to be read, rather than performed." It includes a foreword by Lin Yutang. It is one of several renderings of this famous drama into English. Another, also bearing the title *The Romance of the Western Chamber,* is by S. I. Hsiung. Originally published in 1936, it was reissued by the Columbia University Press in 1968.

Yan Dunyi. *Yuanju zhenyi* [*Consideration of doubts in Yuan dramas*]. Zhonghua shuju, Beijing, 1960. A vast, painstaking, often rigorously skeptical reappraisal of material and traditions about the stories and editions of Yuan *zaju*, with many new slants and theories and some debunking of common oversimplifications.

CHAPTER III

MING DYNASTY DRAMA

John Hu

THE MING DYNASTY (1368–1644) marks a most important chapter in the history of Chinese drama and theater. More than four hundred playwrights produced over fifteen hundred plays, ranging from one-act skits to works with more than fifty scenes.[1] As a performing art, Ming theater, with its polished singing, intricate choreography, and splendid costumes, has been rarely, if ever, surpassed. This chapter proposes to present this rich heritage in five sections.

1. General introduction.
2. *Chuanqi:* The predominant dramatic form of the age, including its structure, development, and major representative authors.
3. *Kunqu:* The various forms of the accompanying music for *chuanqi* underwent dramatic changes until the refined *kunqu* (the music of Kunshan) became dominant.
4. *Zaju:* The major dramatic form of the Yuan dynasty, *zaju*, continued to be popular during the Ming, but, after a series of bold experiments, came to mean only a short play.
5. Theater and performance.

GENERAL INTRODUCTION

The Ming was one of the most despotic of all Chinese dynasties. It continued many of the suppressive practices of the alien Yuan dynasty it had overthrown. Furthermore, it introduced many policies and systems aimed at enhancing the power of the emperor. The position of prime minister, leader of government servants, was abolished in 1380. The emperor headed directly the various ministries of the central government, *de jure* if not *de facto*. Never in the previous thousand years had there been such a structured concentration of power in China.

The government controlled also thought and learning more systematically than ever before. The literati, who regained their prominent position and enjoyed many statutory and extended privileges, had to pass the civil service examination to enter this exclusive class. The subjects for the examination were now limited to a few books of the Confucian school, from which extensive passages that seemed offensive or subversive to the emperor had been deleted. Worse still, the aspiring officials had to write their essays in a particular form, the "eight-legged essay." With both the content and the form thus restricted, the examination was a means of the most stringent thought control and ideological indoctrination.

During the Ming it was the literati who effectively monopolized the writing of plays in the two major genres that are to be discussed below. Indeed, a few men of low social status wrote some plays early in the dynasty, but their works were harshly condemned. The fashion of the Ming was such that only men of immense learning and great knowledge of music could produce acceptable plays. Of the great number of playwrights, three were princes, and some thirty held high government office, including several ministers. In contrast to Yuan drama, that of the Ming may be regarded as essentially the product of the aristocracy and the learned for their followers. Its language and sentiments were fundamentally those of the literati, not of the common people. By extension, we may say that few Ming playwrights were professionals in the sense that they made a living from playwriting as many Yuan dramatists had done.

The aristocratic tendency on the part of the playwrights was intensified further by government regulation. In 1373, a criminal law declared:

> Players and musicians, in their performance of *zaju* and southern plays, are prohibited from impersonating emperors and kings, queens and imperial concubines, loyal courtiers and noble patriots, and sages and worthies of all dynasties. The offender shall be beaten with 100 strokes; officials and civilians permitting any such performance shall be guilty in the same way.[2]

Explicitly exempted from the prohibition were sagacious and exemplary characters regardless of their position or pursuits. Obviously, the government wanted to use theater and drama to propagate conventional morality as well as to instill loyalty. This stern attitude was extended later from performance to printed works. In 1412, a court official recommended arrest and punishment of those who held, circulated, or printed plays and scripts that slandered kings and sages. The emperor decreed subsequently: "All such plays and arias must be submitted to the officials for burning within five days after the proclamation of this order. Kill all people and their families who dare keep their collections of such works."[3] Though the government does not seem to have enforced its restrictions vigorously, Ming drama, in contrast to Yuan, refrained generally from direct political and social criticism.

Other important factors that conditioned Ming drama were economic and demographic. Ming society was affluent and trade was vigorous. An inequitable share of the wealth, however, fell into the hands of corrupt officials, eunuchs, literati, merchants, and landlords. It was these people who supplied and maintained most of the known private troupes. Their taste and outlook differed naturally from that of the general populace, a fact that accounts substantially for the rise and development of various theater forms. Related to this was the fact that the population and wealth in south China long before had outstripped that in the north. It was thus only natural for the melodies and drama of the south to influence and eventually outshine those of the north.

CHUANQI

Chuanqi originally referred to the "marvel tales" of the Tang dynasty (618–907) (see chap. I). Literally meaning "the transmission of the marvellous," *chuanqi* was used as a reference to drama at the end of the Yuan dynasty. It does not seem to have made any distinction between the then well-established *zaju* and the still evolving new forms. It became accepted generally as the antithetical designation to *zaju* during the early Qing dynasty (1644–1911) after the form had already passed its zenith.

The forerunners of *chuanqi* were the southern plays, the origins of which are discussed in chapter II. Their development was arrested by 1280, when the Mongols conquered the whole of China and their *zaju* reigned supreme. As the country gradually became more settled, however, many *zaju* playwrights migrated to the south and settled in the Hangzhou area, where they wrote both southern plays and *zaju*. Their contributions helped bring about a revival of southern plays during the reign of Shundi (1333–1368), the last Yuan emperor.

Three complete southern plays are extant, plus the titles of more than 170 plays, many of which are preserved only as fragments. There is no way yet to ascertain their authorship or the date of their composition. Two of these three extant plays, *Top Graduate Zhang Xie (Zhang Xie zhuangyuan)* and *Little Butcher Sun (Xiao Sun tu)*, were each composed by a "writing society," a kind of private and small organization engaged in popular education and entertainment. The third one, *The Wrong Career of an Official's Son (Huanmen zidi cuo lizhen)*, was written by "the talented man [or men] of ancient Hangzhou." A "talented man," was different from a "famous gentleman," in that he was a man without a high social or political position.[4] He could be a low-ranking official, a merchant, a physician, an actor, or even a male prostitute. He usually joined a "writing society" in his literary and theatrical activities. Together, these "talented men" contributed more than their social betters to the development of Chinese drama.

All three plays bear unmistakable marks of a new form still at a very flexible and formative stage. None of the three plays had any marked internal divisions; only on the basis of internal structure can each play be divided into scenes, which vary from ten to more than forty. As was the case with *zaju*, or for that matter with all major forms of traditional Chinese drama, each scene had three components: rhymed poetry for all librettos; prose to be spoken, declaimed, or recited; and stage directions indicating entrance, exits, laughter, fighting, and other movements of the characters. However, unlike the practice of *zaju*, singing in any scene no longer was limited to the leading character, but could be carried out by any character in any way; solos, duets, chorus, or a combination of them. Furthermore, southern plays also used an offstage chorus that would join the singer or singers either in the middle or at the end of an aria.[5] Even the audience might have participated in these choral sections. While *Top Graduate* obviously used both stringed and wind instruments, the other two plays most probably did not use instruments to accompany the singing. A further difference is that, whereas *zaju* used only one rhyme through the entire act, different rhymes could appear within a single scene of southern plays. The tunes for the arias of southern plays are taken from northern as well as southern sources, including those from folk songs, *ci* lyrics, and "various modes" (see chap. I).[6] The total number actually used amounted to four hundred. These tunes did not lend themselves readily to the harness of modes, as did those in *zaju*. Even the concept of having them arranged into modes according to their inherent musical qualities does not seem to have occurred. At the inception of this new drama form, the obscure playwrights simply composed new lyrics for these popular preexisting melodies to fill the people's need for entertainment.

As exemplified by the three preserved plays and the extant fragments, southern plays possess both the strengths and weaknesses of a new folk art. They could be very effective on the stage with their fast-moving events, powerful and genuine emotion, and unselfconscious delight in buffoonery and bawdy jokes. Their sentiments obviously were those of the common people instead of the literati. Their literary quality is uneven at best, and amounts to little more than doggerel in many passages. Their plots, moreover, have serious and obvious loopholes. They obviously were in need of the cultivation of men of learning and talent, in the same way that pre-Elizabethen drama needed the "university wits."

The greatest writer of southern plays was Gao Ming (c. 1301–1370), the dramatist of *The Lute Song (Pipa ji)*. Also known as Gao Zecheng, he was a native of Yongjia, Zhejiang province, not far from Wenzhou, home of the southern plays. While still a student of a famous neo-Confucian philosopher, Gao started the draft of his immortal play. By nature a recluse, he shunned the civil service examinations till the need to support his widowed mother induced him to take them in 1345, and with success. His resultant official career was marked with humanity and lasted ten years. The Yuan dynasty was then disintegrating fast; rebellion was spreading like wildfire in south China, where he held office. When one of the rebel leaders tried to force him to join the ranks, he quit office in 1355, shut himself in an upstairs room for three years, and finished *The Lute Song*.[7]

The play is about Cai Boxie, a historical scholar who had been presented as an ungrateful son in earlier popular songs and literature. Gao's play begins when Cai is living happily with his parents and his newly wedded wife, Zhao Wuniang (Fifth Maiden). When the time for the civil examination approaches, his father forces him to take it, despite Cai's reservation that once far away from home he may not be able to serve his parents in any crisis. He comes out top graduate, and Prime Minister Niu immediately seeks his hand for his daughter. Cai declines and offers to resign, but he is overruled by imperial order on both counts. Famine and the bitter feeling of betrayal soon bring death to his parents. Zhao buries them and sets out for the capital to find her husband. With Prime Minister Niu, the couple spends three years mourning beside the elders' grave. At the end of the mourning period, Prime Minister Niu personally brings the royal decree which praises the filial piety of the younger generation and rewards them with court position and honors.

Despite the happy ending, there is a serious and even a tragic tone underlying most of the action in the play. Against a background of famine, robbery, and the insolence of office, Gao attempts to define a code of behavior that can ensure human happiness.[8] Gao Ming must have been fully conscious of the significance of the issues involved, for he wrote in the prologue of the play:

> Of times past and present
> How many are the stories recorded!
> No lack of tales of fair ladies and men of talent
> Nor of the gods and spirits,
> But all so paltry as would not bear reading,
> Thus is seen; where the subject concerns not moral example
> Though good the tale, yet it is told in vain.[9]

Confident of its values and achievement, Gao Ming compares his play to a celebrated steed, while regarding other plays as merely ordinary horses. The founding emperor of the Ming dynasty, while a commoner, was so touched by a performance of the play that after he ascended the throne he ordered daily performances for a long, indefinite period of time. He compared the play to a precious delicacy that no truly noble family should forego, while the classical works of ethics and philosophy were like daily necessities that every household must possess.[10]

Many Ming critics ranked *The Lute Song* among the highest dramatic works ever written. Xu Wei, for example, credited Gao for having used elegant and polished poetry in what had been merely a crude art of villagers and men of the streets.[11] He agreed also with others that many scenes in the play were truly great, but added that certain scenes simply overflowed from the heart and lay beyond the pale of rationality. A later critic, Lü Tiancheng, thought the supreme achievements of the play were found in Gao's description of the situation and revelation of emotions. Its arrangement of scenes, in which happy ones alternated with sad, could serve as models for imitation, but its marvellous achievements stood beyond emulation.[12]

As to adverse criticism, the most recurrent, and what seems to us relevant, kind was related to music or prosody. Many critics faulted its songs and song sets, the sequence in which one song followed another, as being disharmonious. As evidence, they pointed to Gao's request, made in the prologue, that his audience and readers "not look for 'modes' and count the tunes in the play."[13] In the context, Gao really was saying that moral and thematic ideas were more important than musical qualities. As Xu Wei pointed out, the songs and song sets in the play were quite congenial in nature. What the critics implied was that these song sets should be arranged in particular ways. This criticism helped bring about the standardization of song sets, consequently a stricter requirement for playwrights to follow some conventional or prescribed song sequence. In retrospect, this kind of standardization seems the most crucial difference between southern plays and *chuanqi*.

There are many other differences between southern plays and *chuanqi*. Before we attempt any generalizations, we should remember that there was no sharp break between, but a gradual evolution from one form to the other. The largest collection of *chuanqi* plays for more than three hundred years was drawn together by Zang Maoxun (d. 1621), discussed in chapter II as the compiler of the *Selection of Yuan Songs,* who apparently standardized the structure of the plays. Using this standard structure of a *chuanqi* play, we may observe its differences from that of southern plays.

A southern play does not have any marked internal divisions, whereas a *chuanqi* play is divided into scenes, numbering from at least thirty to as many as over fifty. Each scene bears a subtitle. A southern play has a title poem, usually a quatrain, which summarizes the story and serves as the complete title of the play. This poem appears in the beginning of the play (in Yuan *zaju* it appears at the end). In *chuanqi* it is attached to the end of the first scene. The first scene of a *chuanqi* play is routinely a prologue consisting of two poems. The first is an argument of the plot. In between are sometimes inserted a question for the title of the play and the answer given by an offstage voice. To recapitulate, the standard first scene of a *chuanqi* play proceeded as follows: first poem, optional question and answer about the title, second poem, title quatrain. The dramatic action itself begins to unfold in the second scene. A southern play was more flexible: it might or might not follow this procedure.

In its Yuan editions, *The Lute Song* comes very close to the structure of a southern play. It was changed to conform to the standard structure of *chuanqi* by Ming editors.[14] These changes were not substantial, since *The Lute Song,* though without marked scores and subtitles, had incidents organized clearly around one episode after another. It thus marked a transition from southern plays to *chuanqi.* From this time onward, *chuanqi* became the dominant form of drama not only of Ming, but well into the next dynasty.

During the transitional period from Yuan to Ming, several *chuanqi* plays appeared. Four of them were famed as the "four great *chuanqi* plays." These were *The Thorn Hairpin (Jingchai ji), The Moon Prayer Pavilion (Baiyue ting), The White Rabbit (Baitu ji),* and *Killing a Dog (Shagou ji).* They were either based on legends, historical fact, or adapted from Yuan *zaju* plays.

The first two plays are stories of love and success of an originally humble man or persecuted noble, the "man of talent." While seeking success in the civil service examination, he is forced to leave behind his beloved, the "lady of beauty." During the absence of the man, his beautiful lady would rather suffer maltreatment and persecution than betray her husband or lover. Eventually, the man achieves great success and becomes happily reunited with her. This story pattern was to become the most prominent archetype of Ming *chuanqi* plays. Particularly noteworthy is that passing the civil service examination and acquiring the title of the top graduate was the turning point in the development of the plot.

After the appearance of these early *chuanqi* plays, there was a lull of almost half a century in dramatic activity of all sorts. A major cause must have been the disorder and change following the civil war for the throne that took place between 1399 and 1400. As an effort at reconstruction and appeasement, more than two thousand scholars were engaged in the compilation and editing of three monumental literary enterprises. This was followed by the relocation of the national capital from Nanjing to Beijing in 1421. The political and learning center of the nation was thus moved from the south to the north. *Zaju,* the favorite form of the north, flourished, but only for a short while before it too disappeared. Another explanation was offered by He Liangjun (fl. 1550), essentially in terms of shifted government policy and public taste:

Since the founding fathers upheld Confucianism in great honor, the scholars and gentry were ashamed to indulge themselves in poetry and drama. Thus, *zaju* and the stories of the old southern plays were not made accessible to the general public. Though professionals performed them, the ancient tunes sounded unpleasant to vulgar ears, nor were the southerners knowledgable of northern sounds. The listeners were thus displeased. The learners (of drama) gradually decreased. It accidentally happened that printed copies of *West Wing* and *The Lute Song* were available. People were delighted to read them, and knew nothing else.[15]

A more basic reason was that ever since the early *chuanqi,* playwriting required a high literacy and extensive knowledge of music and cultural tradition. Only the literati were capable of writing plays that the literati would appreciate and care to preserve for posterity. Yet, this class was preoccupied with the civil service examinations. If we remember that denial of government services to the intellectuals counted heavily in the flourishing of Yuan *zaju,* the reverse policy would naturally exert an adverse effect on Ming drama.

Following the lull, the first noticeable playwright of *chuanqi* was Qiu Jun (1421-1495), a native of the south. He held preeminent government offices and enjoyed great respect for his scholarship in philosophy, rites, and rituals. His creative writing, however, was overburdened with pedantry and a philistine morality. His only extant play, *Five Human Relationships (Wulun quanbei),* has been harshly but accurately termed "rotten."[16] However, the very fact that such an eminent scholar-official cared to use *chuanqi* for the propagation of moral principles encouraged others to imitate his style.

No fewer than twenty-four playwrights and forty plays appeared during the half a century that extended from the appearance of Qiu Jun's play to the end of the Zhengde reign (1506-1522). Generally speaking, the playwrights were deficient not only in lofty perceptions, but were also weak in creativity and original ideas. Their stories were based mostly on early Yuan *zaju* plays, Tang short stories, or such popular novels as *The Three Kingdoms (Sanguo zhi yanyi)* and *The Water Margin (Shuihu zhuan).* Since the playwrights had little of their own to offer, they chose to demonstrate their wide learning in the plays. But these amateurish playwrights—none of the Ming playwrights were professional in the sense of making a living from their writing—failed more frequently than succeeded in fusing their learning with the stage or the dramatic situation of the plays. As a result, the plays were often closet drama, pedantic and tedious. Historians have often accused Qiu Jun of having started the trend, but a careful reading of earlier plays will show that the practice was actually discernible from the very early *chuanqi* plays. He merely intensified the trend and made it respectable by virtue of his political and scholarly position.

There were of course delightful exceptions; one was in *Embroidered Jacket (Xiuru ji)*, traditionally attributed to Xu Lin (1462–1538). Faithfully adapted from a Tang short story, the play tells the love story of a young scholar and a beautiful prostitute. It is neatly organized, with few digressions or overstuffed demonstrations of pedantry. The love between the hero and heroine moves from sensuality to gain a spiritual depth through their mutual sufferings. The suspense is sustained until the very end, for the prostitute contemplates suicide so that her lover may win glory and success. Finally, the happy ending stems from a new and humanitarian perception with which the once arrogant and upright father welcomes into his family a member of the downtrodden class.

During all the centuries of their development, the southern plays and *chuanqi* were constantly in search of a perfect musical form for their librettos and performances. When the founding emperor ordered the performance of *The Lute Song,* court officials resorted for musical accompaniment to the four-stringed plucked lute *pipa* and other stringed instruments used for *zaju,* but the result was not quite satisfactory. This method of "playing southern drama in the northern way" did not go far beyond the court throughout the dynasty. It was called "official stringed music."

During the second half of the fifteenth century several regional musical styles appeared to fill the gap. They gradually attracted an increasing number of followers until southern music eventually prevailed over northern music. Chief among these regional music forms were those of Haiyan, Yuyao, Yiyang, and Kunshan.[17]

REGIONAL DRAMA AND *KUNQU*

Haiyan was a trade port and salt manufacturing center in Zhejiang province dating from the Song dynasty onward. Also from that time its people were reputed for their excellent singing, and during the Yuan dynasty, its music was further enriched by northern music. The Haiyan music began to spread to other parts of Zhejiang province no later than the middle of the fifteenth century and reached northern China a century later. Its singing was soft and quiet, not accompanied by any instrument, except a clapper or a fan to beat the time at small-scale performances, or a drum and clapper at large-scale ones. In short, it used only percussion instruments. Many earlier writings about its using such instruments as the *pipa* have been challenged recently. The confusion probably resulted from identifying it with "official stringed music."

The Yuyao music was obscure in origin, but circulated widely in Zhejiang and Jiangsu provinces between 1465 and 1521. Its central characteristic was the insertion of "parenthetical" songs or speeches. They were actually explanatory passages written in the colloquial language of the people and attached at proper places to the original scripts, whose literary language might be beyond their comprehension. Mostly in seven- or five-character lines, these songs were sung in a very fast tempo and would not much retard the action. We do not know much else about this musical style except that the practice of inserting parenthetical songs was adapted by the Yiyang style.

Yiyang music may trace its origins to the rice planting songs. It began to spread at the beginning of the sixteenth century from its home in Jiangxi province. It had no instruments to accompany the singing, except drums and gongs that beat out the time. Like the southern plays, it used an offstage chorus that joined the singing at the end of a song. This practice was dropped around the middle of the sixteenth century in favor of the parenthetical songs. As a result, the Yiyang style spread gradually to Beijing in the north and Guangzhou in the south (see plate 12).

While these original forms were prevalent everywhere, in the early decades of the sixteenth century *kunqu* was in circulation mostly at Kunshan, near Suzhou in Jiangsu province. Probably it was a soft and simple kind of music. Then in the middle of the sixteenth century it underwent important changes under the direction of Wei Liangfu. A native of Jiangxi province, Wei lived sometime between 1522 and 1573. He first attempted to distinguish himself in northern music, but found himself eclipsed by a great northern musician. He then turned his attention to studying the music styles of Yiyang and Haiyan. After having familiarized himself with all the major forms of his day, he devoted ten years to the innovations and refinements of the local music of Kunshan, in the neighborhood of which he lived. Particularly helpful to his work must have been Zhang Yetang, an expert on northern songs and string music whom Wei admired so much as to give him his daughter in marriage. With the assistance and consultation of other local musicians, Wei created a new Kunshan music that was so smooth and delicate that it acquired the appellation "water polished tune." For a simple performance, only a side-blown bamboo flute *(dizi)* was needed to accompany the singing with a wooden clapper to keep the beats. Its full orchestra, however, included percussion, and string and wind instruments including side-blown and straight flutes, *sheng* (a reed or bamboo wind organ), lute, and moon guitar *(yueqin)*. Since most of the instruments had been in use in other forms, Wei's major contribution lay obviously in adding such instruments as the flutes and integrating them all into one harmonious unity.

Along with instrumental music, Wei also expounded new approaches and techniques that stressed accuracy in enunciation and propriety in delivery. These ideas were succinctly put down in the *Rules of Prosody (Qulü)*, a treatise of about a thousand words.[18] An excellent singer himself, he was able to teach and demonstrate vocal music with the accompaniment of the innovative and enriched instrumental music. He won wide acclaim and stimulated many imitators. As a result, *kunqu* began to spread to other parts of the country by the end of the sixteenth century.

The first playwright to use the revised *kunqu* with immediate and lasting success was Liang Chenyu (c. 1520–1594). He was a famous music teacher and interested in experimenting with both northern and southern music. A native of Kunshan, he came into contact early with Wei Liangfu's work. After some successful collaboration, he wrote *Washing Gauze (Huansha ji)* for the new music form. This epoch-making play dramatizes a love story against the background of the historical struggles between the kingdoms of Wu and Yue. Fan Li, a prominent Yue official, is on an excursion in the countryside when he finds Xishi washing gauze by the stream. He falls in love with the beautiful village girl at first sight and proposes to marry her. Soon afterwards, their country is conquered by Wu. To please the Wu king and lead him into a life of dissipation, Xishi is trained in music and dance and then presented to the victors. This beautiful spy, together with other shrewd strategies, finally brings defeat and suicide to the Wu king. In his hour of triumph, however, Fan Li becomes very apprehensive that the king of Yue harbors suspicions against him and is likely to mistreat him. He thus leaves the country with Xishi to live a hermit life.

The play was an instantaneous success. The libretto and music dovetailed and reinforced each other. Propelled by this success, *kun-qu* gradually became a national music form. Since *chuanqi* afterwards generally used *kunqu* for accompaniment, and since the *"qu"* in *kunqu* could mean tunes, poems, and drama, *kunqu* became a common reference for *chuanqi* also. What had happened was that a simple musical style, *kunqu,* had undergone great development at the hands of Wei and Liang and had been applied to the existing drama form *chuanqi* to make a new form of theater, also termed *kunqu.*

Just as the success of *The Lute Song* led to efforts to standardize *chuanqi*'s literary form, so did that of *Washing Gauze* stimulate many critics to try to codify a new music prosody for *kunqu,* which, by extension, meant also *chuanqi*'s musical form. One of the most influential in this regard was Shen Jing (1553–1610). A native of Wujiang in Jiangsu province, Shen worked for the government while young, but retired in his prime. He spent the rest of his life writing plays and dramatic theories. His fame rests on the *Complete Table of Southern Prosody (Nan jiugong pu).* His primary concern was with rhyming, intonation, and the correspondence between libretto and music. Xu Fuzuo (1560–c. 1630) commented on his works: "They point out the directions for playwrights, like a shining compass in the forest of poetry."[19]

Naturally, a playwright pays close attention to the intonation of his lyrics for it is inconceivable that a word with a falling tone could fit with ascending musical notes. But Shen Jing compounded the problem. For each of the tunes used in southern drama, he selected a model lyrical verse and pointed out the intonation of each word in it, expecting aspiring playwrights to follow it word by word. It never occurred to him that if a misfit appeared, changing the melody rather than the lyrics would solve the problem. Nor did he acknowledge the fact that China had many dialects with differing pronunciations. He dogmatically insisted that lyrics be in harmony with preexisting tunes. He revised part of *The Lute Song,* among many other plays, to harness its excellent diction to these tunes. Shen Jing had a large number of followers. They formed the Wujiang school of dramatists, since Shen was a native of Wujiang. For their insistence on the priority of music over diction, they were also called the school of prosodic regulations. During the remainder of the Ming, the school dominated dramatic criticism.

As a playwright, Shen Jing was a victim of his own theory, and so were many of his followers. Of the nineteen plays that he wrote, all except one were failures. This successful play, entitled *An Upright Hero (Yixia)*, was adapted from chapters in the famous novel *Water Margin*. It is still popular today in its Beijing opera form. But it might have perished along with so many of his other plays, for Shen, unable to see its stage potential, particularly requested that the play should not be given wide circulation.[20] The unexpected success of the play shows its author's poor judgment of the appeal of drama. Generally speaking, the Wujiang school of playwrights overstressed musical harmony at the expense of poetic spontaneity. Their plays are pleasant to hear, but have little else to offer to readers or audience.

Fortunately, many playwrights held a different view and stressed artistic ingenuity and spontaneity. The most successful and influential of them all was Tang Xianzu (1550–1617), a native of Linchuan in Jiangxi province. From his childhood, he was torn between his desire to earn distinction in officialdom and his longing for freedom from its humdrum and transient life. Though justly acclaimed as a man of immense learning, he failed the civil service examinations at the capital three times. He was thirty-three years old already when he finally passed it. His resultant official career was marked by poverty, demotion, exile, and disillusionment with the court, fraught with corruption and factionalism. He abandoned office in 1598 and lived the rest of his life in great poverty and chronic sickness. Through his association with a great Chan master, particularly after the tragic death of his eldest son in 1600, he moved steadily to embrace Buddhist views and other-worldly values. In the twilight of his life, he was able to face death with tranquility and serenity, as magnificently reflected in his last poems and will.[21]

Tang Xianzu left behind him five plays: *The Purple Flute (Zixiao ji)* (1577–1579), *The Purple Hairpin (Zichai ji)* (1587), *The Peony Pavilion (Mudan ting)* (1598), *The Dream of Nanke (Nanke ji)* (1600), and *The Dream of Handan (Handan ji)* (1601). Usually they are referred to collectively as the *Four Dreams of Linchuan (Linchuan simeng)*, because of the first two plays overlap, while dreams play a critical role in all four plays. Of the four, *The Peony Pavilion* is by general consensus the greatest of all *chuanqi* plays.

The heroine of the play is Du Liniang, the beautiful daughter of a high-ranking official. After having had a love affair with a handsome young scholar in her dream, she pines away and draws a self-portrait before her death. Compassionate and sympathetic, Judge Hu of the underworld frees her soul and has her body preserved. She soon begins to have nocturnal trysts with Liu Mengmei, a young scholar, who has discovered and admired her self-portrait. Then, at her ardent pleas, he exhumes her body and brings her back to real life. They marry and travel to the capital, where he takes the civil service examinations. Due to the Tartar invasion, the disclosure of the result is postponed indefinitely. In sheer poverty, Mengmei visits his father-in-law seeking help, merely to be thrashed as a fraud. He is rescued in the nick of time because the invaders are defeated and he is selected as the top graduate. Du, however, can neither believe in the resurrection of his daughter nor forgive her for her self-contracted marriage. Only imperial intervention makes reconciliation and family reunion possible. In a treatise published in 1610, Lü Tiancheng wrote:

> The affair of Liniang is quite marvelous. The deliberate elaboration of a young woman's longing for love and marriage is evocative to the heart and disturbing to the soul. Furthermore, every dramatic situation is a novelty, with one ingenious stroke after another. The play is really a work for all times.[22]

Two centuries and a half later, another eminent critic wrote in England: "Without a shadow of doubt, *The Peony Pavilion* is the richest and maturest product of the Chinese stage."[23] In between, there were many similar comments, and sustained theatrical successes (see plate 13).

After Tang Xianzu and Shen Jing, *kunqu* was established firmly as a respectable literary genre, and as a decent pursuit for literati as well. Generally speaking, with the revival of classical literature in the middle of the sixteenth century, literature was regarded as the highest of human achievements. Over the years, government restrictions on the theater were gradually allowed to lapse. Thus, the remainder of the Ming dynasty saw the appearance of some 330 playwrights, who produced approximately 900 *kunqu* plays. Many of these were very popular then and have remained so till recent decades. They include *The Eight Righteous Men (Bayi ji)*, which elaborates on *The Orphan of Zhao (Zhaoshi guer ji)* and particularly on the hero's growth into manhood, avenging the wrongs his family has suffered and being reunited with his parents. Another adaptation, *The Incense Burning (Fenxiang ji)*, retells the sad story of the ungrateful Wang Kui and his wife Guiying, who commits suicide in earlier versions, but here has a happy ending through the intervention of the Sun God. Another play, parts of which are still performed today, is *The Jade Hairpin (Yuzan ji)*. It dramatizes the love affair and eventual marriage between a scholar and a nun. One of its scenes, subtitled "Qiujiang" ("Autumn River"), shows the nun in her lay dress taking a ferryboat in pursuit of her lover. It never fails to delight the audience whenever well performed.

The plays just mentioned show a number of general characteristics of *kunqu* at this stage of its development. Few of the playwrights were original. They were content to adapt and to combine what had been already in existence and in great esteem. The fashion and expectation of the age were such that the playwrights were almost forced to give their plays a happy ending, even if the original versions finished tragically. With their ready sources and foregone conclusions, the playwrights were left to concentrate on the diction and prosody of their works. They strove for novelty in expression rather than originality in perception. In other words, they cared less about what they said than how they said it. As a result, their language became increasingly ornate, their episodes repetitive, their characters blurred and stereotyped. While a few of the plays stood out as good examples of *kunqu*, many others became closet drama, ignored and forgotten even by their contemporaries.

To conclude our survey of *kunqu*, two outstanding dramatists may be mentioned for their artistic achievements and also for their outlook, which reflects on the destruction of the Ming dynasty. Ever since the formation of the Wujiang school and the school of prosodic regulations, efforts had been made to reconcile and integrate them. People expected new playwrights able to follow the standard prosody of *kunqu* and simultaneously maintain poetic eloquence and beauty. Both these playwrights lived up to this expectation.

The first one was Ruan Dacheng (1587–1646). After he earned his advanced degree in 1611 at the age of twenty-four, he ingratiated himself with the then powerful eunuchs and became their protégé. When the eunuchs lost power, Ruan also fell into disgrace. In his retirement, he maintained a private troupe and personally trained the performers in enunciation, singing, dance, and other stage movements. He also lavished money on their costumes, hand properties, and scenic units. As a result, his contemporaries judged his troupe the most outstanding. Aside from personal entertainment, Ruan also lent his troupe to others to curry favor with them. When the Qing army advanced to the south, he surrendered, joined the invaders, and soon died in an accident while leading them to conquer the rest of China.

Ruan wrote nine *kunqu* plays. The best known are *The Swallow-Carried Message (Yanzi jian)* and *The Spring Lantern's Riddles*

(Chundeng mi). In the first, a handsome young scholar courts and finally marries two beautiful girls; one is a prostitute he loved in his frivolous days, the other a virtuous girl from a noble family. In the second play, two brothers marry two sisters after no fewer than ten incidents of mistaken identity caused by misunderstandings and changes of sex and name. Essentially comedies of situation, these and other plays are remarkably adroit in their technique. They repeatedly use mistaken identity for complication and an object, such as a portrait or a poem, to achieve clarity and continuity of action. While technically superb, the plays manifest mere hedonism and escapism from the internal and external problems that soon would destroy the dynasty.

The second of these outstanding playwrights was Wu Bing (d. 1646). A contemporary of Ruan Dacheng, Wu also at one time held ministerial rank. Unlike Ruan, he committed suicide after capture by the Qing army. He left five *kunqu* plays, which are imitative of the four dream plays of Tang Xianzu. His *The Remedy for Jealousy (Liao-du geng)* evinces both his own dramaturgy and Tang's influence. The story is about how Yang Qi takes Xiaoqing (Little Green) to be his concubine through an arrangement made by his wife who is barren but wants to have a son in the family. The dramatic incidents, particularly in outline form, would appear absurd and incomprehensible if one were unfamiliar with Tang Xianzu's masterpiece. For example, Little Green is so frustrated with her love for Yang that she pines away and dies, only to be brought back to life by a friend soon afterward. When she visits him at night, he is moaning before her portrait, which she has prepared in her last days. Mistaking her for the portrait come to life, Yang releases his pent-up passions. This reverses the situation in *The Peony Pavilion* in which Liu Mengmei makes love to the ghost of Du Liniang believing her to be a real woman. Yang feels ashamed when his wife breaks into the chamber and charges him with infidelity, but his shame is changed into great joy the next day when he learns that he can formally marry Little Green. Eventually, his wife and concubine each give birth to a son.

Wu Bing won great admiration from his contemporaries. They praised him for the harmony that he created between his diction and music.[24] They also recognized his ingenuity in twisting familiar dramatic situations to generate delightful surprises. However, they failed to realize the decadent taste and weakness of his dramaturgy. Gone is the genuine and humane sensibility of the characters in *The Lute Song*. Vanished also are the passion and compassion we find in *The*

Peony Pavilion, in which the gods champion a girl's normal desire for marriage. Vehement social and political protest is also muted. Plays with such qualities admittedly were unique and rare in Ming drama, conditioned and made effeminate by dictatorship and thought control. The works of Wu Bing, Ruan Dacheng, and their contemporaries, then, merely intensified the trend. They mirrored a dynasty's decline and foreshadowed its destruction.

THE *ZAJU*

While *chuanqi,* including *kunqu,* was the mainstream of Ming drama, *zaju* was its major tributary. About a hundred playwrights produced 520 *zaju* plays, a very impressive record for any age.[25] While many of the playwrights wrote in the same *zaju* form established in the preceding age, many others made a sequence of changes which transfigured totally the familiar form. This section will trace the most significant changes, while attempting to present representative playwrights and their important works.

Since most of the early playwrights grew up in the Yuan dynasty, they naturally tended to write in the *zaju* form. This tendency was further strengthened by two early Ming princes who wrote *zaju* plays themselves and encouraged others to write in the same form. The first one was Zhu Quan (1378–1448), the seventeenth son of the first Ming emperor. He received the title of prince at the age of thirteen and two years later headed a border garrison with eighty thousand soldiers and six thousand chariots and horses. He lost command of his army during the coup d'état in 1399 and began to lead a quiet life devoted to studies, writing, and entertainment. In his old age, he occupied himself increasingly with Taoism and the cultivation of immortality. About fifty works are now ascribed to him, including twelve plays. Only two of these plays are extant. One traces a recluse's attainment of immortality, reflecting its author's aspiration. The other, entitled *Zhuo Wenjun's Elopement with Xiangru (Zhuo Wenjun siben Xiangru),* is based on a historical event. In it, a talented young scholar attracts a beautiful widow, elopes with her, and finally marries her with her father's blessing. While both plays deal with familiar subjects of Ming drama, they are praised particularly for their elegant and polished style.[26]

Another work traditionally ascribed to him is *The Table of Correct Sounds of the Great Peace Era (Taihe zhengyin pu).* The preface to this work is allegedly dated 1398, when Zhu Quan was only twenty

years old and busily engaged in government duties.[27] Both its authorship and the authenticity of the preface have been challenged recently. Based on internal evidence and cross references, a historian has
argued that the work was composed by one of Zhu Quan's subordinates sometime between 1429 and 1448.[28] Whatever the authorship
or date of composition, *The Table of Correct Sounds* is an important
and monumental work of *zaju*. First, it contains a title list of 689 *zaju*
plays written between the Yuan dynasty and Zhu Quan's own age,
providing valuable information for drama historians. Second, it gives
a series of impressionistic and summary comments on the dramatic
poetry of many outstanding dramatists. Third, and most important,
is certainly its "Table of Correct Sounds." It lists titles of 335 musical
tunes for *zaju* and arranges them into twelve "modes." For each of
these tunes, a libretto is provided to exemplify the tonal demand on
the Chinese characters (words) accompanying the melodies at certain
intervals. The *Table* is tantamount to a handbook for *zaju* writing.
The first of its kind, it also stimulated such men as Shen Jing to compose similar works regulating the prosody for *kunqu*.

Another Ming prince interested in drama was Zhu Youdun (1379–
1439). Filial and kindhearted, he never played an active role in politics but devoted his leisure time to gardening, calligraphy, and theater. He left behind him thirty-two plays, all extant. More than half
of them feature Buddhist and Taoist priests or immortals involved in
either the celebration of festivals or the salvation of fallen people. The
rest of his plays are about courtesans and prostitutes, patriotic warriors, virtuous women, righteous brigands, and peonies, the flower he
particularly loved.

One of the plays is entitled *The Sorrow of the Perfumed Sachet
(Liu Panchun shouzhi xiangnang yuan)*. Based on a true contemporary incident, the story is about a *zaju* actress who has a love affair
with a young scholar and commits suicide when forced to marry a rich
salt merchant. At her funeral, her body and clothing are burned to
ashes, but her perfume sachet, containing her lover's letter and
poem, remains intact. Her lover, thus far barred by his father from
seeing her, arrives at the funeral and swears celibacy in return for her
fidelity and sacrifice. This play has long been an audience favorite. It
presents forcefully the steadfast love and deep sorrows of an actress of
that time. It also shows the duress and humiliation experienced by
those of her profession in general.

In his plays, Zhu Youdun experiments frequently with the *zaju*
form, influenced apparently by the increasing popularity of *chuanqi*

drama. Instead of the regular four acts with an optional "wedge," an introduction to the main action or a brief extension of it, he once used five acts and two wedges. Instead of assigning all the arias in one act to one character, he followed the practice of *chuanqi* and distributed the librettos in any way he saw fit. The tunes of *zaju* had always been taken from the vigorous and sonorous northern music repertoire, but in one play he contrasted the hero's northern tunes with the heroine's soft and mellifluous southern tunes. In short, he departed from all the characteristic practices of Yuan *zaju*. While for him these departures were occasional and experimental, they would later become normal. With these far-reaching innovations and thirty-two plays to his credit, Zhu Youdun stands foremost among the Ming *zaju* dramatists.

Contemporary with the two princes were sixteen *zaju* playwrights mentioned in *The Table of Correct Sounds* and credited with thirty-three plays. Of these surviving plays, two are particulary noteworthy. One is *The Pilgrimage to the West,* written by Yang Na, a sinicized Mongol playwright with eighteen plays to his credit. *The Pilgrimage* is divided into six "parts," each containing four acts, the length of a regular *zaju*. This long play traces Tripitaka's travels to India in quest of Buddhist sutras, accompanied by his three famous disciples (Monkey, Sandy, and Pigsy). The first volume shows how Tripitaka is born an orphan, raised by a monk, and how his father is restored to life after his murderer has been punished. The next five volumes retell the various dangers, trials, and temptations that Tripitaka and his disciples encountered and overcame, sometimes through divine intervention. The last volume records his final success and ascension to the Buddhist heaven. This play manifests the continuing Chinese fascination with the Tripitaka story. It also forms a link with later variations of the same story. These later versions, however, tend to stress the histrionic episodes of the disciples, whereas Yang's focuses on the trials and spiritual ascension of the master.[29]

The second interesting *zaju* play of the early Ming period was *The Golden Boy and the Jade Girl (Jintong yunü jiaohong ji)*, by Liu Dongsheng, about whose life we know practically nothing. In the play we find a curious combination of two trends prevalent in works of this period: on the one hand a strong interest in the occult and mysterious, particularly in Taoist or Buddhist cultivation of immortality, and on the other hedonism and eroticism. *The Golden Boy and the Jade Girl,* in eight acts, parades before its audiences a prolonged and repeated sequence of rendezvous, separation, love-sickness, and gratification of desires between the hero and heroine. In the wedge at the beginning, which serves as a prologue, they are presented as two fallen Taoist deities. Their love affair is supposed to effect the purging of their carnal desires. In the concluding part of the play, after their marriage, they are welcomed back to the Taoist heaven.

After Zhu Youdun's death in 1439, half a century passed before any noteworthy playwright appeared. *Zaju* declined during this period for the same reasons that *chuanqi* declined: disorder and change, the shift in government policy and public taste, and the preoccupation of the literati with civil service examinations. The long silence in *zaju* was broken by two playwrights, Wang Jiusi (1468–1551) and Kang Hai (1475–1540), who were close friends living in the same area. Both lost their offices because of involvement in court factionalism and their dubious connections with a powerful but corrupt eunuch. Both were good at playing the lute, the major accompanying instrument of *zaju*. To vent their anger at their ungrateful friends or unappreciative superiors, each wrote a *zaju* entitled *The Wolf of Mount Zhong (Zhongshan lang)*. They tell how a philanthropist-scholar rescues a wolf from its pursuers at the risk of his own life, and how, once safe but hungry, the wolf threatens to devour him until it is killed by a passerby. Kang's version is in the strict *zaju* form, while Wang's version has only one act.

The one-act *zaju* form was used by another playwright, Xu Chao, in a more interesting way. We know little about him except his authorship of eight extant plays, plus fragmentary arias from five others. Each of these plays has only one act, showing an immortal or a man of letters on an occasion that is historically celebrated. For example, in *Poem Reciting at Noon (Wuri yin)* an official pays a visit to Du Fu (712–770), one of the greatest Chinese poets, during the Dragon Boat Festival, which commemorates the tragic drowning of Qu Yuan (340–278 B.C.), the first great known poet of China. The highlight of the play shows the official and Du Fu reciting poetry and singing songs, while attractive ladies dance in the dragon boat. Similar occasions are chosen for other plays, so that each takes place in a different month of the year. Contemporary records show that Xu Chao originally composed twenty-four plays under the collective title *Songs of Great Peace (Taihe ji)* for celebrating the same number of festivals in the Chinese lunar calendar. While interesting in themselves, the *Songs* were the forerunner of the Qing court drama celebrating various festivals.

One of the most famous Ming playwrights to continue the trend was Xu Wei (1521–1593). A most versatile and eccentric genius, he was driven several times to the verge of insanity and suicide. In one of these outbursts, he killed his wife and was imprisoned for seven years. He died in great poverty despite the fact that he was an excellent calligrapher, painter, poet, and dramatist. He left behind two dramatic works. One was *The Four Shrieks of a Monkey (Sisheng yuan)*, which consists of four separate plays. In one of them, a humiliated and persecuted scholar accuses the usurper, Cao Cao, by beating a drum at a banquet. In another, a monk deliberately seduced by a prostitute commits suicide and becomes a prostitute through reincarnation until he gains enlightenment. In each of the last two plays remarkable women are presented who disguise themselves as men and win high recognition—one (Hua Mulan) in military affairs and the other (Huang Chongku) in literary circles. Each of these four plays reflects its author's defiant spirit; he was prepared to overcome any restraint, whether political, religious, or biological.

The form of Xu Wei's plays is also remarkably unconventional. One of them has only one act, two others have two acts each, and the last one has five. The tunes in the acts were selected from both the northern and southern repertories and arranged in boldly novel sequences. This drastic departure from standard practice won universal acclaim. Wang Jide (d. c. 1623), a famous playwright and theoretician, commented: "Mr. Xu's *Four Shrieks of a Monkey* is really a marvelous literary work in the world. The northern tunes of Mulan and the southern tunes of Huang Chongku are marvels of all marvels."[30] His opinion was widely shared by others.

After the innovations of Xu Chao and Xu Wei, the only drastic change that could be made was to use southern tunes only for *zaju*. Wang Daokun (1525–1593) was one of the earliest, if not the earliest, playwright, to make this last change. A great reader with a distinguished official career, Wang wrote five plays, four of which are preserved. Each of them dramatizes an imaginary situation involving a famous historical figure. *The Song of Five Lakes (Wuhu you)*, for example, shows Fan Li and Xishi boating and exchanging their wine for fish from a fisherman and woman. The whole play is like an idyllic poem. While the tunes in this play are taken from both the northern and southern repertoires, the other three plays use southern tunes only. Furthermore, each play has a short prologue and a poem to conclude the action, which had once been distinctive features of the southern plays. To differentiate this kind of *zaju* from their prototype in the Yuan, some historians prefer to call them "southern *zaju*."

Indeed, at this stage of development, a *zaju* might come very close to a southern play in its earliest stage. Since the length of a southern *zaju* was shorter than that of a *zaju*, not to mention *chuanqi*, some historians referred to them simply as "a short play."

After these various experiments, *zaju* became a very flexible form of dramatic expression. During the last eighty years of the dynasty, some eighty playwrights produced more than two hundred plays. To provide better models, Zang Maoxun published in 1615–1616 his *Selection of Yuan Songs*. Other anthologies followed, and their availability stimulated aspiring playwrights to imitation. As a result, the traditional *zaju* form also flourished.[31]

Even if the tunes used in *zaju* were northern, they were so in title only, not in their musical qualities. So pervasive were *kunqu*, the "water refined" tunes, that northern music gradually but steadily lost its distinct quality. In an important treatise on northern and southern music, prefaced 1639, Shen Chongsui (d. c. 1645) wrote:

> Ever since Wei Liangfu, the sound of southern music has been fully explored to enhance its beauty. The sound of northern music became increasingly submerged through long neglect. A title may exist, but its musical notation is untraceable; the notation may exist, but its beats are unverifiable; the notation and beats may exist, but hardly has anyone understood how to handle such critical techniques as "stressing the beginning" or "tumbling down" in the original melodies. . . . As to the lute-accompanied vocal music, vulgarly known as "northern tunes," it is northern only in name but not in actuality. Its melodies are too effeminate and its pronunciation and direct melodies have only brought it closer to the "water refined" tunes. It has lost its northern characteristics.[32]

In the same treatise, Shen Chongsui, a southerner, wrote how he had gone to northern China to search for genuine northern music, but in vain. The few tunes that seemed to him close to northern music moved him deeply. As time went by, even those few tunes were lost in the ravages of time.

THEATER AND PERFORMANCE

When the Ming dynasty established its capital in Nanjing in 1356, it followed the practice of previous dynasties and founded an institute, the Imperial Academy of Music, to be in charge of musical and dramatic entertainment at the court. Selected actors and actresses in the capital were registered and assigned to live in a compound provided by the government. They performed at the court only on special occasions. At other times, they presented plays to the public also. The government erected two theaters for them. At least one of them was a large, storied building, richly decorated. This "Imperial Theatre" must have been the first state-managed public theater in the history of the Chinese empire.[33] It was highly esteemed during the fourteenth century. A similar establishment might have existed in Beijing, after the capital moved there from Nanjing, until the beginning of the sixteenth century.

At the court, a eunuch agency was founded in 1390 to provide regular dramatic and other entertainment on short notice. Its repertoire initially consisted mainly of *zaju* and southern plays and other forms from the Yuan dynasty. Most of the extant *zaju* scripts have come down to us from this agency. The court repertoire was expanded later to include such fashionable theater forms as *kunqu*. From the sixteenth century on, many emperors were extremely fond of variety shows, puppet shows, and comic skits that poked fun at their vulgar and often mischievous subjects.[34] The courtly performances were very large in scale and complex in nature, but since their connection with popular theaters is not clear, there is no way to ascertain their influence.

Outside the court, there were two kinds of basic acting troupes.[35] The first kind was domestic, organized and maintained by households of the rich or the powerful. The masters might be merchants, nobles, officials, or landlords. For example, Princes Zhu Youdun and Zhu Quan, Minister Shen Shixing (1536–1614) and Ruan Dacheng each maintained an outstanding family troupe. The status of the actors and actresses was either that of servants, born slaves, concubines and mistresses, or contracted employees engaged for a period of time. These troupes performed at the master's command. The occasion might be a wedding, a birthday party, or any of the festivals held throughout the year. Just as frequently, a private troupe performed at small private parties to please its master or to entertain his family and friends (see plates 14 and 15). Ruan Dacheng even lent his troupe to influential people for political advancement.

The other kind of troupe was professional. Some were stationary in a city large enough to support them through paid attendance. The attractiveness of the troupes depended to a large extent on their lead-

ing performers, male or female. Other professional troupes were itinerant, travelling from one place to another to seek an audience. These
troupes were mostly small companies, consisting of members of the
same family. Both kinds of professional troupes could be invited to
perform at temples, restaurants, and private homes. It was their duty
to act at the summons of local magistrates with or without previous
arrangement. Delay in appearance might lead to a reprimand or punishment.

Obviously, each troupe had to have enough actors and actresses to
play the basic role types demanded by the plays. The names of role
types underwent certain changes in the various genres of drama, but
the basic types were essentially similar. Those of the southern plays,
sheng, dan and so on, as explained briefly in chapter II, were taken
over and in some cases slightly changed and subdivided in the *kunqu*,
which increased the number to twelve or as many as twenty-five according to certain historians.[36] The categorizing of roles is merely a
broad indication of the sex, age, national inclination, and temperament of the characters. It serves as a general guidance for specialization in singing and acting styles. On the other hand, since each character in a play is an individual, his emotions and thoughts inevitably
vary from one play to another. Characters can be unique and quite
distinct, and although the division of roles is very useful, can be overstressed.

Our knowledge of the training of the actors is inadequate in view
of the tremendous variety of regional theaters that arose and inter-
mingled during the 260 years of the Ming period. Even with the
kunqu theater, we do not have sufficient information on how those
most intricate and exquisite dances and movements were taught.
Judging by the frequency with which new plays appeared and saw the
stage, the choreography must have been designed for each production. What the performers needed then was the basic training and
control of their bodies, similar to modern dancers. To achieve distinction, they must have had a strong will to excel and resort to whatever
means were appropriate and available to them. Several anecdotes
tend to confirm this observation.

A certain actor by the name of Ma Jin once felt inferior to and
humiliated by another actor in impersonating a powerful but corrupt
official. He therefore went to the capital and worked as a servant to a
powerful official for three years. Through close observation and imitation of this official, Ma acquired the understanding and techniques

for his role. He eventually outshone his rival in acting and won his sincere admiration, not to mention the high esteem of the audience.[37]

Another actor, Yan Rong, acquired his performing ability through self-imposed hard drill and practice. He originally failed to move the audience in his role in *The Orphan of Zhao,* in which one of the secondary characters (the *mo*) substitutes his son for the Zhao orphan in death. Yan subsequently punished himself by slapping his face until it became red. Then he rehearsed the same role before a dressing mirror for days, holding a doll in his hand. Subsequent performances moved spectators to tears. He then returned home, bowed to his image in the mirror, and said, "Yan Rong, now you are really worth watching."[38]

Contemporary records similar to those above indicate that anyone could learn certain acting and singing fundamentals through hard work and practice. The performer could then select a certain type of role suitable for his or her natural voice and body-build. Tutoring and coaching were not hard to come by. Besides, there were numerous books on voice, enunciation, and elocution. Many masters of the domestic troupes were well versed in singing; so were many playwrights, and they often taught troupes or actors closely associated with them.

A performance in the Ming period and, for that matter, for any traditional Chinese drama, could take place anywhere with a flat area for a stage. Scenery was unnecessary; it could be a hindrance, since the location for the dramatic action shifted fast at short intervals. In many cases, a character or characters would have journeyed scores of miles in an aria or a few lines of dialogue. The place for performance during the Ming could be and often was a boat, a rice-threshing floor, a hall, a temple, or of course a permanent or temporarily erected theater. Wherever it might be, a red carpet spread on the flat place would be sufficient for "the stage." Stage right was normally used for entrance and stage left for exit. The scale and arrangement for a performance were extremely flexible (see plate 16).

An example of a production on a grand scale was the public performance of *Mulian Saves His Mother (Mulian jiumu).*[39] For the performance that lasted three days and nights, a large but temporary stage was erected. It was surrounded by about a hundred raised booths for the female members of the audience. In addition to the regular performers, some thirty to forty actors were hired to demonstrate somersaults, tumbling, tightrope walking, jumping the hoop, and leaping through fire and over swords. In the play itself, Mulian goes down to hell to save his mother who has been sent there for her sins on earth. He passes various regions in hell and witnesses the horrible tortures the condemned sinners suffer. The apparatus for torture included a mountain of knives, boiling cauldrons, trees that grow swords, trenches of blood, saws, and grinding stones. Along with the guarding ghosts of the underworld, these scenes were represented on the stage in a most realistic manner. The audience was so discomforted that their faces took on a ghostly hue under the lamplight. During certain particularly exciting and terrifying episodes, "more than ten thousand people roared in unison. Prefect Xiong was frightened awake from his sleep and sent his subordinates to investigate, suspecting that the pirates had suddenly arrived."[40]

Scenery must have been used in the production, otherwise it would not have created such a strong impact on the audience. In the production of one drama about the Tang emperor Minghuang's travels to the moon, not only was scenery used but lighting and sound effects as well. In the course of the production, "the stage was plunged into pitch darkness. A sword was raised and swung, producing a thundering rumble. With the dark curtain suddenly withdrawn, a moon appeared, as round as if drawn with a compass."[41] Surrounding the moon were clouds and mists in five different colors. Inside the moon flames from hidden sources emitted an opaque blue light, like the hue of early dawn, through a light gossamer screen. While these productions were certainly marvelous, we must remember that they took place late in the dynasty and that even then they were exceptions rather than general practice.

The flexibility and variety found in the arrangements of a performance applied to the use of costumes. Elaborate and lavish costumes were used; for example, in the production of Zhu Youdun's *zaju* plays.[42] On the other hand, the costumes commonly used had barely more than ten different basic patterns and designs.[43] They included the *mang* (python robe) with pythons embroidered on it for high-ranking officials; the yellow *mang* was for emperors only.[44] *Pei* was also an embroidered dress, but less elaborate, to be worn by officials on informal occasions or by retired officials and gentry. *Xiezi* was the daily wear for all men—officials and military officers, scholars and merchants. On formal occasions, military officers wore *kai*. Finally, there was *chaiyi,* a plain upper garment for such lower-class people as woodcutters, waiters, and pages. Each of these costumes had counterparts for women. In addition, women could wear skirts.

The designs of the Ming costumes were based on patterns found in divergent sources from preceding dynasties. No effort was made at historical authenticity; anachronism in costumes was the general practice. Nor was there any attempt at realistic representation: the same *mang*, for example, could be used for all seasons and various weather conditions. Rather, the costumes aimed primarily at establishing the identity and social status of the characters. Costumes could also indicate the occasion on which the characters appear. Playwrights often indicated in the stage directions the costumes to be used. For example, in *The Lioness Roars (Shi hou ji)*, the *sheng* role wears "informal dress" in scene two, when he leaves his domineering and suspicious wife. The stage directions stipulate that he reappears in "gorgeous dress" in scene five, in which he is with his newly acquired mistress.[45] The playwright obviously expected that his costumes should suit the dramatic situation and atmosphere.

If costumes were used primarily for establishing characters' social status, face painting was used chiefly to denote a character's moral qualities and temperament. In its simplest practice, face painting was merely makeup, the application of rouge and powder to enhance the physical beauty of the actors. But more elaborate painting that changed considerably the natural hue and appearance of the face was a long practice in the performing arts of China. It remained, however, rudimentary until the early Ming. Designs preserved from that time show that face painting was limited by the eyebrows and eye sockets. It was only gradually that designs were applied to other parts until the whole face was colored. The hues used were few, but each had a symbolic significance. Red was used for generals of outstanding loyalty and patriotism, while purple was for distinguished officials, known for their loyalty and tranquil temperament. Characters with a black face were honest, fierce, or serious-minded. Mischievous and arrogant characters, often rebels or bandits, had their faces painted blue. A yellow face denoted that the character was scheming or calculating. These were the most important colors used during the Ming.[46] Variegated designs were known, but would have to wait until the rise of Beijing opera to become generally adopted.

In summarizing the Ming period's theater, the observer is struck by the rise of new forms of drama and the fall of others. The *chuanqi* flowered in the transitional period between the Yuan and Ming. It then developed into the newly integrated *kunqu* in the sixteenth century and continued strongly as an aristocratic form. In the meantime the mass local theater was beginning to take a clearer shape, with richer variety than ever before.

At the same time the *zaju,* which had reached its apex under the Yuan, declined sharply in the Ming. This is not to say that nothing new or inventive emerged in the *zaju* theater. On the contrary, changes were made in its structure and style by daring authors. But this did not arrest its failing appeal in the face of competition from the *kunqu* and new regional styles.

These processes laid a strong basic framework for the later development of Chinese theater. The same is true of the developments, continuities, and changes in the Ming dynasty's theater practices, costumes, face painting, acting and singing techniques, and staging methods. These were assimilated into the succeeding theater forms, particularly Beijing opera.

Taking them as a whole, a leading historian of Chinese theater has summed up the achievements of Ming theater as follows:

> Even though hundreds of years have passed since the Ming dynasty, few significant changes (with the exception of spoken drama) have occurred in our theater until recent years. By and large, we have continued and inherited the practices of Ming theater. The performing arts of Ming, therefore, occupy a pivotal position in the performing arts of today. The Ming theater achievements provide models for posterity; the serious attitude of its artists really surpasses that of many of the present followers.[47]

NOTES

1. Luo Jintang, *Mingdai juzuojia kaolue* (Longmen shudian, Hong Kong, 1966), pp. 1–17.

2. Quoted in Zhou Yibai, *Zhongguo xiju shi* (Zhongguo shuju, Shanghai, 1953), p. 310.

3. Quoted in Wang Xiaochuan, *Yuan Ming Qing sandai jinhui xiaoshuo xiqu shiliao* (Zuojia chubanshe, Beijing, 1958), p. 10.

4. Feng Yuanjun, *Guju shuohui* (Zuojia chubanshe, Beijing, 1956), pp. 57–58.

5. Zheng Qian, "Dong Xixiang yu ci ji nanbeiqude guanxi," in *Jingwu congbia* (Zhonghua shuju, Taibei, 1972), vol. 2, pp. 374–410.

6. Ye Dejun, "Mingdai nanxi wuda qiangdiao ji qi yuanliu," *Xiqu xiaoshuo congkao* (Zhonghua shuju, Beijing, 1979), pp. 9–14.

7. A succinct account of Gao Ming's life and work in English can be found in

H. C. Chang, *Chinese Literature: Popular Fiction and Drama* (Edinburgh University Press, Edinburgh, 1973), pp. 79–87. Translation of certain scenes of the play appears on pp. 88–121.

8. I have written two articles on the subject, "The Lute Song: An Aristotelian Tragedy in Confucian Dress," *Tamkang Review* (October, 1971–April, 1972):344–358; "The Lute Song Reconsidered: A Confucian Tragedy in Aristotelian Dress," *Tamkang Review* (October, 1975–April, 1976):449–464.

9. As translated by H. C. Chang, *Chinese Literature*, p. 88.

10. Xu Wei, *Nanci xulu*, in *Zhongguo gudian xiqu lunzhu jicheng* (Zhongguo xiju chubanshe, Beijing, 1959), vol. 3, p. 240.

11. Ibid., pp. 239–240, 243.

12. Lü Tiancheng, *Qupin* in *Zhongguo gudian xiqu lunzhu jicheng* (Zhongguo xiju chubanshe, Beijing, 1959), vol. 6, p. 224.

13. Gao Ming, *Pipa ji*, p. 1.

14. See the preface to *Pipa ji*.

15. *Qulun* in *Zhongguo gudian xiqu lunzhu jicheng* (Zhongguo xiju chubanshe, Beijing, 1959), vol. 4, p. 6.

16. Aoki Masaru, *Zhongguo jinshi xiqu shi*, trans. Wang Gulu (Shangwu yinshuguan, Shanghai, 1936), p. 119.

17. Colin Mackerras, "The Growth of the Chinese Regional Drama in the Ming and Ch'ing," *Journal of Oriental Studies* 9, no. 1 (January, 1971):58–91; Ye Dejun, "Mingdai nanxi," pp. 1–67.

18. Wei Liangfu, *Qulü* in *Zhongguo gudian xiqu lunzhu jicheng* (Zhongguo xiju chubanshe, Beijing, 1959), vol. 5, pp. 5–7.

19. *Qulun*, p. 240.

20. Lü Tiancheng, *Qupin*, p. 229.

21. Tang Xianzu, *Tang Xianzu ji* (Renmin shuju, Shanghai, 1973), vol. 1, pp. 659–662.

22. Lü Tiancheng, *Qupin*, p. 230.

23. H. C. Chang, *Chinese Literature*, p. 271. A succinct and precise biography of Tang Xianzu and translation of parts of *The Peony Pavilion* can be found on pp. 263–302.

24. Aoki Masaru, *Zhongguo jinshi*, pp. 314, 319.

25. Luo Jintang, *Mingdai juzuojia*, p. 4.

26. See for example, Zheng Qian, "Guben Yuan Ming zaju duhou ji," in *Jingwu congbian*, p. 392.

27. Zhu Quan, *Taihe zhengyin pu*, in *Zhongguo gudian xiqu lunzhu jicheng*, vol. 3, p. 11.

28. Zheng Yongyi, "Taihe zhengyin pude zuozhe wenti," in *Shuo xiqu* (Lianjing, Taibei, 1976), pp. 93–98.

29. A scene-by-scene synopsis of the play can be found in Glen Dudbridge, *The Hsi-yu chi, A Study of Antecedents to the Sixteenth-Century Chinese Novel* (Cambridge University Press, Cambridge, 1970), pp. 193–200.

30. *Qulü*, in *Zhongguo gudian xiqu lunzhu jicheng*, vol. 4, p. 167.

31. Zheng Yongyi, "Mingdai zaju yanjin de qingshi," *Chung Wai Literary Monthly* (October, 1972):15–18.

32. *Dugu xuzhi*, in *Zhongguo gudian xiqu lunzhu jicheng*, vol. 5, pp. 198–199.

33. W. L. Idema, "Stage and Court in China: The Case of Hung-wu's Imperial Theatre," *Oriens Estremus* (December, 1976):179–183, 186.

34. Zhou Yibai, *Zhongguo xiju shi,* p. 469.

35. Wang Liqi, "Yuan Ming Qing tongzhi jieji duidai xiaoshuo xiqude taidude kaocha," *Wenxue yichan zengkan* (Zuojia chubanshe, Beijing, 1957), vol. 5, pp. 217–218.

36. Zhang Jing, *Ming Qing chuanqi daolun* (Dongfang shudian, Taibei, 1961), pp. 122–125.

37. See *Zhuanghui tang wenji* (*Wenji* section), chap. 5, pp. 13a–13b.

38. Li Kaixian, *Cixue,* in *Zhongguo gudian xiqu lunzhu jicheng,* vol. 3, pp. 353–354.

39. Zhang Dai, *Taoan mengyi,* in *Yueya tang congshu* (Zhonghua shuju, Taibei, 1965), vol. 2, p. 881.

40. Ibid., p. 48.

41. Ibid.

42. Zhou Yibai, *Zhongguo xiju shi,* pp. 452–453.

43. Qi Rushan, *Qi Rushan quanji* (Lianjing, Taibei, 1979), vol. 1, p. 70.

44. Color plates of the basic costumes along with explanations in English and German can be found in Qi Rushan, *Qi Rushan quanji,* pp. 78–89. The first important study of costumes used in the Yuan and Ming theater was made by Feng Yuanjun in 1944 from fifteen Yuan *zaju* plays in Ming editions rarely seen before her time. She finds forty-seven kinds of dress for male characters and seven for female (see Feng Yuanjun, *Guju shuohui,* pp. 346–351). While her discovery seems to contradict Qi Rushan's observation, which is not documented, a careful analysis of her list of costumes indicates otherwise. She lists, for example, nine kinds of robes for males, including "robe," "yellow robe," "red robe," "black robe," and "tiger skin robe" (p. 348). Apparently they differ only in color or design patterns and belong to one kind in Qi Rushan's category. Since she admits that most of the names of the dresses are no longer identifiable, I have followed Qi. Furthermore, Qi's categories enable us to see the continuity and development of costumes used in traditional Chinese theater.

45. Wang Tingna, *Shi hou ji* (Kaiming shudian, Taibei, 1960), pp. 1, 11.

46. Qi Rushan, *Qi Rushan quanji,* p. 90.

47. Zhou Yibai, *Zhongguo xiju shi,* p. 461.

SELECTED READINGS

Aoki Masaru. *Zhongguo jinshi xiqu shi* [*History of recent Chinese drama*]. Translated from Japanese to Chinese by Wang Gulu. Shangwu yinshuguan, Shanghai, 1936. A pathbreaking general treatment of theater in China since the Song (960–1279), but with a particular focus on later periods.

Birch, Cyril, trans. *Anthology of Chinese Literature, Volume 2: From the 14th Century of the Present Day.* Grove, New York, 1972. This includes a translation of four scenes from *The Peony Pavilion.*

Hung, Josephine Huang. *Ming Drama.* Heritage Press, Taipei, 1966. A descriptive general study in English of Ming dynasty theater. The emphasis is primarily literary, though social aspects are not ignored.

Luo Jintang. *Mingdai juzuojia kaolue* [*A general investigation of the Ming drama-*

tists]. Longmen shudian, Hong Kong, 1966. A thorough treatment of Ming drama in general, the *zaju* writers, the *chuanqi* authors, and the various materials on Ming theater. The material is rich more for its information than for its analysis.

Mackerras, Colin. "The Growth of the Chinese Regional Drama in the Ming and Ch'ing." *Journal of Oriental Studies* 9, no. 1 (January, 1971):58–91. A useful discussion of the various styles of regional theater, including their music and how they related to each other.

Scott, A. C., trans. *Traditional Chinese Plays, Volume 2.* The University of Wisconsin Press, Madison, 1969. A translation, with copious annotation and explanation, of two *kunqu* dramas, *Longing for Worldly Pleasures (Sifan)* and *Shiwu guan (Fifteen strings of Cash).* The first was originally staged in the Ming period, the second in the seventeenth century, but the texts here used as the basis of translation are modern adaptations. Another translation of the second drama is that by Yang Hsien-yi and Gladys Yang, published under the title *Fifteen Strings of Cash* by the Foreign Languages Press, Peking, 1957. For play translations, see also the chapter II Selected Readings under Dolby.

The Peony Pavilion by T'ang Hsien-tsu, Indiana University Press, Bloomington, 1980.

Wang Gulu, ed. *Mingdai Huidiao xiqu sanchu jiyi* [*Collection of rare drama scenes of the Anhui music of the Ming dynasty*]. Gudian wenxue chubanshe, Shanghai, 1956. A fascinating collection of unusual regional theater excerpts from the Ming dynasty, with a brilliant interpretive introduction by Wang Gulu.

Wang Xiaochuan, ed. *Yuan Ming Qing sandai jinhui xiaoshuo xiqu shiliao* [*Historical material on the banned and burned novels and dramas of the Yuan, Ming, and Qing dynasties*]. Zuojia chubanshe, Beijing, 1958. A collection of edicts, central and local, on the drama and novel of the three dynasties listed in the title, together with an interpretive introduction by Wang Xiaochuan. Very useful for work on the social place of theater.

Zhao Jingshen. *Ming Qing qutan* [*Discussions of Ming and Qing drama*]. Zhonghua shuju, Beijing, 1959. A collection of papers on drama by one of the foremost Chinese theater scholars of contemporary times.

Zhao Jingshen. *Xiqu bitan* [*Notes on drama*]. Zhonghua shuju, Beijing, 1962. This work covers specific aspects of the Yuan, Ming, and Qing periods, but the major emphasis is on the Ming. The author treats specific styles of drama at length, including *kunqu,* as well as particular authors and works, e.g., Tang Xianzu and his *Peony Pavilion.*

CHAPTER IV

THE DRAMA OF
THE QING DYNASTY

Colin Mackerras

DYNASTIC CHANGES rarely form sharp breaks from a sociocultural point of view. The year 1644, which marked the accession of the Qing dynasty, is no turning point in the history of Chinese theater. On the other hand, dynasties often provide convenient general headings under which to discuss aspects of culture or society. The 267 years from 1644 to 1911 did collectively witness substantial, even fundamental, changes in the Chinese drama. They can be summarized as follows:

1. The sophisticated and aristocratic *kunqu* drama declined from what was possibly its highest point in the late Ming and very early Qing dynasty to almost total neglect and oblivion.
2. The regional theater of the masses rose from a period of already considerable importance and prosperity to dominate the Chinese stage.
3. The period saw the gestation, birth, and growth to maturity of the best known of the regional styles, still the most important of forms of traditional Chinese theater: the Beijing (Peking) opera.
4. Theater became a highly politicized form of art of which the relations with society were as tight as at any period in Chinese history.

THE WANING AND FALL OF *KUNQU*

Aoki Masaru, who has written what remains to this day one of the principal works on Chinese theater of the late imperial period, has divided the *kunqu* of the Qing dynasty into two broad periods. One lasts from the mid years of Kangxi (1662–1722) to the end of the

Qianlong era (1736–1795) and he has called it the "waning of *kunqu.*" The second covers the period from the Jiaqing era (1796–1820) to the end of the Qing dynasty; this he terms "the period of decline and fall."[1]

In neither of Aoki's two periods did the *kunqu* produce any major new literary style, such as it had done in the Ming. The music underwent very little change. As time went on the style became increasingly stereotyped. The classes that had created and patronized the *kunqu* during the Ming dynasty, that is to say the educated and ruling classes, continued their sponsorship, although, as the Qing period wore on, with decreasing enthusiasm and firmness. In fact, by the end of the "waning" period they had even begun to switch allegiance to other forms of drama. Although these classes continued to hear and watch *kunqu* at their banquets and to hire companies, the ownership of *kunqu* troupes within private mansions contracted sharply during the "decline and fall" period. During the latter half of the nineteenth century the pinnacle of society, the court, also began to transfer its attention away from this old style and toward greener pastures.

Although *kunqu* spread throughout the whole of China mainly through the movement of its patrons, especially officials, from area to area, the Yangzi valley region of Jiangsu and Zhejiang remained the heartland of its performance. Partly for this reason the mid-nineteenth century was a particularly disastrous time for this form of theater. The Taiping revolutionaries occupied the Jiangsu capital Nanjing for eleven years (1853–1864) and Suzhou and other Lower Yangzi cities for substantial periods. They were bitterly hostile to this aristocratic art, more so even than to other forms of theater, just as they were to its educated patrons. The economic disruption and human holocaust caused by the uprising contributed substantially to the decline and fall of the *kunqu*.

Of the *kunqu* dramas and dramatists of the Qing dynasty, all the most important belong, not surprisingly, to Aoki's waning rather than decline and fall period. Two dramas stand out: *The Palace of Eternal Youth (Changsheng dian),*[2] completed in 1688, and *The Peach Blossom Fan (Taohua shan),*[3] finished in 1699, composed respectively by Hong Sheng (1645–1704) and Kong Shangren (1648–1718). One nineteenth-century author says: "During the Kangxi reign *The Peach Blossom Fan* and *The Palace of Eternal Youth* were completed one after the other, so at the time people talked about

'Hong in the south and Kong in the north.' "[4] This saying has remained well known to this day.

The southern Hong Sheng came from Qiantang, Zhejiang province, but went to Beijing in his twenties. There he held a job in the Imperial College but he never attained prominence as an official. His main connection with the bureaucracy was perhaps through his wife, the granddaughter of the distinguished Huang Ji, who was grand secretary from 1682 to 1683.

Hong's *The Palace of Eternal Youth* gained immediate popularity on its completion, including the strong approbation of the Emperor Kangxi himself. This fact did not save him when in 1689 the opera was performed within two months of an empress' death, thus breaking an official taboo. Hong was dismissed from the College and forced to leave Beijing. He lived the latter part of his life in retirement, devoting himself to poetry, drama, and wine. The last of these three was an indirect cause of his death: during a boat journey he fell overboard while drunk and was drowned.

Hong Sheng wrote altogether eleven dramas. The only one to survive in full is *The Palace of Eternal Youth*. This opera deals with the famous Emperor Minghuang (713–756) of the Tang dynasty (618–907) and his love for his favorite concubine, Yang Guifei. The story is the subject of several well-known poems, including one by Bai Juyi, and earlier dramas. When the An Lushan rebellion breaks out in 755 the emperor flees the court and on the demand of his mutinous troops orders his favorite concubine to commit suicide, which she obediently does. Later, however, the drama ends happily when the two are reunited in the moon.

This opera is regarded by the Chinese as among their finest. Contemporary writers of varying political persuasions have continued the favorable appraisal. One professor of drama in Taiwan comments that "the merit of this play lies in the refinement and beauty of its lines, the elaborateness of its showmanship, perfect harmony of its musical compositions and the intricacy of its romantic and touching story."[5]

Scholars of the People's Republic of China are equally enthusiastic. One of them, Tu Pien-pu, draws attention to the aptness with which the tunes and the words are married to each other and to the opera's variety, especially in the alternation of tragic and humorous scenes. He is also struck by its political virtues, in particular its national spirit and its author's defense of Yang Guifei against the feudal charge that as a woman she was responsible for the dynasty's disastrous fate. Tu goes on, "Hung [Hong] Sheng invariably takes the side of the people. He attacks the shameless license of the court and the nobility, and pillories the corrupt and turncoat officials, but he shows great sympathy for the humbler characters in the drama and for the hard lot of the people."[6]

Kong Shangren was similar to Hong in that he too fell foul of the authorities over his drama. Initially all seemed favorable for him. He was a descendant of Confucius, and so had a good family background and, like his famous forebear, was a native of Qufu, Shandong province, hence the reference to him as a northerner. Like Hong he went to Beijing early and held official posts there, but of far greater importance and prestige than those of his older fellow dramatist. In 1699, the same year as the completion of *The Peach Blossom Fan*, Kong Shangren was relieved of office. The sources are silent on the reason why, but considering that the opera is strongly pro-Ming and consequently anti-Manchu, we may well agree with Harold Acton's verdict "that it was the reading in the Manchu Imperial palace of this threnody for the Ming which led to K'ung Shang-jen's [Kong Shangren's] dismissal from office."[7]

The Peach Blossom Fan is set in the last years of the Ming dynasty in Nanjing. It is similar to *The Palace of Eternal Youth* both in being strongly historical and a love story. All the main characters in it are drawn directly from history, and every scene is accurately dated. The hero is Hou Fangyu (1618–1655), a Ming loyalist in love with Li Xiangjun (Fragrant Princess). The two swear eternal love, and as a betrothal pledge Hou gives her a fan, on which, later, peach blossoms are painted in Fragrant Princess's own blood. Hou's enemies try to force her into marriage with a high official. The lovers are separated and do not meet again until after the Manchus have taken Nanjing. By that time each is living in a different Taoist religious house; a priest forces them apart forever to become a monk and a nun. This drama differs from most *kunqu* in its tragic end; there is no doubt that in the mind of the dramatist the religious life under the circumstances of Manchu occupation is indeed a tragedy.

The characterization of this drama is perhaps more effective than that of *The Palace of Eternal Youth*. The reader or audience can feel more sympathy for the lovers in *The Peach Blossom Fan*. In the former, the emperor's surrender to his mutinous soldiers' demand and the fact that the heroine is but a spirit for half of the opera detract from its human quality. One modern Chinese scholar concludes of

The Peach Blossom Fan that "in literary quality this drama ranks among the greatest in the Chinese language."[8] Cyril Birch makes a similar assessment: "Buried among the hundreds of southern-style plays, hardly ever performed and seldom even read today, are scenes of great verbal beauty, lively passion, or effective comedy. There are only a handful of plays, though, which taken as a whole can match *The Peach Blossom Fan* for quality."[9] It is in fact its literary value which is this drama's strongest point. The music has come under criticism for being inappropriate to the words, and some regard the plot as much too complicated for dramatic intensity.

There were no full successors to the mantle of Hong Sheng or Kong Shangren. The latter part of Aoki Masaru's waning period of *kunqu* produced comparatively few dramatists of stature. The foremost of the Qianlong period was Jiang Shiquan (1725–1785), whose works rank far below those discussed earlier.

Jiang Shiquan came from Jiangxi province and enjoyed a modestly successful official career. As a literary figure he was more remarkable, especially in his versatility. He took part in the compilation of several important historical works and was also recognized as being among the best poets of his time. He was a friend of Yuan Mei (1716–1798), certainly the most famous of the poets of eighteenth-century China.[10]

Nine of Jiang's dramas survive, the earliest dating from 1751, the latest from 1780. Their themes tend to be Confucian and moral. According to one modern authority, "he leaned towards realism, preferring themes from historical or contemporary events in which he could demonstrate the virtuous qualities in human nature."[11] Jiang was an ardent admirer of the Ming dramatist Tang Xianzu, discussed in chapter III, and consciously strove to imitate his style.

His realism and his admiration for Tang Xianzu both expressed themselves in *The Dream of Linchuan (Linchuan meng),* which dates from 1774 and is in *kunqu* style. Linchuan in Jiangxi is Tang Xianzu's birthplace. The drama concerns Tang's career, his drama *The Peony Pavilion,* and the woman Yu Erniang's admiration for this, Tang's most famous work. Jiang clearly aimed to extol Tang Xianzu, but one contemporary critic, in an apparent reference to Jiang's rigidly Confucianist approach, carps that all he does is "to show how upright he [Tang] is as an official and how he sits chatting with his many friends that have gathered around him with piles and piles of books scattered all over his study."[12]

In contrast to the attempted realism of Jiang stands the *Leifeng*

Pagoda (Leifeng ta), an anonymous eighteenth-century *kunqu* on a famous ancient fairy story about a white snake that turns into a beautiful woman. Over the centuries the story has been used in ballad and other forms. This drama is worth mentioning because the story was adapted as a Beijing opera by Tian Han, under the title *The White Snake (Baishe zhuan)*, and is among the most popular of all traditional operas in the People's Republic.[13]

The drama takes place in Hangzhou at the beautiful West Lake. The snake-turned-girl marries a scholar and lives happily with him, bearing a son. She is recognized as a snake by the monk Fahai, and after a famous reunion with her scholar-husband at the Broken Bridge, Fahai changes her back into a snake, burying her under the Leifeng Pagoda. There she will stay until the pagoda collapses and she is released. In Tian Han's version the drama concludes with this event, but in the anonymous Qing version the monk is a positive character, the snake negative, so the pagoda's destruction would not be a fortunate ending.

Josephine Huang Hung has suggested that Fahai symbolizes the spirit of opposition to the Manchus, represented by the white snake, and that this is a political protest.[14] Since we do not know even the name of the drama's author, it is difficult to be sure of his intentions. It appears, however, that the Manchus themselves did not object to this work. If there was protest against them in it, they were unaware of the fact.

One last facet of *kunqu* under the Qianlong Emperor deserves note: the court drama. Early in his reign the emperor ordered Zhang Zhao (1691–1745) to adapt some old dramas for performance at court. The result was seven enormously long works with musical scores mainly by Zhang. The stories were diverse, including those based on *The Romance of the Three Kingdoms (Sanguo zhi yanyi)* and Mulian and his mother as well as some depoliticized ones from *The Water Margin (Shuihu zhuan)* (see plate 17). About 1740 Qianlong set up schools to train eunuchs as actors to perform such dramas for the court. Both in the Beijing palaces and at the emperor's summer residence in Jehol (plate 18), theater was an important part of court life.[15]

Kunqu dramas survived both at the court and outside after the end of the Qianlong era. But it comes as no surprise that Aoki Masaru's period of decline and fall produced very little worth comment, and there are virtually no representative dramatists of note.

THE GROWTH OF REGIONAL DRAMA

Concurrent with the waning and decline and fall of the *kunqu* came the proliferation of different regional theatrical styles. By the time the Qing dynasty fell there were several hundred different types, each of them catering to a particular area or areas of China. Some were confined to only one or several counties within a single province; others were popular over an entire province or larger region. They differed from each other in the dialects of their librettos and in their music; for instance, the instruments which accompanied the singers varied from style to style.

One of the main methods whereby regional drama styles proliferated was that each area adapted to suit its own taste styles imported from other districts by wandering companies. These troupes would move from village to village, staying at each place for only a few days before proceeding to the next. They often followed trade routes, for the Qing dynasty was a peak period of Chinese internal interregional commerce.

The stories in the operas performed by wandering companies were usually similar to those of the *kunqu* or of popular novels. The custom was to extract a particular incident from a chapter of a novel and adapt it into a short opera lasting probably less than an hour. This was an appropriate practice because Chinese novels normally consist of incidents, each interesting in itself, rather than of a chain of episodes leading to a climax. Although the stories of the regional operas tended to remain constant from style to style, there were some particular stories with local flavor that were especially popular in one region but hardly known in others. In the same way, some acting techniques, stage properties, and costumes were peculiar to one region or style, but in general they did not differ much from one area to another.

The people who performed the regional operas were very low in social status; they were regarded by the law as slaves and suffered serious discrimination. It was a symbol of the contempt of society towards them that they were forbidden to sit for the official examinations, but of course very few of them wanted to or would have thought of doing so anyway. Like the performers, the audiences of the local drama were ordinary people. Indeed, this was truly popular theater and among the most genuine forms of mass traditional art that China produced.

Regional theater styles were able to spread so widely throughout China because they depended for expansion neither upon fixed per-

formers nor upon the patronage of the rich. Indeed, the upper echelons of society were at first rather unhappy about this development
and reacted to it with contempt. For any educated person of the early
Qing period to show interest in regional popular theater was tantamount to social suicide. As the dynasty wore on, however, attitudes
began to change. By the latter part of the Qianlong period we find
examples of officials, scholars, and well-to-do merchants who were
prepared to take an interest in, and even develop a liking for, the various styles of regional drama. A particular example of such a scholar-
official was Yan Changming (1731–1787), who in about 1780 published a detailed exposition on why he believed the regional opera of
the Shaanxi capital Xi'an should be taken seriously.[16] At about the
same time, Jiang Chun (1725–1793), one of the most distinguished
salt merchants of the city of Yangzhou, the hub of China's largest salt
administration, was prepared to devote considerable effort to founding and maintaining his own regional opera troupe.[17] While it is true
that merchants were traditionally not a high class in Chinese society,
the salt merchants of Yangzhou were so rich that they were able to
buy their way to social prestige, among other ways, by procuring education for themselves and their families.

Most of the several hundred styles of regional opera that developed
under these circumstances belonged to a limited number of systems
or broad categories. One of the earliest of these was that of Yiyang
(Yiyang qiang), called after its place of origin, Yiyang in Jiangxi province. The system had arisen during the Ming dynasty (see chap. III),
and by the early Qing period, numerous of its variant styles were
found in different parts of China, including Beijing itself, where it
was called the Capital style. In fact, during the eighteenth century
this particular variant became popular not only among the masses of
the city but even among the aristocracy. In the 1770s one of the most
famous theater troupes in Beijing was the Great Company of the
Princely Mansions, which specialized in the Capital style of local
opera.

A little later to develop than the Yiyang system was that known as
clapper opera *(bangzi qiang).* Since its growth to maturity and proliferation through much of China were features of the Qing dynasty, it
merits more detailed treatment here.

The actual place of origin of the clapper opera is not known exactly.
However, the signs point to a core area of development in adjoining
regions of Shaanxi and Shanxi provinces, specifically Dali in eastern

Shaanxi and nearby Puzhou in the southwestern corner of Shanxi (see plates 19 and 20). When clapper opera was first heard is likewise uncertain. The first precise references date from the early years of the Qing period; but since the educated elite, who wrote the works on which our knowledge depends, certainly would have needed time to sense the development of a new system of popular drama, the likelihood is that the seeds of clapper opera were already germinating in the late Ming dynasty.

A good point at which to begin a general discussion on the clapper opera is the following observation by the contemporary scholar Xia Ye:

> Just like the other theatrical styles, when the clapper opera gradually spread from Dali to every northern and southern region, because of the continual influence of the folk and theatrical music of each particular region, the melodies underwent varying degrees of alterations and formed quite a number of different kinds of clapper opera. Take, for example, the Shaanxi clapper opera as a representative of the clapper opera; there are also the different versions called "Eastern Road," "Western Road," and "Middle Road." However, apart from the somewhat great changes in the melodies of clapper operas of certain particular regions such as the Henan clapper opera, the other clapper styles are fairly similar to each other.[18]

The observations about where clapper opera spread need expansion. A work on Hunan and Hubei by Liu Xianting (1648–1695) mentions, "the new sounds of the actors of Qin."[19] Liu is clearly referring to the clapper opera here, since Qin is the standard name for Shaanxi, suggesting that the system of clapper operas had already spread to central-southern China fairly early in the Qing period. Most unusual evidence is found also in the diary of the coauthor of one of Kong Shangren's dramas, Gu Cai, who visited the rather remote city of Hefeng in the far southwest of Hubei in 1703 and found clapper opera widely performed there.[20] Wandering companies appear to have brought the clapper opera to the southwestern province of Sichuan also, where by the late eighteenth century a truly magnificent tradition of clapper actors had developed.

But it was above all in the north of China that clapper opera became so popular and important. From Shaanxi and Shanxi it spread to Henan, Hebei (then called Zhili) and Beijing itself. It may be that the Shanxi bankers who dominated Beijing finance created the demand for the regional opera of their home province. In addition, the more northwesterly provinces of Qinghai and Gansu abounded in different styles of clapper opera.

Xia Ye comments that most styles of clapper opera are actually rather similar to each other. There are several important characteristics all of them share. In the first place they are, as their name implies, dominated by the clapper. In Chinese opera there are two quite different types of clapper. One, termed *ban,* consists of three strips of wood, two of which are fastened to each other; with a flick of his wrist the player induces two of the three strips to strike together making a sharp wooden sound. The other type of clapper, *bangzi,* is a block of datewood which the player strikes with a stick. It is the latter kind that is characteristic of the clapper opera.

A second feature common to all styles of the clapper opera system is the division of the music into "happy sounds" and "weeping sounds." The peculiarity of the latter is its use of quarter-tones; the 4th of the scale (termed "subdominant" in European music) is a little sharpened, whereas the 7th ("leading note") is slightly flattened. The interval between the 7th and the tonic is thus just over a semitone but less than a tone.

The rhythm of the clapper opera is also fairly constant from style to style; indeed it is very close to that of other styles of Chinese regional opera, including the Beijing opera. The basic rhythm is termed "one beat, three eyes" *(yiban sanyan)* and corresponds to the quick, simple 4/4 time of Western music. Some sections are in 2/4 time or free rhythm. For tragic scenes the slow 4/4 is particularly important.

In terms of content, all clapper opera styles, like those of other systems, can be divided into "civilian" and "military," the former chiefly love stories, the latter tales of heroism and battles. Although the librettos of popular operas were but rarely written down until recent times, examples of eighteenth-century clapper operas do survive in the famous collection *Zhui baiqiu,* its preface written in 1770, in the sixth and eleventh volumes of a total of twelve. The most famous clapper item recorded there is probably *Selling Cosmetics (Mai yan-zhi),* in volume six. Very much in the civilian category, it is a short love story about a scholar who falls in love at first sight with a girl selling cosmetics. The piece is typical of its kind in its brevity and simplicity and in the flirtatiousness of its content.

In the clapper opera of Shaanxi the civilian items include in their accompanying orchestra a range of stringed, bowed intruments as well as the side-blown Chinese flute. The leading instrument is the stringed *ergu xuan,* which is "in shape the same as the two-stringed Chinese fiddle but with a shorter neck; the two strings are made of cattle tendons; the player wears iron guards over his fingers; the sound is sharp, fine and ear-splitting."[21] The military scenes use far more drums, cymbals, and other percussion instruments.

As the Qing dynasty progressed and the clapper opera spread, famous actors of its various styles flourished. By far the greatest of them was Wei Changsheng (1744–1802), an exponent of Sichuan clapper opera. Like so many well-known actors of regional styles, he fell foul of the authorities through his bawdy acting. This undoubtedly was a sign that he was good in the civilian drama and made him popular with the masses, whatever the government's view. He was also proficient in the acrobatics that have thrilled Chinese audiences for so long and are very characteristic of military scenes.

A much later distinguished actor was Tian Jiyun (1865–1925) of the Hebei clapper opera. He also was an object of suspicion to the government, not for his bawdiness but for something much more serious— his progressive political opinions. An active supporter of the Hundred Days Reform in 1898, he was arrested by the Empress Dowager, though later released through the good offices of the Beijing opera actor Sun Juxian. He consciously espoused revolution in the dramas he performed both in Beijing and elsewhere in the first decade of the twentieth century and spent time in prison for so doing. One of his artistic contributions was to "create the precedent of performing clapper and Beijing opera together, so that Hebei clapper opera absorbed nourishment from Beijing opera."[22]

BEIJING OPERA

Wei Changsheng and Tian Jiyun form a suitable bridge leading to consideration of the Beijing opera, the most widespread of the regional styles.

Together with numerous followers, Wei arrived in Beijing in 1779, probably in order to take part in the celebrations for the Qianlong Emperor's seventieth birthday the following year, and stayed there for six years, creating a tremendous impact. Wei Changsheng's sojourn on the Beijing stage once again made the city the capital of China not only in politics but also in theater. Although he was a clapper actor, the Beijing opera even today retains aspects of the music, actions, and stories he performed. One may regard his stay as the prelude to the birth of Beijing opera.

Wei Changsheng and his followers were banned from the Beijing stage in 1785, but other groups of actors came to take their place. In 1790 Qianlong's eightieth birthday attracted to the capital a number of theater troupes from Anhui province; they were performers of the styles *erhuang* and *xipi*. Since these two collectively form the basis of the Beijing opera even today, the year 1790—the first that they were heard on the Beijing stage—has come to be popularly regarded as the birth of Beijing opera.

Of course, both styles already had a history outside Beijing. *Erhuang* originated in Yihuang county, Jiangxi province, in the Ming dynasty and spread to many southern provinces, especially Anhui, in the early part of the Qing. *Xipi* was a variant of the clapper opera. Actually, although the two were thus initially separate, the unity of *erhuang* and *xipi* is now a characteristic not only of Beijing opera, but of Cantonese, Hubei, and many others as well. It was probably in Anhui in the Qianlong period that the dual combination began.

The Anhui actors who had introduced the two styles to Beijing were followed by many others from the southern provinces, especially Anhui, Jiangsu, and, from about 1830 onward, Hubei as well. In the minds of the public Anhui remained the most significant. This is evident from the use of the term "the Four Great Anhui Companies" to apply to those groups that dominated the Beijing stage through most of the nineteenth century. The four were the Chuntai, the Sixi, the Sanqing, and the Hechun. The first of them lasted the longest and disbanded finally only because of the Boxer Uprising in 1900.

Indeed, the Boxers and the eight-power foreign invasion of China and occupation of the capital to suppress them caused considerable destruction in Beijing city and resulted in the demolition of several of its major theaters. None of the major companies of the nineteenth century survived the holocaust, and from 1900 onward new and different companies, usually attached to specific actors, were in control of the theaters of Beijing.

Beginning with the emergence of the Anhui companies, the Beijing opera showed a number of important development characteristics. As far as the records tell us, all the most important performers of the early period were *dan*, that is to say, male actors who impersonated women on the stage. Wei Changsheng had belonged to this category and was noted for devising a technique for imitating the gait of a woman's bound feet (see chap. V). Gao Langting, the best-known actor of the early Anhui companies, was also a *dan*.

In the last years of the eighteenth century a custom grew up that provided a large supply of *dan* actors to the Beijing stage and, for a while, kept the *dan* art dominant. This was the purchase of little boys in the southern provinces, especially Jiangsu and Anhui, to be trained and put on the stage in Beijing. Specially employed managers were sent to selected cities in southern China to seek willing parents, mainly those whose poverty gave them very little chance to reject any offer of an agreement which would profit them financially. A typical contract stipulated the return of the child after a given period, but in fact, the parents had no way whatever of ensuring fulfillment. Even more powerless was the boy himself. Once in Beijing he joined a training school that was itself attached to one of the major companies of Beijing, especially the Four Great Anhui Companies. Although their treatment there was harsh, including severe corporal punishment for minor omissions or mistakes, those boys who did well achieved a reasonably high standard of living and sometimes even wealth and fame.

These boys fulfilled another function besides that of actor. Wei Changsheng had been a homosexual lover to several eminent men in Beijing, including Heshen (1750–1799), the most powerful minister of the day. The little boys who followed him enjoyed less choice in such matters, and many of them became boy courtesans. Although homosexuality among actors had been common since long before the rise of the Beijing opera—the poet Yuan Mei (1716–1798) was only one among many men to have love affairs with young actors—it appears to have become unusually prevalent in nineteenth-century Beijing. One scholar, writing in 1876 under the pen name Shuxi qiao ye, tells us the main reason why: "I particularly feel that there are no flowers [female courtesans] left. If one is choosing smiles or fine songs, one needs to go to the acting companies."[23] Legal constraints against female prostitutes had led to their decline. Yang Moujian, a writer and Beijing opera enthusiast, noted in 1842 that one area of town had formerly flourished as a female brothel area, "but now there are no wine shops and as for the houses of debauchery, everyone covers his nose and passes them by."[24]

The fact that the young actors were substituting for women, both in social life and on the stage, carried an important implication for the themes of the dramas they performed. As long as *dan* actors dominated the stage, the Beijing operas were largely civilian; very few were military. Love stories, short and simple items about marital fidelity, and religious pieces were of prime importance. A typical example was *Selling Cosmetics,* already mentioned as a clapper opera; it is not surprising that it was taken into the Beijing opera repertoire. Another popular example of the early period was *Longing for Worldly Pleasures (Sifan)* about a nun in search of love who escapes from a convent.[25]

In about the third decade of the nineteenth century the themes began to change. Military scenes based on novels, especially *The Romance of the Three Kingdoms,* reasserted themselves. Heroism replaced love as the dominant force of the Beijing stage. Acrobatics came back with a vengeance.

What made all this possible was the rise of the *sheng* actors, who were mature and performed the parts of men, including ministers, generals, and various heroes. The most famous of these *sheng* actors was Cheng Zhanggeng (1812–c. 1880), who performed to great perfection many of the standard heroic roles of *The Three Kingdoms* and other novels. He is described in the sources as extremely honest, upright, and hardworking; in some ways a somewhat Confucian type of character. The boy actors did not of course disappear, although the system for recruiting them began to change at the turn of the century. Many continued to act as *dan* as they matured. It became possible as the nineteenth century wore on to train equally well all categories of actors and thus produce a balanced fare of civilian and military theater. Cheng Zhanggeng may have been the most famous, but there were many actors who approached his stature. The second half of the nineteenth century was the real heyday of the Beijing opera.

Another factor in its triumph at this time was that the imperial court, for so long a bastion of conservatism and thus a patron of *kunqu,* began to espouse the cause of the Beijing opera. In 1860, for the first time, the emperor invited actors from the city of Beijing to perform in his own palaces. As on several occasions before, it was an imperial birthday, the thirtieth of Xianfeng (1851–1861), that brought about this change in the fortunes of the Beijing opera. This was a very traumatic time for the emperor, however. Only two months after the first performance, British and French troops occupied Beijing and Xianfeng fled to Jehol, where he died the following year. The practice he had begun was suspended.

In 1884, the Empress Dowager Cixi (1835–1908) revived Xianfeng's plan. In order to celebrate her own fiftieth birthday she brought several well-known actors in from the city to perform in the imperial palaces. From that time until the fall of the Qing dynasty they came in a continuous stream, some to take up residence at court, some for individual performances only. The Empress Dowager and other members of the court thus were able to enjoy the Beijing opera and they patronized it with enthusiasm. The Dowager would transmit commands to actors on how they should perform particular sections. She also offered encouragement to favorite actors, including the famous Tan Xinpei (1847–1917), a constant visitor to the court in the last decade or so of her rule, on whom she even bestowed an official rank.

THE BEGINNINGS OF THE SPOKEN PLAY

The last years of the reign of the Empress Dowager saw a considerable increase in the pressures for reform and modernization. In particular, China's defeat at the hands of Japan in the Sino-Japanese War of 1894–1895 and the aftermath of the Boxer uprising brought about a situation such that even the Empress Dowager herself was forced to issue decrees in favor of reform.

It was in this context that a completely new form of theater, based on a foreign model, took root in China; namely, the spoken play *(huaju)*. Up to this point all drama had been sung, and the nearest approach to a spoken play had been a form of stylized semichanted dialogue. The idea that actors might talk to each other on the stage, rather than sing, was a new one for the Chinese tradition. Tian Han, one of modern China's foremost dramatists, describes the beginnings of the spoken play as follows:

> After the Sino-Japanese War of 1894 [*sic*], in order to demonstrate their anger against the corrupt rule of the Qing dynasty and the imperialist aggressors and in order to arouse the consciousness of the broad suffering people, the patriotic intellectual youth often made use of [traditional] artistic forms . . . to carry on enlightened patriotic propaganda. This had a definite function, but it was not until the discovery and the first stages of adoption of the spoken play form that they found a new sharp tool for the direct expression of their political feelings. Before this, through the missionary schools of Shanghai, Guangzhou, and Suzhou, they had introduced some Shakespeare and Molière and at the same time a few folk theater workers had begun pioneer

activity in a form similar to plays. But this still did not have too great a social influence, and for the response to the nationalist Chinese movement of the beginning of this century it is more appropriate to count from the Chunliu (Spring Willow) Society, which introduced the European play form in a regular way and was organized by Chinese students studying in Japan.[26]

In other words, the Chinese spoken play was in fact first performed in Japan, where the new form, as in China based upon a European model, had been introduced not long before. The Norwegian Henrik Ibsen (1828–1906), the Briton George Bernard Shaw (1856–1950), and other contemporary European playwrights were already influencing the Japanese scene, and some of their works had been translated into Japanese. Dramas with explicit social or political commentary were common and fairly popular.

Tian Han's reference to the Chunliu (Spring Willow) Society requires explanation. This was the first Chinese drama troupe to perform a Chinese spoken play. Established in Japan early in 1907, it put on, in February of that year, one act of the drama *Chahua nü,* a translation of *La dame aux camélias* by Alexandre Dumas *fils* (1824–1895), as part of a more general program to aid disaster relief. Parts of China, in particular northern Anhui and Jiangsu, were at that time suffering unusually acute famine, and Chinese students in Japan hoped through their activity to raise money towards the alleviation of the disaster.

On the first and second day of June of the same year, the Spring Willow Society gave successive performances of the first full-length formal Chinese spoken play in history: *The Black Slave's Cry to Heaven (Heinu yutian lu)*. The play was adapted from a Chinese translation of *Uncle Tom's Cabin,* the influential novel by the American Harriet Beecher Stowe (1811–1896). The central theme of the play, like the novel, was the evil of slavery and, by extension, of oppression of the masses in general.

These pioneering spoken plays exemplify two important points. One is that many of the early works were translations of Western dramas or novels; they were not originally Chinese, and their social context and setting were not Chinese. The second point is the emphasis on social commentary. As Tian Han observed, this was a specifically political activity; it was seen as such both by the young actors and, in particular, by the authorities. Ouyang Yuqian, himself a member of Spring Willow, writes that "at that time, the Chinese Legation [in

Tokyo] was very much opposed to the performance of dramas by the Chinese students studying in Japan; there were a few people who had for a time been happy to take part in the Spring Willow Society but because they feared this might have an effect on their own future gradually stopped coming."[27]

For this and a number of other reasons the Spring Willow Society did not remain in existence very long. Its last major performance was in 1909, of a play called *Hot Blood (Rexue)*, an adaptation of Victorien Sardou's (1831–1908) *La Tosca*. The Chinese play came from a Japanese version of Sardou's work, which was already much better known in the form of an opera by Puccini. *Hot Blood* was not a success. "Unlike *Uncle Tom's Cabin*, *Tosca* received not a single notice from Japanese critics, but only brought a final threat from the Chinese Legation, . . . that performers would lose their scholarships."[28]

Along with Ouyang Yuqian, one of the leading lights of the Spring Willow Society in Tokyo was Ren Tianzhi. He had earlier suggested that the company should go to Shanghai to perform, but this proved impossible because of the students' other commitments. Later in 1907, however, he, Wang Zhongsheng, and others succeeded in organizing the Chunyang (Spring) Society in Shanghai, which performed *The Black Slave's Cry to Heaven* there for more than a month. Like its Tokyo counterpart the Spring Society did not last long, yet its production of this adaptation of *Uncle Tom's Cabin* does enjoy a certain importance in Chinese history, being the first spoken play to be performed in China itself.

The years following 1907 saw the performance, mainly in Shanghai, of a number of spoken plays, or "civilization dramas" as they were also called, and the establishment of several societies to organize and carry out the productions. By far the most important of them was the Jinhua (Progress) Troupe that Ren Tianzhi set up in Shanghai in October 1910. Its repertoire included plays adapted from foreign drama as well as from Chinese and foreign novels. Shortly after its founding the Progress Troupe went on tour. In January 1911, for instance, it visited Nanjing, which thus saw a spoken play for the first time. Indeed, within a few years after the establishment of the Progress Troupe there were a number of cities outside Shanghai that enjoyed the services of "civilization drama" companies.

Nevertheless, the spoken play had enjoyed but small beginnings in China up to the time of the 1911 Revolution. Its scope remained minute by comparison with the traditional Chinese theater. Yet its significance cannot be ignored, either in its newness or in the very conscious and specific propaganda role against the Manchus that its molders attempted to play. The civilization dramas did exert a certain degree of influence among urban intellectuals, and to that extent may have played a role, albeit a very small one, in creating the kind of political and social climate that resulted in the collapse of the Manchu dynasty.

THE POLITICIZATION OF DRAMA

The propaganda function of the civilization dramas is part of a more general tendency in Qing theater, namely its politicization. It is possible to relate the decline of *kunqu,* the rise of the popular mass theater, and the beginnings of the spoken play to the deterioration of China's Confucian ruling classes and the rise of the anti-Confucian rebellious movements of the late Qing period. The precise role of theater was to influence the attitudes of the people—and the general direction was against the Qing rulers and against Confucianism.

As background to this general theme it will be useful to note the tight integration of drama into the lives of the people at this time. One local historian of late nineteenth-century Zhili makes the following comments on the ways theater functioned in the villages:

> When it came to the appointed days [during temple fairs] various drama performances were given and all kinds of goods displayed [for sale]. Men and women mixed in confusion and, taking hold of incense and flowers, would go to the temples in search of good fortune. . . .
> The village would give opera performances on the gods' feast days and hold fairs. In this way they made known regulations, such as forbidding chickens, lambs, oxen, or sheep to harm the green crops, and women and children to steal grain or other types of things. The prohibitions were written up in large characters, and anyone who infringed them was liable to punishment. . . . On occasion, when people went to the temples to pray because of drought, locusts, or torrential rain, and no disaster followed, opera performances were given by way of thanksgiving. No particular dates were set.[29]

Several points stand out from this passage. The first is the tight connection with commerce; to hold a drama performance was a necessary and useful part of buying and selling. Second, drama performances were inevitable companions of religion and religious festivals.

One part of this is the use of drama to give thanks to the gods. Another point is that drama was used to communicate necessary information—to make known village regulations and prohibitions.

The specific connection between theater, society, and politics lay in drama's being the most important means of communication with the people. In an age without such modern mechanisms as radio or television the only form of art with a genuine mass basis was bound to assume great importance as a transmitter of the standards of morality, both social and political.

The relationship between theater and religion is illustrated by the guildhalls common in Qing China. These were social and religious bodies containing members of a single craft, trade, or profession. It was common for the guildhall to have its own stage (see plate 21) and for performances to accompany festivities in honor of the craft's patron god or other social or religious occasions.

As for social morality, we find throughout the records of the Qing dynasty constant references to a slackening of "proper" family life resulting from drama performances. "Men and women mix in confusion" is a common phrase in the records, not merely in the extract from Zhili quoted above. The modern sociologist C. K. Yang notes that some families even prohibited their womenfolk from attending temple fairs and such occasions, which of course included drama performances, because of the feared impact on family life.[30]

The religious life of the Chinese involved both social and political morality. C. K. Yang has observed: "It is clear that the theater served the function of assembling the community for religious worship and keeping community recreation under religious influence."[31] Yang is no doubt right, but "religious influence" over "community recreation" may actually not have been so welcome from the point of view of the authorities. The fact is that the Manchus were very sensitive to the ability of religions to influence secret societies and, consequently, rebels. Virtually all the Manchu emperors were obsessed with the threat of rebellion. They were, of course, not alone in this, but the fact that they were foreigners whose rule had been imposed upon an initially reluctant China only served to heighten their nervousness.

If the Manchu authorities treated religions with suspicion, the same feeling extended to its companion, the theater. The government was afraid lest the mass theater should operate more in its opponents' interests than in its own. The Manchus imposed strict censorship on all forms of theater during the whole of their dynasty. Again, there was nothing peculiar about that, but we may well agree with the modern scholar Wang Xiaochuan, who has collected all the edicts against novels and dramas, of the Yuan, Ming, and Qing periods, that the Qing was substantially fiercer with regard to censorship than its predecessor, the Ming.[32]

Wang claims that the severity of the Manchus' attitude aroused considerable opposition among the people; he cites as evidence the example of an official called Zhang Binzuo who, in 1758, "prohibited drama performances among the peasants and, as a result, was beaten up and bound by the people."[33] Wang is probably correct, but the extent of resentment against censorship is quite impossible to judge simply because such matters do not usually find their way into the official works on which so much of our historical knowledge depends. Moreover, censorship is likely to be only a part—and a not very important one at that—of the concern of rebellious movements. What is beyond doubt is that the number and scale of rebellions in the latter part of the Qing dynasty was very great.

The most important particular work that the authorities found offensive politically was the novel *The Water Margin (Shuihu zhuan)*; they issued numerous edicts against it because of its praise and support for rebels. The Manchus certainly knew that incidents taken from the novel were dramatized in performances that departed from the desensitized version of their own court. Witness the following statement from a censor called Hu Ding appealing (successfully) for censorship in 1754:

Shuihu zhuan regards cruel and violent people as good Chinese, and rebels as remarkable and able people; those who revolt escape punishment, which is belittled. . . . Actors have adapted it into dramas and in the marketplace worthless people watch them. . . . In 1714 it was suggested to forbid bookshops to sell lewd dramas and novels, so I, your subject, beg you to issue a severe prohibition, to have the book blocks of the *Shuihu zhuan* destroyed and to forbid its performance on the stage.[34]

It cannot have escaped Hu Ding that performances on the stage reached a wider audience than the novel did simply because illiterates, who constituted the great majority, could watch and understand a theater show. Just as important is the fact that, unlike novel reading, a drama performance creates a collective mass atmosphere; this enables it to exercise a greater unconscious influence on the minds of the people than does any novel.

It is not difficult to find specific cases of rebellion that the government believed were to some extent incited by dramas or novels known to have been dramatized. In 1851 a group of Hunanese and Sichuanese secret societies or "religious bandits," as the official documents calls them, were accused of owing many of their ideas to *The Water Margin,* with the result that yet another edict against the novel was promulgated.[35] This particular action was of great importance because of the considerable power that many affiliated secret societies had been able to accumulate. Indeed, the famous Triad rebellion of Guangdong and other southern provinces flared up in 1854, only three years after this edict, and it was influenced by the theater not only in its ideology but also in the fact that one of its principal leaders, Li Wenmao, was an actor who actually led an army of others of his trade.

The Triad rebellion was distinct from but yet connected with the greatest of all rebellions against the Manchu dynasty, the Taiping, which lasted from 1850 to 1866 and covered virtually every province in southern China. Its ideology was very carefully worked out and initially bitterly anti-Confucian and strongly egalitarian. Ironically, the Taiping government actually banned theater altogether in 1859. However, the records illustrate clearly that actors operating in Taiping-controlled areas continued their trade and felt no compunction or fear at so doing. The Taipings were influenced by the ideas of the rebels in the *The Water Margin,* and it appears that their followers used theater performances to espouse the religious, egalitarian, anti-Manchu, and anti-Confucian aspects of their ideology, despite the formal ban.[36]

Similarly, actors propagated from the stage the revolutionary ideas rampant in the Qing dynasty's last decade. Tian Jiyun has been mentioned already, as well as the whole phenomenon of the spoken play. One of the main exponents of this form, Wang Zhongsheng, was even arrested, interrogated, and executed in 1911 by the Manchu authorities for sedition, a charge he proudly accepted. "Quite a few members of the Progress Troupe were sacrificed in the 1911 revolutionary movement."[37] Moreover, a number of actors and theater producers took part militarily in the action that seized the Jiangnan Arsenal in Shanghai for the revolutionaries on November 3, 1911.

The leaders and followers of the revolution were conscious of the influence that drama could exercise. Even outside China itself theater performances successfully encouraged support and donations for the revolution among Overseas Chinese.

Apart from direct political influence, much of it derived from passages inserted into operas or plays themselves not directly on revolutionary subjects, there is another very important aspect of the politicization of drama. It is the question of attitudes, value systems, and images. In every society people tend to derive their values from fictional people with whom they identify and whom they regard as heroes worthy of emulation. They may not realize that this process is going on, and in many cases would be prepared to deny it if it were pointed out to them. What happened in Qing China was that the moral, social, and political values that were projected by drama performances gradually tended to change. Confucian virtues such as loyalty, filial piety, and uprightness shrank in impact as the dynasty progressed and were replaced by others hostile to the ideals of the Manchus and Confucianism.

The Manchu government evidently was aware that this was happening. In an edict of January 11, 1814, we find the following statement:

> As for the performance of drama among the people, this has never been prohibited. But every time [actors] delight in performing the roles of good and brave people or dramas about fighting, not knowing the lesser people, many of them mistakenly treat robbers as heroes, and rebellion as righteousness. The people become familiar through long exposure and the harm it causes is particularly extreme.[38]

The author of this edict does not use words like "value system" or "image," but his statement could hardly be more explicit all the same. The authorities were aware that influence is best exerted in unconscious ways while the targets do not know it is happening.

The Qing dynasty forms a decisive period in the history of the modern Chinese theater. Mass drama achieved a position of great importance when the ruling classes began to abandon their own declining *kunqu* in its favor. A process had gathered some momentum which was to lead to an even more vital mass theater in the People's Republic. At the same time, both the authorities and their opponents could see how popular opera could be used as a weapon for their own particular political purposes. Especially after the West began to make its presence felt in China and brought with it new possibilities in terms of armaments, value systems, and educational and governmental methods, the emperors and their ideology faced increasing challenge and threat. Obviously, they fought for survival with every means at their disposal, including the attempt to influence the attitudes of the people through drama. Conversely, those who sought to undermine the imperial system were in many cases just as aware of the need for popular support and the potential of drama in winning it. The political consciousness of both the imperial court and the people at large rose enough so that no government could hope to remain in power for long without some kind of mass support. Communicating with the masses, either directly or indirectly, thus assumed a significant political function. It is, consequently, possible to argue that the decline of the aristocratic *kunqu*, the simultaneous rise of the mass drama, including the Beijing opera, the beginning of the spoken play, and the general politicization of drama during the Qing dynasty were factors both contributing to and reflecting the overthrow of the Manchus and that of the Confucian system as a whole.

NOTES

1. Aoki Masaru, *Zhongguo jinshi xiqu shi,* trans. Wang Gulu, (Shangwu yinshuguan, Shanghai, 1936), pp. 376, 468.

2. Translated under the given English title by Yang Hsien-yi and Gladys Yang; published by the Foreign Languages Press in Peking, 1955.

3. Translated under this English title by Chen Shih-hsiang and Harold Acton with the collaboration of Cyril Birch; published by the University of California Press in Berkeley, 1976.

4. Yang Enshou, *Ciyu conghua,* in *Zhongguo gudian xiqu lunzhu jicheng* (Zhongguo xiju chubanshe, Beijing, 1959), vol. 9, chap. 2, p. 251.

5. Josephine Huang Hung, *Ming Drama* (Heritage Press, Taipei, 1966), p. 214.

6. " 'The Palace of Eternal Youth' and Its Author," in *The Palace of Eternal Youth* (Foreign Languages Press, Peking, 1955), p. 320.

7. *The Peach Blossom Fan by K'ung Shang-jen,* trans. Chen Shih-hsiang and Harold Acton (University of California Press, Berkeley, 1976), pp. xi–xii.

8. Tu Lien-chê, in Arthur W. Hummel, ed., *Eminent Chinese in the Ch'ing Period (1644–1912)* (United States Government Printing Office, Washington, 1943–1944), p. 435.

9. "Introduction: *The Peach Blossom Fan* as Southern Drama," in *The Peach Blossom Fan,* p. xvi.

10. For a full-length study of Jiang Shiquan, see Zhu Xiang, "Jiang Shiquan," in Zheng Zhenduo, ed., *Zhongguo wenxue yanjiu* (Zhongguo wenxue yanjiushe, Hong Kong, 1963), pp. 467–488.

11. Tu Lien-chê, in Hummel, ed., *Eminent Chinese*, p. 142.

12. Hung, *Ming Drama*, p. 227.

13. See the translation by Yang Hsien-yi and Gladys Yang in *The White Snake (A Peking Opera)* (Foreign Language Press, Peking, 1957).

14. Hung, *Ming Drama*, pp. 232–233.

15. I have discussed the Qing court theater in *The Rise of the Peking Opera, Social Aspects of the Theatre in Manchu China* (Clarendon Press, Oxford, 1972), pp. 116–124, 154–161.

16. *Qinyun xieying xiao pu, in Shuangmei jing'an congshu*, pp. 9b–12b.

17. Li Dou, *Yangzhou huafang lu*, Qingdai shiliao biji congkan ed. (Zhonghua shuju, Beijing, 1960), chap. 5, especially pp. 107, 131.

18. *Xiqu yinyue yanjiu* (Wenyi chubanshe, Shanghai, 1959), p. 52.

19. *Guangyang zaji*, Qingdai shiliao biji congkan ed. (Zhonghua shuju, Beijing, 1957), chap. 3, p. 152.

20. *Rongmei jiyou*, in *Xiaofang huzhai yudi congchao* (1891–1897), vol. 6, p. 5a.

21. An Bo, *Qinqiang yinyue*, Minjian yinyue congshu (Xin wenyi chubanshe, Shanghai, 1952), p. 6.

22. *Zhongguo difang xiqu jicheng, Hebei sheng juan* (Zhongguo xiju chubanshe, Beijing, 1959), "Qianyan," p. 2.

23. *Yantai huashi lu*, in *Qingdai Yandu liyuan shiliao* (Suiya zhai shudian, Beiping, 1937), vol. 2, preface, p. 1a.

24. *Menghua suobu*, in *Qingdai Yandu liyuan shiliao*, vol. 2, p. 19a.

25. See a translation of this drama by A. C. Scott in *Traditional Chinese Plays, Volume 2* (The University of Wisconsin Press, Madison, 1969), pp. 21–37.

26. Tian Han, "Zhongguo huaju yishu fazhan de jinglu he zhanwang," in Tian Han et al., eds., *Zhongguo huaju yundong wushi nian shiliao ji, diyi ji* (Zhongguo xiju chubanshe, Beijing, 1958), pp. 3–4.

27. Ouyang Yuqian, "Huiyi Chunliu," in Tian Han et al., eds., *Zhongguo huaju*, p. 22.

28. A. R. Davis, "Out of 'Uncle Tom's Cabin,' Tokyo 1907: A Preliminary Look at the Beginnings of the Spoken Drama in China," *The Journal of the Oriental Society of Australia* 6, nos. 1 and 2 (1968–1969):39.

29. *Luanzhou zhi* (1896 ed., Taibei, 1964), chap. 8, pp. 24a–25a. See alternative translation in Kung-chuan Hsiao, *Rural China Imperial Control in the Nineteenth Century* (University of Washington Press, Seattle, 1967), pp. 278–279.

30. *Religion in Chinese Society: A Study of Contemporary Social Functions of Religion and Some of Their Historical Factors* (University of California Press, Berkeley, 1967), p. 85.

31. Ibid., p. 84.

32. *Yuan Ming Qing sandai jinhui xiaoshuo xiqu shiliao* (Zuojia chubanshe, Beijing, 1958), "Qianyan," p. 16.

33. Ibid., p. 30.

34. *Dingli huibian*, chap. 3, quoted in Wang Xiaochuan, *Yuan Ming Qing*, pp. 40–41.

35. *Da Qing Wenzong Xian huangdi shilu* (Huawen shuju, Taibei, 1964), chap. 38, pp. 12b–14b.

36. I have discussed this problem in greater detail in "Theatre and the Taipings," *Modern China, An International Quarterly* 2, no. 4 (October, 1976):473–501.

37. Ouyang Yuqian, "Tan wenming xi," in Tian Han et al., eds., *Zhongguo huaju,* p. 54.

38. *Da Qing Renzong Rui huangdi shilu* (Huawen shuju, Taibei, 1964), chap. 281, p. 13a.

SELECTED READINGS

Gee, Tom. *Stories of Chinese Opera.* Liberal Arts Press, Taibei, 1978. This book gives detailed accounts of 202 stories of Chinese opera. They are arranged in alphabetical order according to Chinese title. There is a very brief introduction.

Hatano, Kenichi. Translated from Japanese to Chinese by Luyuan xueren. *Jingju erbainian zhi lishi* [*Two hundred years history of the Beijing opera*]. Taidong tushuju, Shanghai, 1926. A much-quoted source for the biographical details of the best-known actors who were active in the nineteenth and early twentieth centuries.

Liu Wu-chi. *An Introduction to Chinese Literature.* Indiana University Press, Bloomington, 1966. An excellent introductory study that covers early theatrical activities.

Mackerras, Colin P. *The Rise of the Peking Opera 1770–1870: Social Aspects of the Theatre in Manchu China.* Clarendon Press, Oxford, 1972.

Mackerras, Colin. *The Chinese Theatre in Modern Times from 1840 to the Present Day.* Thames and Hudson, London, 1975.

Ouyang Yuqian, ed. *Zhongguo xiqu yanjiu ziliao chuji* [*First collection of research material on Chinese theater*]. Zhongguo xiju chubanshe, Beijing, 1957. A collection of articles by prominent scholars on particular forms of regional theater, including Guangdong opera, Hubei opera, and Beijing opera.

Tanaka Issei. "Development of Chinese Local Plays in the 17th and 18th Centuries." *Acta Asiatica, Bulletin of the Institute of Eastern Culture* 23 (1972):42–62. A summation in English of some of the excellent work Tanaka has done in Japanese to explain the growth of regional theater in social and economic terms.

Tanaka Issei, ed. *Shindai chihō geki shiryō shū* [*Collection of material on the regional drama on the Qing*]. 2 vols. Tōyō gaku bunken sentā sōkan II, III [*Series of the Center for Eastern Studies and Documentation II, III*]. Tōkyō daigaku Tōyō bunka kenkyūjo, Tokyo, 1968. Here Tanaka has collected numerous administrative documents relating to regional theater. The materials are arranged by province. Despite its lack of introduction this is a tremendously valuable work.

The Palace of Eternal Youth. Translated from Chinese to English by Yang Hsien-yi and Gladys Yang, Foreign Languages Press, Peking, 1955. Includes an introduction and sections of musical score.

The Peach Blossom Fan by K'ung Shang-jen. Translated from Chinese to English by Chen Shih-hsiang and Harold Acton. University of California Press, Berkeley, 1976. The translation of Kong Shangren's masterpiece includes a brief preface by Acton and an introduction by Cyril Birch.

Tian Han et al., eds. *Zhongguo huaju yundong wushi nian shiliao ji, diyi ji* [*A collection of historical material on fifty years of the Chinese spoken play movement, first collection*]. Zhongguo xiju chubanshe, Beijing, 1958. A collection of articles, including many reminiscences, on the spoken play from the beginnings to the early period of the People's Republic; the most essential primary material on the subject.

Zhang Geng, Guo Hancheng et al., eds. *Zhongguo xiqu tongshi* [*General history of Chinese theater*]. 3 vols. Zhongguo xiji chubanshe, Beijing, 1980–1981. The latest research on Chinese drama history from the People's Republic. The work covers all aspects of theater and all periods from the earliest antiquity to the middle of the nineteenth century. The major focus is on the Qing dynasty; part of the second volume on *kunqu* and Yiyang drama and the whole of the third volume on regional theater cover that period.

Zhou Yibai. *Zhongguo xiju shi* [*History of Chinese drama*]. 3 vols. Zhonghua shuju, Shanghai, 1953. Still among the best general coverage of Chinese drama history. This work covers all periods, but with greater focus on the later. The whole of vol. 3 is devoted to the Qing dynasty.

CHAPTER V

THE PERFORMANCE
OF CLASSICAL THEATER

A. C. Scott

THE WESTERN WORLD'S KNOWLEDGE of Chinese theater has largely
been derived from the old Beijing style of performance, commonly
known as Beijing opera *(jingxi* or *jingju),* and it is the production
methods and aesthetic principles of this form, as it was staged before
1949, which provide the basis for description in this chapter.

The term "classical" has been used in the dictionary sense of "long
established," since all traditional styles of Chinese theater conform to
fundamentally similar principles of production and performance, ir-
respective of the literary content of the plays.

It was explained in the previous chapter that the Beijing opera
attained a supreme popularity in China as the result of transposing
and adapting the production methods of other regional styles. It
could further be said that theater people, by nature a peripatetic
community, have never scrupled to borrow and transform anything
new or novel which added to the drawing power of their own performance. Actors thus become the effective instruments of change, and
they have certainly been crucial to the developing and shaping of the
Beijing opera, which can with reason be described both as the creation of actors and an actor's theater. It is a presentational style in
which the conjoined elements of song, dance, mime, music, and dialogue are bound by set compositional and choreographic rules, to
produce a total rhythmic flux realized through the self-sufficiency of
the actor's skill at all levels.

The actors from Anhui who prepared the way for the emergence of
the Beijing opera style during the nineteenth century were distinguished by a common versatility only possible among men who had
thoroughly mastered a craft in which a high standard of individual

competence was mandatory, since repertory troupes depended on a tightly structured system of ensemble relationships for their organic unity and survival. The old nineteenth-century actors in particular devised fresh ways of interpreting the traditional character roles, investing them with a new popular appeal as a result of their vocal innovations and inventive stage business.

There are four principal role categories in the Beijing opera: male, *sheng;* female, *dan;* painted face, *jing;* comic, *chou;* and a number of variants on the parent role in each of these categories. These are indicative of sex, age, social standing, and occupation rather than any concern with the psychology of the individual; that is to say, they are archetypal presentations by which a surface contrast between positive and negative, good and evil, is established through the stage action. The actor or actress playing such roles is concerned with creating imagery that draws upon the collective concepts of a society schooled in a Confucian code of values and behavior, theatrically transmuted from popular historical novels and the themes of the public storytellers. Two rich sources of invention were *The Romance of the Three Kingdoms (Sangyo zhi yanyi)* and *The Water Margin (Shuihu zhuan).* Stories from both these popular works were familiar to Chinese people from childhood and many knew them by heart. They depicted a familiar assembly of characters representative of all segments of Chinese society and provided a fertile source for creating larger-than-life characterizations presented through aesthetically distanced acting forms.

A typical Beijing opera playscript is little more than a skeletal indicator which tersely notes the entry or exit of a character and the points at which song replaces speech, followed by the literary name of the stock model pattern to be used for developing the musical mood of the particular dramatic situation. The actors with their instinctive command of form and content require no script to set a live performance in action, or detailed stage instructions for disposing themselves on stage. However, the most expressive acting in the light of Chinese critical acumen is the product of something more than sheer assimilation of technical forms by rote. Within the progression of the rhythmic permutations which provide the basic structure of any play, the actor's total physical being is keyed to a pitch of instantaneous response at several levels, a transcendent deployment of his own dynamism, and it is to achieve this prized state that every actor is submitted to long and merciless training.

TRAINING OF ACTORS

Teaching has always been by direct transmission. The apprentice learns his craft from practicing professionals, whether in an institutional or private capacity. The aim of the instructor, at least in the past, was to ensure an unbroken supply of trained personnel for a theater in which continuity was vital and a common high standard of technical competence essential, and for a vocation in which competition was fierce.

The deliberate social segregation of theater people in China tended to make acting a family profession carried on from father to son. Many actors, while being the descendants of generations of performers, customarily married into other acting families. As noted in chapter IV, the alternative way to become a professional actor in former times was through an old, established system whereby boys were selected for training and, after a contract was drawn up with parents, sent to Beijing where they were attached to one of the big troupes or contracted out again to an established actor, who then became responsible for the upkeep and training of a boy as his disciple. There were also many smaller private training troupes run by actors or ex-actors who travelled the country looking for boys suitable for the stage. There are many accounts of ill-treatment of these boys that find their parallel in the examples of child exploitation exposed in Dickens' novels. It was common practice to use boy apprentices as male prostitutes in Chinese intellectual circles.[1]

On the other hand, the stagestruck amateur, as common in China as elsewhere, could work privately with actor-teachers and if he had real talent, gain acceptance into the professional world. A number of notable Beijing actors commenced their careers in this way, while amateur performers were a prominent feature of life in the capital during the nineteenth century. They had their own organizations and premises for performances and were a useful source of income to the professionals they employed as instructors. Needless to say, when an amateur turned professional, known in theatrical jargon as "diving into the sea," he could only be admitted by approval of a hierarchy whose preserves were jealously guarded, following a ritualistic initiation ceremony in the presence of his teachers, when he forswore further involvement with the world of amateurs.

Training methods for professional actors were undoubtedly harsh, with no compromises made, but they must be judged in the light of their times. Not every acting instructor was a sadistic monster or a procurer. The good teachers knew their jobs.

An augury for improved professional training conditions was the founding of the Xiliancheng school at Beijing in 1903.[2] It later changed its name to Fuliancheng and gained a reputation as a model of its kind. During its forty years' history the school graduated more than seven hundred students, many of whom became China's best-known Beijing opera actors in the first half of the century.

A revolutionary step was the founding of a coeducational Conservatory of Dramatic Art in 1930.[3] During its first three years it was directed by the actor Cheng Yanqiu, one of the most popular performers of leading women's roles.[4] He travelled in Europe during the whole of 1934 in order to study European methods, the better to develop the school's curriculum. One innovative feature was the provision to continue the student's general education while he underwent professional stage training; a comprehensive syllabus of subjects was offered in addition to the customary rigorous theater routines. War brought this ambitious undertaking to an end. The first graduating class, fifteen boys and six girls, earned their diplomas in 1937, by which time the work of the school had been favorably received by professionals and public alike. Students were selected by open interview and, if accepted, given six years training, with board and lodging, at no cost to themselves. No vacations or outside contacts were sanctioned, but parents were allowed to visit weekly. On completing their training, students were required to give their professional services to the school for one year. The old system of discipline prevailed, there were no short cuts to the tried methods of the past.

As soon as they entered the school, students were called at 5 a.m., summer or winter, to start the day with voice practice. Led by instructors, they were marched to the city walls and there went through their vocal exercises against the stone "sounding board" of the wall. First came what were termed the "tight or narrow sounds," *i* and *ah,* the correct intonation of which is important in Beijing opera vocalization. Increasing emphasis on volume of projection was practiced for about thirty minutes. Next came singing to instrumental accompaniment, again with progressive intensification of volume and pitch, and correction of individual faults. The students were then marched back to the school for breakfast. At no point in their training were they free from the observation of their tutors, who were quick to correct any relaxation of deportment or behavior.

After breakfast all beginners practiced dance movements to make waists and limbs supple. One elementary routine involved alternately lifting each leg vertically, with the foot braced against the wall for support, and raising it progressively higher in a crescentlike curve. It was designed to eliminate flections of the knee. This was succeeded by the students walking in single file and raising each leg vertically and alternately. These exercises were done at the command of the instructor. Following progress in these routines, the pupils learned to do handstands, and after that came training in bending the torso backward from the waist, so that the head nearly touches the ground. In a description of his own early training, Mei Lanfang speaks of one particularly difficult exercise:

> The two legs were placed firmly apart at a distance of twelve inches. Both hands were lifted over the head, palms outward with eyes focused on the thumbs. The body was then gradually bent over backwards; if you could grasp your ankles with both your hands your technique was considered good.[5]

Then came choreographic work with bamboo staves in order to develop footwork and combat postures, with the students working solo and in ensemble. Long hours were also spent with the instructors in attaining postures of total immobility, first with the legs and arms raised and then the whole body, for increasing periods of time, a preparation for those sculptural poses vibrant with constrained energy that are so characteristic of Beijing opera stage movement. Both while the students worked and relaxed, their legs were encased in cloth binding padded with fine-grained sand. This conditioned the limbs to support weight which when discarded gave an added lightness to the leaps and bounds associated with many of the more vigorous acting forms.

All students underwent this grueling basic training, whatever their later area of specialization. Beginners spent their mornings in this way, with the afternoons devoted to their general education. The advanced students worked with individual instructors on specific roles and the more advanced techniques relating to their particular needs. Preliminary singing exercises were given without musical accompaniment, the instructor providing onomatopoetic guidance and beating out the time with his hand on a table, while students sang in a low voice following the changes in rhythm, striving to attain correct pitch and intonation. Criticism of students in all areas of their study was constant and severe, while strict attention to deportment was enforced throughout their long day.

After the evening meal there was further individual practice and study, with lights out at 9 p.m., unless in the case of senior students they had to perform in a city theater, where they still remained in charge of an instructor who escorted them to and from their engagement.[6] From the day they entered the school until the day they left, students lived as a community apart, disciplined, conditioned, and guarded from outside distractions until initiation in their craft was finished.

THE CATEGORIES OF ROLES

On the completion of training, a student was equipped to begin a professional career as a specialist in one of the precisely categorized character roles of the Beijing opera stage. The comprehensive nature of instruction encouraged a versatility that enabled the young actor or actress to meet working contingencies by playing more than one of the major role categories, but specialization in a single role and its related variations was the universal practice for everyone once launched on a professional stage career. In a majority of cases this specialization was predetermined by teachers and theater family members at a very early stage of instruction. Decisions were based on physical build, facial characteristics, and the instinctive appraisal of potential from those who had spent a lifetime in the profession.

The standardized role categories of the Beijing opera had their antecedents in Yuan times, when the structured four-act play, a prototype for later theater, was devised to incorporate a fixed role system with the four main categories *mo, dan, jing,* and *chou:* male, female, evil, and comic characters (see chap. II). Each category had its further classifications, and the system approximated the *sheng, dan, jing,* and *chou* divisions of the Beijing opera, which categories, however, came to assume a more minutely descriptive definition of age, status, and occupation.

The first role category in its broadest sense symbolizes the mature, literate, orthodox man; a scholar, official, or civilian of good standing, who conforms to the tenets of society (see plate 22). The prototype for this concept, *laosheng,* was created by Cheng Zhanggeng (1812–c. 1880), popularly known among the Chinese as the "emperor of the Beijing theater." Distinguished as an actor, teacher, and

leader of a prestigious troupe, he developed a style of acting and singing that was seminal to future developments and became designated
Chengpai. The term *pai* is used to describe an artistic method and is
preceded by the name of the particular practicing artist regarded as its
innovator. In this case it refers to the way the actor has developed the
expressive qualities of his dramatic enunciation in song and dialogue,
particularly the individual treatment of stress and tonal sequences
which are all important in Chinese lyrical expression.

Other character types covered by the *laosheng* classification are
older men frail in body but eloquent and strong in spirit, emperors,
princes, and men of high civilian status. Military leaders and warriors
in combat are designated *wusheng*, or "military" *sheng*. Fighters of a
different kind also included in this type are the outlaws and sworn
brothers in adversity depicted in *Water Margin*. Brilliant swordsmen
and wrestlers, they match their skill in the cause of rough justice.

Young men are classified as *xiaosheng*, a name first used in Ming
times for secondary characters but given more positive definition in
Beijing opera (see plate 23). The actor Xu Xiaoxiang (1832–1888), a
member of Cheng Zhanggeng's troupe and originally from Suzhou,
the home of the *kunqu* style, is today regarded as the artist who set
the precedent for the interpretation of this role as it has been performed in Beijing opera. The type of personality portrayed is the
young scholar, refined, cultivated, sometimes delicate in constitution,
and very often involved in amorous intrigues. A variation on the
theme is the impoverished but ambitious young man of talent who
emerges from his tribulations to a happy and frequently romantic
conclusion of his affairs. A third type is the young hero of high rank
skilled in military affairs, often seen in plays with historical themes.

The second category, *dan*, embraces all the women's roles for which
there are several classifications. An important one, *qingyi*, symbolizes
women of virtue, dignity, and strong character, loyal to their family
obligations and often portrayed in moods of anguish and adverse situations. Faithful wives, filial daughters, and distressed lovers are the
subjects here (see plate 24). A pioneer in the development of this
genre was the actor Shi Xiaofu (1837–1901), who was a distinguished
exponent of both the *kunqu* and Beijing opera acting styles.

A contrasting type is the young woman of bold and extrovert character, full of charm and seduction, most commonly depicted as a
maidservant or ladies' maid, who captivates the audience with her
mischievous and flirtatious byplay. This role, classified as *huadan*,

provides lighter entertainment in the general scheme (see plate 25). It is complemented by that of the young woman who is skilled in fighting and riding and accustomed to vigorous action while not dispensing with her feminine appeal. Designated *wudan,* the role provides opportunities for dazzling displays of acrobatics and combat forms on stage.

The matriarchs of the Beijing opera stage are called *laodan.* Halting in step but firm in spirit, forceful in expression and emotional in their grief, they are constantly concerned with the honor of family life and the unity of the clan (see plate 26). This particular role was given new interpretations by Hao Lantian (1820–1872), a versatile actor who joined Cheng Zhanggeng's troupe where he created technical precedents for a generation who followed him.

The third role category, *jing,* is distinguished by the use of polychrome makeup covering the whole of the actor's face and brow, to symbolize through color and design the particular nature, talents, and destiny of the character portrayed (see plates 27 and 28). In general this role suggests power, whether in thought, word, or deed. The types represented are men of action, warriors, swashbuckling outlaws, crafty ministers, upright judges, and loyal statesmen, as well as gods and supernatural beings. The bravura style of performance they engender was given impetus during the Daoguang era (1821–1850), a seminal exponent being the actor He Guishan (1843–1913). He began his career as an amateur but turned professional and joined Cheng Zhanggeng's troupe.

Last of the four role categories are the *chou,* or comic actors. Their forerunners were the public storytellers and fairground entertainers who have colored the history of popular entertainment in China. The comic actor of the Beijing opera is not necessarily limited to playing the buffoon but serves a catalytic function by depicting corrupt or stupid officialdom, shrewish women, petty criminals, and haunted men, as well as a Shakespearean galaxy of woodcutters, boatmen, household servants, jailers, and the like. The nineteenth-century actor Liu Guisan, a member of Cheng Zhanggeng's troupe, like others of the period mentioned above, brought great luster to the comic role. He delighted Beijing audiences by his playing of old servant women, tavern mistresses, and similar characters. His interpretation of the role of a shrewd marriage go-between became a model of its kind that has been emulated by actors ever since. Although his personal facts are scanty he left a legend of performance behind.

The comic actor on the Chinese stage is the one performer sanctioned to use colloquial speech, indulge in personal or topical allusions, and identify himself with the crowd out in front. Nevertheless, the techniques, costumes, and makeup are no less formalized in this than in the other roles; the actor's presentation here too is ruled by the single principle of submitting individual creative energy to the restraint and order of stereotyped patterns and modes of expression through which the actor alternately shifts his audience's focus from the visual to the aural by devices that treat speech and song as more than direct rational statement, and sound itself is used to raise spontaneous associations in the spectator's mind. The formalized devices instrumental to the symbolic realization of character conform to common technical and aesthetic principles for all the roles, only their usage differs for the various categories in the elements of production touched upon below.

THE MUSIC AND VOCAL EXPRESSION OF BEIJING OPERA

The musical style of the Beijing opera is called *pihuang,*[7] a telescoped term derived from the collective function of the two parent modes discussed in chapter IV. It serves a strictly theatrical function and has no place as concert music. Prior to 1949, the orchestra was always seated downstage left, and their playing was both aurally and visually integrated with the placing and rhythm of the actors. The terms *erhuang* and *xipi* define two principal styles, each of which serves as a prototype for a prescribed number of metrical arrangements that are defined in terms of *ban,* the accented, and *yan,* the unaccented beat within the measure. For example, an actor's song may be shown in the script as *xipi yuanban;* the theater musician at once knows this signifies a time signature comparable to 2/4—one *ban,* one *yan*—that is to say, with the rhythmic pattern of the measure defined within a total of two quarter notes, approximating andante, a moderate movement. The Chinese theater musician requires no printed notation and reacts instinctively to a particular rhythmic combination described by its *ban/yan* structure.

The leader of the ensemble is responsible for the timing, which he beats out on a pair of hardwood clappers, *ban,* held in the left hand and used rather in the manner of castanets, and on a small hardwood drum with a skin head, beaten simultaneously with the *ban* using a single stick, or two when the *ban* is not in use.

PLATE 1. "Horn butting game," or wrestling, of the second century. Source: *Han Tang bihua (Murals from the Han to the Tang Dynasty)* (Foreign Languages Press, Beijing, 1974), pl. 38.

PLATES 2, 3. Scenes from an aristocratic banquet of the second century. Source: Ibid., pl. 39.

PLATE 4. A wall painting from a tomb of about A.D. 145 to 220 in Holingol, Inner Mongolia. It depicts an acrobatic display, dancing, and musical accompaniment. Note the audience at the top left. Source: Ibid., pl. 24.

PLATE 5. Detail of plate 4. The principal figures here are a man and a woman dancing as partners. Source: Ibid., pl. 25.

PLATE 6. Song dynasty wall painting of performer accompanied by an orchestra. Source: *Zhongguo yinyue shi cankao tupian*, eighth collection (Yinyue chubanshe, Beijing, 1959), pl. 29.

PLATE 7. Song dynasty theatrical costumes. Source: *Xiqu yanjiu*, no. 3 (July 10, 1958): facing table of contents.

PLATE 8. A picture of the famous Yuan dramatist Guan Hanqing. Source: Ibid., front cover.

PLATE 9. Scene from a Yuan drama. This is a wall painting in the Guangsheng Temple in Hong-zhao county, Shanxi province. It is dated the fourth month of 1324 at the left, just above the rear curtain. Source: *Xiqu yanjiu,* no. 2 (April 10, 1957): facing p. 66.

PLATE 10. Yuan dynasty pottery figurine of a vaudeville actor, unearthed in Henan province. Source: *Historical Relics Unearthed in New China* (Foreign Languages Press, Beijing, 1972), p. 193.

PLATE 11. Yuan dynasty pottery figurines of a dancer and a flutist. Source: Ibid., p. 192.

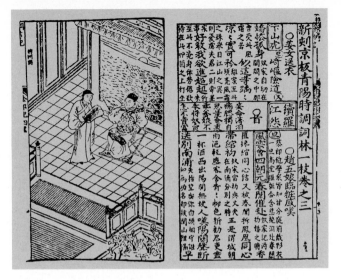

PLATE 12. Two pages from a very rare Wanli (1573–1620) edition of dramas of the Qingyang style, an early variant of the Yiyang drama. The lower half of the right-hand page is the first passage of a scene from *The Lute Song,* a *chuanqi* adapted to the Qingyang style. The left-hand page shows a scene from a drama based on contemporary political affairs. Such dramas were rare in the Wanli era. Source: Wang Gulu, ed., *Mingdai Huidiao xiqu sanchu jiyi* (Gudian wenxue chubanshe, Shanghai, 1956), before p. 1.

PLATE 13. Scene from a film of the Ming *kunqu The Peony Pavilion.* The actors are the famous Mei Lanfang as the heroine Du Liniang and Yu Zhenfei, the best-known twentieth-century *kunqu* performer of scholar-lover roles, as Liu Mengmei. Source: New China News Agency; Myra Roper.

PLATE 14. Theatrical performance at a private dinner party in traditional China. The original is from a late Ming edition of the novel *Jin Ping Mei*. Source: *Xiju luncong*, no. 1 (February 27, 1957): facing p. 2.

PLATE 15. Theatrical performance at a private party. Note the drummer and flutist to the left rear. Source: *Xiqu yanjiu*, no. 4 (October 10, 1957): front cover.

PLATE 16. Ming actors dressing for a performance. Source: *Xiqu yanjiu*, no. 3 (July 10, 1958): facing p. 120.

PLATE 17. Early Qing *kunqu* performance of a *Water Margin* drama. The audience was seated on three sides of the stage—audience members can be seen in this drawing behind the balustrade to the right of the two stage performers. Stylization of stage costume is evident in the wires connecting the performers' beards to their ears, in the manner of eyeglasses. Source: Ibid.

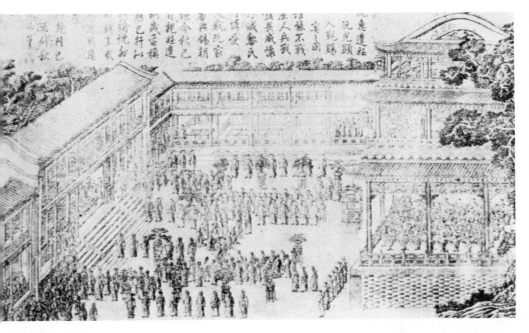

PLATE 18. Watching drama at the emperor's residence in Jehol during the Qianlong period (1736–1795) of the Qing dynasty. Source: Zhou Yibai, *Zhongguo xiju shi,* vol. 2 (Zhonghua shuju, Beijing, 1953), p. 670.

PLATE 19. Scene from the Puzhou clapper opera *Killing a Clan (Shafu)*. The king of Chu plans to kill all the Wu clan members because the father of the clan has criticized the government. Wu Yun (center), after ordering that his wife commit suicide, sings of his feelings while two servants look on, one of them holding Wu Yun's baby. Puzhou clapper opera is among the most ancient of all clapper styles. Photo by Colin Mackerras, Beijing, January, 1980.

PLATE 20. Scene from the Puzhou clapper opera *Xu Ce Runs on the City Walls (Xu Ce paocheng)*. The aged Xu Ce helps avenge the Xue clan's suffering at the hands of an evil official during the Tang dynasty by ascending the city wall to keep watch; his reports result in the clan's military victory. Here Xu Ce is on the right with the wall behind him. On the left is a young member of the Xue clan whom Xu Ce saved thirteen years earlier. Photo by Colin Mackerras, Beijing, 1980.

PLATE 21.   A permanent stage in a guildhall in Qingdao, Shandong province. Guildhalls were a common venue for theater performances. Source: National Library of Australia; Colin Mackerras.

PLATE 22.   A *laosheng* character. The double-winged headgear, magnificent embroidered robe, and large hoop belt show him to be a scholar-official. In his left hand he carries a tablet which is an order from the emperor. Source: Zhongguo xijujia xiehui (Chinese Theater Association); Colin Mackerras.

PLATE 23.   A *xiaosheng* character pleading for his life in the play *The White Snake*. The role type is immediately identifiable by the soft, elegant robes and beardless face. Source: Zhongguo xijujia xiehui; Colin Mackerras.

PLATE 24. Liu Xiurong as an immortal white snake spirit who has taken the form of a beautiful *qingyi* in the play *The White Snake*. Her headdress in this scene is typical of the *qingyi* role. In later scenes from this play, a headdress more indicative of the White Snake's reptilian nature is worn, as can be seen in plate 23. Watersleeves—the long white silk extensions to her sleeves that enhance hand gestures—are an important feature of the costumes for the *qingyi* role type, and are worn throughout the play. Source: Zhongguo xijujia xiehui; Colin Mackerras.

PLATE 25. Yang Paifeng, a maidservant in the Beijing opera of the same name, is a *huadan* character with fighting skills. Source: *Shaanxi xiju*, no. 1 (January 25, 1979): back cover.

PLATE 26. Zheng Ziru as the *laodan* character Jiang Guizhi in the Beijing opera *Flower Spear Fight (Dui huaqiang)*. Source: Zhongguo xijujia xiehui; Colin Mackerras.

PLATE 27. The *jing,* or painted face, character on the right is a general in the Beijing opera *Reconciliation of the General and the Prime Minister (Jiangxiang he)*. Source: *New China* (Foreign Languages Press, Beijing, 1953), n.p.

PLATE 28. Sun Wukong, the Monkey King, stealing heavenly peaches in the Beijing opera *Disturbance in Heaven (Nao Tiangong)*. Although this role uses elaborate painted makeup similar to that of *jing* characters, it is classified as a *wusheng* role because of the complex pantomime and acrobatic sequences that are featured. Source: Zhongguo xijujia xiehui; Colin Mackerras.

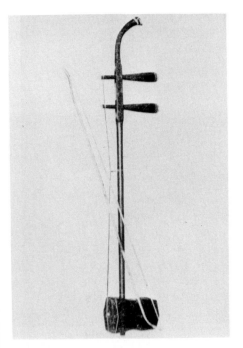

PLATE 29. An *erhu*. Source: *Zhongguo yinyue shi cankao tupian*, vol. 2 (Yinyue chubanshe, Shanghai, 1954), no. 12.

PLATE 30. Relief of a dancer from the tomb of the ruler Wang Jian (846–918) in Chengdu, Sichuan province. Note the extended sleeves. Source: Ibid., vol. 7 (Yinyue chubanshe, Beijing, 1958), no. 13.

PLATE 31. Scene from *Peach Blossom Fan (Taohua shan),* a spoken play by Ouyang Yuqian, as performed by students at the Central Drama Institute in Beijing, 1959. Ouyang Yuqian, one of the founders of the spoken play movement in China, based this play on the *kunqu* of the same name by Kong Shangren. Costumes for this production were strongly influenced by those of traditional theater. Source: Central Drama Institute; Colin Mackerras.

PLATE 32. *Yangge* dancers in Tiananmen Square, Beijing. Source: *New China* (Foreign Languages Press, Beijing, 1953), n.p.

PLATE 33. A simply staged open-air performance for the masses in Yan'an. Source: Myra Roper.

PLATE 34. A travelling opera company giving an open-air performance of a traditional work. Source: New China News Agency; Myra Roper.

PLATE 35. Members of a caravan troupe performing for herdsmen and their families. Source: *Wudao,* no. 4 (August 30, 1978): front cover.

PLATE 36. A scene from the modern Shanxi opera *Going Up Peach Peak Three Times,* as performed by the Shanxi Provincial Shanxi Opera Company. The opera was denounced in 1974, shortly after its Beijing premier, but rehabilitated in 1978. Source: Myra Roper.

PLATE 37.   In the model revolutionary opera *Taking Tiger Mountain by Strategy*, the Communist forces led by Yang Zirong are fighting the Guomindang in northeast China in 1946. Here Yang ascends the mountain on horseback to infiltrate the enemy stronghold. Source: *China Reconstructs* 19, no. 2 (February, 1970): 19.

PLATE 38.   *The Xi'an Incident* is among those modern plays that portray famous revolutionaries on the stage. Here Mao Zedong (left), Zhou Enlai (center), and Zhu De (right) are shown together. Source: *Renmin xiju,* no. 3 (March 18, 1979): front cover.

PLATE 39. The Persian plate dance, a scene in the dance-drama *Tales of the Silk Road,* a contemporary work set in the Tang dynasty. Source: *China Reconstructs* 29, no. 3 (March, 1980): 25.

PLATE 40. Huang Xiaoci in the role of Qiu Tong, a provocative young woman who has just entered the Jia household as a new concubine in the play *Wang Xifeng Disrupts Ningguo Prefecture,* performed by the Jiangsu Provincial Beijing Opera Troupe. The costume, inspired by those created for *Tales of the Silk Road* (see plate 39), was designed by Mao Zongliang. Photo by Elizabeth Wichmann, Nanjing, January, 1981.

PLATE 41. Hu Zhifeng as the spirited young singing girl Li Huiniang, and Chen Xiaohua as the young scholar Pei Shunqing, in the newly written historical play *Li Huiniang,* performed by the Suzhou Municipal Beijing Opera Troupe. The scenery, designed by Sun Chang, is essentially traditional—silk-covered tables and chairs set on a carpeted stage. However, this design also makes use of two scenic elements that have become quite common in the staging of traditional and newly written historical plays—a decorative painted screen behind the table, and silk curtains at the sides of the stage held back by thick silk cords and tassels. These curtains are never closed. They are primarily decorative, although they serve the practical function of closing off the side stage area from the audience. Photo by Elizabeth Wichmann, Suzhou, November, 1979.

PLATE 42. Yan Shaoshan as the eldest brother of the Jia family, Jia Zhen, and Li Junqi as his wife, You Shi, in the Jiangsu Provincial Beijing Opera Troupe production of *Wang Xifeng Disrupts Ningguo Prefecture*. This production, directed by Shi Yukun, utilized multiple-set realistic scenery, designed by Xu Kebing, as well as atmospheric lighting and special effects. In the set for this scene, designed to represent the apartments of the eldest son and his family, both wealth and adherence to traditional Confucian values are suggested through the prominently displayed calligraphy carved in stone, the couch for conversation and smoking, and the shelves for books and objects of art. Photo by Elizabeth Wichmann, Nanjing, January, 1981.

PLATE 43. Fu Yiqun as Zheng Jiagui, a doctor persecuted to death by followers of the Gang of Four in the play *A Record of Bloody Injustice (Xue yuan ji)*, performed by the Suzhou Municipal Beijing Opera Troupe. The designers, Sun Chang and Bai Dongwu, created for this scene a somewhat abstract set in which violently skewed walls display accusatory posters, evoking the atmosphere of a world gone suddenly mad. Photo by Elizabeth Wichmann, Suzhou, November, 1979.

The melodies, whose structural patterns are defined by the time-beating instruments, are developed by the *huqin,* a bowed fiddle with two strings tuned in fifths. The body, made from bamboo, consists of a small cylinder covered with snakeskin at one end, the other being left open, while the neck is made from a short length of bamboo with two wooden tuning pegs inserted at the top. The instrument is held vertically on the seated player's knee, and the bow is fixed to the strings, which are stopped with the fingers of the left hand. The *huqin* provides the main accompaniment to the actors' singing, against which it develops a florid, rippling, sometimes divergent line to embellish the central melody of the singer. The bowing is characterized by constant vibrato and glissando effects.

Subsidiary accompaniment to the *huqin* is provided by the *yueqin* and *sanxian.* The first has a circular body, a short neck with four lateral tuning pegs, ten frets with four strings set in double courses, and is tuned in fifths. It is played with a plectrum, as is the *sanxian.* This instrument has three strings, a long redwood neck with three lateral tuning pegs, and a small oval-shaped sound box of redwood, faced on both sides with snakeskin. A third subsidiary instrument is the two-stringed *erhu,* which has a fixed bow. It belongs to the *huqin* family but is made of redwood, has a hexagonal-shaped body, and both the neck and bow are longer (see plate 29).

A large and a small brass gong and cymbals are used to mark entries and exits and to accentuate emotional climaxes in the song and action of a play, the choreographic posturing and timing of combat scenes, and the more tense passages of dance movement. The large gong is one foot in diameter and suspended by a grip with which it is held and beaten with a headed stick; the small gong is six to seven inches in diameter and beaten with a short wedge-shaped piece of wood. There are timing patterns for the percussion instruments no less than the others, and these are onomatopoetically represented in notation.

The *dizi,* a side-blown bamboo flute used in the *kunqu* theater, which was replaced by the *huqin* as the principal accompanying instrument in the Beijing opera, is sometimes used for plays of *kunqu* origin. It has six finger holes, a blow hole, and next to this another covered by a thin membrane of rice paper. It has a fixed pitch, which limits its bravura effect and adaptability to different vocal styles—disadvantages for the Beijing opera, where sustained playing in long performance is required. Around 1840, the Sixi troupe first introduced the *huqin* as a replacement for the two flutes that until then had been used to accompany the actors. The innovation quickly proved popular, in spite of some protest, with consequent changes in the orchestral components, including the addition of the *yueqin*. The *erhu* was a latecomer to the ensemble, being first introduced in the 1920s by Mei Lanfang's *huqin* player, Wang Shaoqing, in order to give variety to the existent arrangement of instruments.

The musical content of the Beijing opera is limited and repetitious in its forms, but it is precisely this factor that endows it with strong appeal. The songs, melodies, and versification are quickly assimilated and easily remembered by the general public. Through transposition of recurrent metrical patterns, the playwright sets the appropriate mood for stage presentation within a matrix of forms devised to stimulate awareness by the most open, readily identifiable means. The audience is thus induced to experience directly the dynamic impact of the actors' transcendental artistry deployed through speech, song, movement, and integrated as a total rhythmic force.

Singing is used to indicate human emotions and psychological reactions, melodramatically conveyed through the range of mood offered by the metrical arrangements of the two principal musical styles. Each role category is vocally identified by specific qualities of pitch, volume, and enunciation, and whether it is the especially high falsetto of the *dan* roles, the *tenore robusto* of the *sheng* parts, or the thunderous quality of the *jing* actor's projection, the method of singing is completely stylized within the patterned relationships created by the string and percussion accompaniment, together with choreographic forms in which every gesture is predetermined.

The use of rhyming patterns, so integral to Chinese lyrical expression, is confined in the Beijing opera to a system of thirteen character groupings which provides a compositional key for the playwrights. Two characters in each grouping define the sounds available for complementing rhyming endings to the actor's lines. A general ruling decrees that when the rhyme of a first stanza occurs within one of the groupings, the next stanza follows the same rhyming patterns. It is possible to change rhyme in a particularly long passage, but monorhyme is in general the preferred treatment throughout. A common verse form consists of lines of ten feet, that is to say, ten Chinese characters, which the actor breaks down vocally into two series of three feet and a group of four, or alternatively into a four-three and three-feet arrangement, so alleviating monotony in the rhyme accentuation and varying the cadences. The rhyming sounds themselves are divided into "sharp" and "rounded" characters, and because Beijing opera idiom is not pure Beijing dialect at all, but contains elements from the dialects of Anhui, Sichuan, and Hubei, the variations in nuance thus provided in the interests of euphony and dramatic intensity give theatrical speech its "bite" and contribute to the larger than life projection of the actor.

Whether it is monologue or dialogue, stanzas of four lines rhyming alternately are the rule in Beijing opera verse. The first two lines are often recited in monotone with the third line rising to a long drawn-out utterance of the final syllable, and the fourth line taken very smoothly, or alternatively given a brisker emphasis as an indication of following action. Rhyming patterns and syllable prolongation serve a characteristic euphonic purpose, and the women's roles especially make great play with steeply rising and descending cadences as the conclusion to emotionally charged passages of monologue. The shrill laughter of the *xiaosheng,* the weeping of the *laosheng,* and the bellow of anger from the *jing* performer in their turn are examples of contrived usage in which the emotive effect of pure sound creates its own dimensions within the quantitative rhythms of song, music, and the controlled progression of movement and gesture.

GESTURE AND MOVEMENT

Gesture and movement, no less than the vocal expression of the actor, are bound by ordered rules of performance. For each role category there are prescribed methods for every kind of physical action pertaining to human behavior. Theater people usually listed them for technical purposes under the following headings: foot movements and pace, leg, hand and fingers, sleeves, pheasant plumes, and beards. In effect this represents a breakdown of the independent choreographic elements basic to the grand pattern of dance at the heart of all Beijing opera acting forms, in which every step, gesture, head movement posture, and combat form is minutely defined. In his extensive studies on the Beijing opera, Qi Rushan (1876–1962) has pointed out the similarities between dance methods recorded in Tang and Song and some of the movements and gestures of the Beijing opera actor.[8] Dance was fundamental to court entertainments, public ceremonies, and temple rituals in former times, and this has been of profound significance for the development of traditional stage techniques in which every kind of expressive physical action is treated as a choreographic unit essential to a total rhythmic harmony.

The relationship between music and the spoken word created by the homonymic nature of spoken Chinese first led to the involvement of musicians and poets with deliberately contrived meters and the accompanying elements of rhyme, alliteration, and onomatopoeia as the tools of formal composition. The words of songs and dialogues were treated as time-movement units for creative purposes. This in turn led to formalized treatment of the stage performer's natural movements and gestures, which preceded, accompanied, terminated, or linked together passages of prose, poetry, and song. Through this synchronization of means the choreographic nature of Chinese acting was established.

Hand gestures are used symbolically to express emotional reactions and provide a continuous pattern of movement while an actor is singing. They are also given great emphasis in expressive mime techniques whereby simple actions like the opening or closing of a door or the threading of a needle become visually attractive interpolations within the total action of a theme played out through the combined elements of music, song, and dance.

A number of Beijing opera hand gestures have been derived from Buddhist temple imagery and suggest an affinity with the Indian *mudra* in their ritualistic origins and unspoken transmission of dramatic story. However, they are neither so numerous nor as symbolically complex as the *mudra,* and their purpose is purely secular and theatrical. They are at all times complementary to the narration and song of the actors.

A characteristic feature of Beijing opera hand gestures is the many different ways of pointing with the fingers, using either one or both hands. In making these gestures the performer keeps his eyes constantly focused in accord with the movement of the fingers. As the performer's eyes follow the gestural phrase through its spatial sequence, his feet move in time to the music if the pointing is carried out during continuing action. Pointing movements are especially developed in the exceedingly graceful movement patterns used in the *qingyi* roles,[9] and they are graphically emphasized in the pure mime of the *huadan* characters when, for example, a developing romantic relationship between two people is suggested solely by means of pointing gestures rhythmically coordinated with the musical timing and accented by an eloquently expressive series of half-glances. Or again, when the comic actor takes a derisory stance and with the admonishing technique of the storyteller analyzes events for the audience with forefingers that move in controlled comparison of himself and "them."

The sleeves, pheasant plumes, and beards, each given separate inclusion in the list of choreographic elements, are costume accessories vital to certain controlled gesture and movement patterns, which accounts for their independent categorization. "Water" sleeves are long cuffs of fine white silk up to two feet long, left open at the seam and attached to the sleeves proper of the actor's robe. They are used in a unique extension of the actor's hand movements and provide the basis of a style of dancing that has had a long history in China. Records indicate the prevalence of dance forms embodying sleeve techniques as early as the Zhou and Han dynasties, and in their early manifestation they were probably used in shamanistic rituals as well as gracing the secular entertainments of the courts. A saying given wide currency in China, "long sleeves and beautiful dancing," underscores a theme that was given considerable emphasis in classical poetry and literary texts. Archaeological sources such as Tang tomb figurines or the wall paintings of the Dunhuang caves provide abundant visual evidence of the popularity of this style of dancing in former times;[10] in both the sources named there are readily discernible similarities between the dance forms portrayed in painting and sculpture and the techniques of the Beijing opera (see plate 30).

The *qingyi* role most notably draws upon an extensive repertoire of sleeve movements which can be readily related to ancient dance forms (see plate 24). The water sleeves are used in all the role categories to a greater or lesser degree, however, except when costumes based on Manchu prototypes are worn or when combat and acrobatic techniques predominate and vigorous movement and weapon play would be impeded by the long sleeves.

The pheasant plumes, which are worn in pairs attached to the headdress of the wearer, are between six and seven feet long and are manipulated in coordinated sweeps of movement with the plumes held lightly between the first and middle fingers of each hand. They had their origins in ceremonial dances and temple rituals such as the annual celebrations for the birth of Confucius. When first introduced into theatrical performances they were used to symbolize warrior characters from the "barbarian" regions beyond China's northwestern frontiers, and they still serve that purpose in the Beijing opera, although no longer exclusively. Because of their decorative potential they eventually became popular with actors for purely aesthetic reasons. The Qing actor Xu Xiaoxiang was particularly responsible for developing many of the dance forms now seen on the stage, and since his day all *xiaosheng* players have made the use of the pheasant plumes a technical feature of the young warrior-hero roles. In more recent times actresses playing the amazon roles have been noted for their skill and virtuosity in dancing with the plumes, a never-failing source of visual gratification for Chinese audiences.

The beards are conventionalized to a degree, being made of hair attached to a flexible wire frame which fits over the ears of the wearer and is supported against the upper lip directly above the mouth, leaving a space between the nose and the beard itself. There are several styles, the two most common being the full beard, a long, broad swath of hair worn by warriors of high rank, and a tripartite version used in the scholar-official roles. Beards can be black, grey, or white to indicate relative age groups, while red beards are worn in some of the *jing* roles to symbolize more tempestuous natures (see, for example, plates 22, 27). Those worn in the comic roles are grotesque in appearance, so serving their own purpose.

In general, beards symbolize maturity and seniority and are therefore not used in the *xiaosheng* roles. In performance the actor strokes them downward, moves them to the right and left with a circling movement, or precisely flicks them aside while singing, to name but one or two of a series of formalized gestures used to stress psychological reactions in the larger-than-life forms of expression seen on the traditional stage. In essence such gestures contribute to the progression of the overall rhythmic theme.

The combat forms that are such a visually engrossing element of Beijing opera performance have been developed and adapted from the fighting arts *(wushu)*, of which there are countless forms dating back through the different periods of Chinese history. Many schools and systems arose, and contradictory claims have been made for several historical personalities as the true originators of physical training methods that have been widely practiced all over China for centuries. These methods had their early origins in Taoist meditative respiratory theories developed in the third and fourth centuries A.D. The basic premise of Taoist belief in breathing disciplines as a therapeutic control of inner energy became fundamental to all Chinese physical training methods. Theories initially developed for medical purposes were applied to systems of inductive callisthenics and combat forms. The dissemination of Buddhism in China resulted in a mingling of Taoist and Hindu theories, including the influence of yogaic principles which also stressed respiratory-psychoid techniques.

This fusion was further extended with the rise of Chan Buddhism and its emphasis on meditation within the immediacy of the active life force. Various Chan communities became renowned as the practitioners of physical training methods and combat forms, which in conjunction with the numerous other styles and methods practiced in more secular environments laid the way for the development of two basic approaches. The first, called the inner, or soft, school taught the exponent to concentrate on rhythmic motion and relaxation and to learn to counter violence through flexibility and resilient strength. The second, called the outside, or hard, school emphasized strength, speed, and powerful action.

Within these two main approaches different styles grew up under the general designation of "the fighting arts," which included bare-handed combat and combat with weapons. Performances of bare-handed combat consisted of boxing, wrestling, and pushing with the hands to fixed steps; combat with weapons was depicted through fencing with swords and with spears. Each style developed its own distinctive rhythms, choreographic patterns, and kinetic variations, such as crouching, twists, turns, and jumping somersaults, whether it was used as training for actual combat or physical exercise and aesthetic display. Today it is the latter two toward which the fighting arts are chiefly directed and which have profoundly influenced the development of stage movement and dance as well as theories of dramatic communication. Although the Beijing opera has developed its own system of physical training to meet special professional needs, it is indisputable that it is in great part both aesthetically and physically an elaboration of the ancient skills.

Mention may be made at this point of acrobatics, which have had a quite independent history from the developments just described. The Chinese are among the world's most superb acrobats, as evidenced in the split-hair timing of the leaping, somersaulting, and diving groups representing Monkey, armies, brigands, or similar supernumerary characters who are introduced onto the Beijing opera stage from time to time solely to provide a visually exciting interlude in the program. Their craft dates from the second century B.C. when acrobatic displays were introduced from Central Asia and developed along various lines to become what was called the "hundred games" (see chap. I).[11] Acrobatics remained a popular feature of court and public entertainments through the centuries, and there is nothing the Chinese public enjoys more than these virtuoso spectacles. The introduction of acrobatic elements in Beijing opera productions was indicative of its catering to a popular audience, and all the old Beijing theaters were fitted with bars above the stage as an aid to the actor's gymnastic leaps and tumbling.

Nevertheless, it is only necessary to see the displays with the scimitar by the "military" *sheng* actors, the hand-to-hand grappling of two stage combatants deprived of their weapons, the airy fencing with spears by two *wudan* actresses, or the pupils in the training school going through their daily paces in group combat exercises to perceive how deeply the theater has drawn upon the ancient fighting arts for its combat style.

THE COSTUMES AND MAKEUP OF THE BEIJING OPERA

Highly stylized and contrived as the movements and gestures of the Beijing opera actor are in every sense, they nevertheless represent an artistic transposition and refinement of movement conditioned by patterns of social behavior and the extension of such movement through the kinds of clothing that were worn. No better example of this could be given than the water sleeves. Their being decoratively flicked back in time to the music while the actor sings and their more extended use in the stage action provide a reminder that garments with long, wide sleeves were once everyday wear. Free movement of the hands created a functional pattern of gesture later transmitted as a dance form.

Chinese stage costume had its origins in the garments worn for the song and dance entertainments of the early courts. Their prime function was to facilitate graceful movement and decorative form without particular consideration for period style. When structured plots were eventually imposed on the old dance forms in their transmutation to performed stories, the basis of the physical presentation remained fundamentally choreographic, with consequent implications for the modification of costumes. The continued use of the water sleeves is a case in point. Thus, although increased attention was given to actual prototypes when stage costumes were devised to meet demands imposed by the changing dramatic content of the plays, the costumes never became authentic replicas. Theatrical effect and choreographic needs continued to be given precedence.

Beijing opera costumes have been considerably influenced by Ming and Qing styles, although these have been modified, exaggerated, or combined in the interests of acting form. To this end, color symbols and common motifs from traditional ornamentation familiar to everyone are important in costume decoration. Each role has its designated styles of garments, headdresses, and makeup, which define social status, occupation, and circumstance at a glance. In former times, Chinese dress was designed to serve such definitive functions in everyday life, and the style of clothing people wore and the quality and colors of the materials they could use were indicative of status, rank, and occupation and conformed to conservative social custom reinforced by edicts imposed by ruling authority. Court edicts decreed the styles, materials, and colors of dress, reflecting an authoritarian and precisely compartmented society. Satins, brocades, and other costly silks were reserved for people of accepted social status, as were the expensive furs like sable and fox used in winter clothing. This was especially true under Manchu rule, when Chinese costume underwent a great change, which is reflected in the historical inconsistencies of stage costume.

The first emperors of the Manchu dynasty compelled the Chinese to adopt some of their styles of dress and personal adornment for official and ceremonial purposes. The most dramatic manifestation of this was the ordering of all males to shave the front of their heads and wear their hair in a long queue, both as a token of submission and also to reduce any racial differentiation in the ranks of the officially employed. Drastic measures were enforced against any Chinese male refusing to wear the queue. A first edict to enforce these changes was issued in 1645 by the emperor Shunzhi. In the winter of 1647 a second edict for regulating the materials to be used for clothing was promulgated. Only officials and public servants were compelled to adopt these changes; the ordinary public was exempt.

In the early years of the Qing rule there were still many ordinary Chinese who continued to wear the clothing and hats of the late Ming period, an early omen of what was to happen on the Beijing opera stage, where Ming, Qing, and other period styles are freely mixed in the costuming of a play. There is no attempt to preserve historic unity in dressing the different roles, theatrical effect and function being the only considerations.

Chinese women's costume underwent no fundamental change between the seventeenth and nineteenth centuries. Women continued to wear the broad sleeves and long pleated skirts used by their ancestors, and these became basic elements of style for so many of the costumes used on the stage. Although Chinese women were not affected by Manchu dress regulations and indeed were left comparatively free from this kind of regimentation, the Manchus did try to abolish the practice of footbinding, without conspicuous success.

Chinese costume in the past was distinguished as being either for ceremonial, official, or everyday wear, a trio of functions which would be readily applicable to the stage wardrobe. In 1694 the Manchus laid down rules and regulations for style and usage in the case of ceremonial and official dress, compiled in exhaustive detail and published in a lengthy series of volumes which were revised during the eighteenth and nineteenth centuries. The many illustrations used in this work make it possible to trace the prototypes of numerous stage costumes.[12]

The Manchus were basically a riding and hunting people who wore costumes suitable for their way of life. Although the official dress they adopted when they conquered China was modelled on that used in Ming times, functional features like tight sleeves, slit hems, high collars, and cloth-looped buttons came in with Manchu styles and were transposed to stage dress.

As a broad generalization it could be said that Ming influences on stage costumes are most obvious in those used to portray men and women in civilian roles, where the old Chinese forms embodying wide sleeves, low necks, and crossover fastenings tend to predominate. A good example is the lined robe for everyday use, used as an informal garment by both male and female characters on stage, where it also serves a universal purpose as a foundation for other stage costumes. It is made in different colors, patterns, and qualities of silk, as well as cotton, and is a loosely cut garment based on the everyday style used in Ming times. Manchu influence is apparent in a costume like the "arrow robe," a long, narrow garment with tight sleeves and a slit down the central hem, which is worn on the stage as a kind of uniform by household guards, jailers, and the like, and in its most elaborate version as the informal military dress of high-ranking personalities.

The stage costume worn to represent armor, made of heavy, embroidered satin, worn by warriors and amazons, bears no resemblance to the steel armor used in ancient times but is derived from the cotton-padded, metal-studded uniforms of Qing military officials at court. The four triangular pennants strapped to the back of the actor below the shoulders, used in the most elaborate version of the armor costume, are a theatrical addition, however, designed to symbolize a person of very high command. They also provide an accessory that adds visual attraction to the gyrations and circumambulations on the stage which characterize the forceful but precisely controlled balletlike dance forms used by the actors wearing armor and engaged in stage combat. These particular costume accessories commemorate the fact that in past times, commanders-in-chief vested authority in a subordinate by handing him a small pennant bearing the leader's insignia.

Although Beijing opera costumes seem complicated at first, in fact they all fit tidily within a limited grouping of basic styles, the variations on a basic style being due to color, pattern, and whether they are to be worn by male or female characters, who frequently use robes of the same name, basic cut, and symbolic function. For example, a stage emperor and empress wear robes derived from the dragon robe styles once used only by the imperial court, although any exact replicas were forbidden under the monarchy.

Apart from the court edicts concerning dress, custom rather than rules decreed that certain garments became standard equipment in the costume chests of a troupe. Every troupe owned the stock costumes used in the four principal role categories, but it depended on the size of the troupe and the extent of their repertoire as to how elaborate their stock wardrobe became. There was always a certain amount of making do and interchange of basic items in the smaller troupes. In the bigger troupes it was customary until 1949 for leading performers to have their own costumes, and the personal stage wardrobe of an actor or actress was always a costly professional acquisition to be treated with care and pride, a contrast to former days when slaves, servants of officials, actors, and entertainers were only allowed to wear pongee silk of rough texture or the lacquered cloth in browns, black, or natural color worn by coolies.

It was forbidden to reproduce official insignia on stage costumes; for example, the dragon roundels on the robes used by the imperial family and sanctioned by a 1759 decree to be used by mandarins down to the sixth rank. The insignia on stage costumes, therefore, were theatrical adaptations with enough visual simulation to serve their purpose. Stage costume was much more restrained in the earlier part of this century than it later became; it was only during the twenties and thirties that the more spectacular qualities of color, material, and pattern were introduced.

Women were freer in the choice of colors and materials than were men in the past, unless they were wives of officials, and were not subject to minute regulations in their attire, but social prejudice and rigid custom confined them to standardized forms of enveloping jackets, trousers, and skirts. Clothing was worn in layers, a practical measure for coping with extremes of climate, among other functions, but for women a necessary total concealment of the figure that was decreed by Confucian prudery. Well-bred women in their deportment were required to keep their eyes lowered, conceal their mouths when smiling, and control their facial expression generally. Their pattern of social behavior was reflected in the *qingyi* roles in which the performer walks demurely, one arm down and the other supporting it across the waist, eyes downcast beneath the heavy makeup disciplining extrovert expression. Bound feet made Chinese women in the old days walk with minute steps, and their skirts were tailored with as many as a hundred pleats in which their gait was expected to cause no more than a perceptible quiver of the pleated lines. Bridal skirts had tiny bells attached to the pleats and the bride was expected to walk so decorously that only a faint tinkling resulted as she swayed gently along.

Chinese women paid great attention not only to their clothes, but to hairstyles and makeup. Powder and rouge were used from earliest times; eyebrows were shaved and penciled and the mouth rouged in with small blobs of color, practices that are reflected in the heavy stage makeup of the women's roles. A common hairstyle that prevailed from the mid-seventeenth to the early twentieth century was one in which the hair was drawn smoothly back to partially cover the ears and form a chignon. The Yangzhou style had a higher chignon; the Suzhou version was set lower in the nape of the neck—Yangzhou and Suzhou being rival towns in the matter of fashion and theatrical activities.

A wide forehead rounded at the temples to complete the oval of the face was regarded as the feminine ideal to which all women conformed and which influenced the design of the all-purpose hairstyle used in the majority of the women's roles in the Beijing opera repertoire. This hairstyle is said to have been devised by the Sichuan actor Wei Changsheng (1744–1802),[13] discussed in chapter IV. It is not a wig but is built up piecemeal for each performance and provides a foundation for the stage jewelry and artificial flowers used as decorations. Special features are the coils and sidepieces of real hair gummed into position by fixative to frame the face and brow, and the long, tightly bound chignon at the back of the head.

Facial makeup on the Beijing opera stage ranges between the highly conventionalized, dependent on a heavy use of powder and paint, to practically no makeup at all, as in the case of the *laodan* roles. With the exception of these and the comic roles, the makeup for women consists of a heavily whitened countenance, the eyes being surrounded by a deep rouge tint extending to the cheeks and the sides of the nose, the bridge of which is left white. The natural mouth and eyebrows are painted out to be replaced by conventionalized forms, the eyebrows and corners of the eyes being penciled with black to exaggerate the upward slant caused by the eyes having been drawn back by a tightly bound tape around the forehead when the hairstyle is being done up. In the past every actor or actress had a special dresser to look after this complex process when making up.

The most unusual facial makeups are those used in the *jing* roles where the actors paint the whole of their faces and brows with either elaborate multicolored or black and white designs, which symbolize the personality and temperament of the character portrayed. White used in a conspicuous way by itself expresses cunning and treachery; black, integrity and straightforwardness; red, loyalty and courage; blue, ferocity and fearlessness; green, evil spirits or supernatural beings; and so on. There were literally hundreds of these designs used at one time but they have become far less numerous today.[14] They are technically classed as "oil face," the colors being mixed with oil to give a sheen, and "powder face," for which the colors are mixed with water to provide a matte surface.

It is a matter for dispute when this style of makeup first developed into the form it has now become, but it was a well-established practice in Ming dynasty times. During the nineteenth century many new designs were introduced for an acting style that had become much admired by theatergoers for its resounding vocal delivery and vigorous physical display.

STAGE PRACTICES

The influence of the old patterns of behavior is traceable in stage techniques. The formalized gait used in the *dan* roles is in effect a theatrical transposition of the old style feminine deportment. The actor or actress playing these roles must keep the feet close together and take very short steps, the quicker the pace the shorter the step. The feet are kept parallel about an inch apart, with the toe of the first foot placed no more than three inches beyond the rear foot.

In contrast, male authority is expressed in the gait of the *sheng* actors, who walk with a dignified strut conditioned by the high, platform-soled knee boots worn in many of the principal roles. The gait commences with the feet planted squarely on the ground six or seven inches apart. The right foot is then lifted forward about fourteen inches with an outward swing before it touches ground, when the left heel is then brought up to the right heel, positioning the left foot at ninety degrees to the right foot. There is a pause before the action is repeated, with the alternate foot leading off for succeeding steps. This pacing is intensified in power, grace, and height of the lifted foot according to the particular role, but is always associated with the statuesque postures characteristic of the genre. The contrast between the commanding gait of the male roles and the softer restraint of the female versions suggests a *yang-yin* concept of stage movement reflecting the old social relationships of the sexes.

In order to simulate the movement and deportment resulting from the custom of bound feet, actors wore small, wooden, stiltlike articles bound to the feet and ankles with wide cotton puttees, so that the wearer was firmly supported in an "on points" stance. They were reputed to be the invention of Wei Changsheng. They were used constantly in the *huadan* and *wudan* roles, and in the latter particularly to perform complex acrobatics of a kind in which no woman with bound feet could ever have indulged, being introduced only to display the actors' gymnastic virtuosity.

The custom of men playing women's roles continued into the twentieth century and was only discontinued after 1949. A result of having to make a virtue out of necessity in the first place, the practice was perfected by generations of actors, not as realistic simulation but as a highly formalized technique for expressing the quintessence of femininity, according to Confucian standards, and as a complement to an acting style that was highly formalized in all its aspects.

The formalized acting techniques constitute a kind of balance to the starkness of the stage itself. Michel Saint-Denis has spoken of the reality of performance being dependent upon the scenic disposition with which it is "naturally, umbilically connected," holding up the Chinese theater among others as a comparative example.[15] It is true that in Beijing opera there is a close visible relationship between the stage area and the acting forms. The uncompromising austerity of the Chinese stage and its properties has become proverbial. A small wooden table, two chairs, a carpet, and a rear curtain through which the actors make their exits and entries are the only scenic necessities for an open area that can be expanded or contracted at will, without minimizing a calculated awareness of space and disregard for illusion that reveals the craft of acting at its source.

The perceptive ability of the Chinese performer to adapt to limited space and constricting stage areas without compromising the precision and integrity of his acting has possibly been strengthened by the long-established custom of performing in private houses, courtyards, and banquet halls, as well as a developed sense of improvisation born of a history of itinerant trouping necessitating overnight erection of temporary stages to be as quickly taken down. The Chinese actor has long been accustomed to adapting his concentrated skills to a wide variety of playing areas.

The traditional Beijing city stage remained constant in design until early in this century and was typified by a low, balustraded platform, open on three sides and canopied with supporting pillars at each corner. It was essentially an intimate stage and one that tested in full an actor's self-sufficiency. It was this quality that stirred Bertolt Brecht to revelation after seeing Mei Lanfang (1894–1961) perform impromptu, wearing formal evening dress, before a crowd of diplomatic guests at a Chinese embassy reception held for Mei at Moscow in 1935. Brecht was full of admiration for the sublime control shown in this extemporaneous presentation.

> The Chinese performer is in no trance. He can be interrupted at any moment. He won't have to "come round." After an interruption he will go on with his exposition from that point. We are not disturbing him at the "mystic moment of creation," when he steps on the stage before us the process of creation is already over.[16]

The provincial and rural counterparts of the old urban theater were the outdoor stages built of stone, conforming to the same kind of spatial dimensions but standing well above the heads of the audience, who stood shoulder to shoulder looking up at the performance from below, a viewpoint conducive to forceful presentation by the players.[17]

It was in Shanghai with its proximity to Western inventions and influences that the changes in theater buildings first came about, including the introduction of lighting, which transformed theater from the daytime entertainment it had been into an evening pastime. The old style gave way to a Western form with footlights, a compromise that retained the spatial integrity of the traditional acting forms and was extended to the smaller teahouse theaters. It was eventually replaced by the proscenium style stage, which continues to dominate theater construction, providing all the temptations for spectacle that modern lighting and scenic effects offer and which audiences have come to expect.

Through all the physical changes, however, the innate Chinese sense of spatial pliancy has remained to dominate stage practices. The unities of time and place are relegated to the domain of mime and dance. Movement and gesture are complete statements in themselves as a communicative force with dimensions beyond the scope of social verisimilitude.

Two of the most common bits of stage business used as interlinking elements in the action of any Beijing opera are the techniques used to portray being mounted on horseback and opening and closing a door, both telling examples of invoking form within space. Riding a horse is suggested through the use of a simple riding switch, ornamented with four silk tassels and secured by a thong to the actor's wrist. This prop is wielded in a structured pattern of movements that are controlled but relaxed, such as kicks, turns, gyrations, and posturings. The movements make up a pantomimic series of images that convey riding, mounting, dismounting, tethering, and backing a horse. Such images are concisely but graphically realized within the expressive choreographic delineation. Similarly, the opening and closing of a door is as potently suggested, and the stage itself can be immediately compartmented into inner and outer playing areas through the sheer mimetic control of space without any demand on credibility.

Michel Saint-Denis in his book on style observed: "The Chinese say it is not doors that are interesting but what happens behind them, so why have doors?"[18] A pertinent comment on a people who have always sought their enjoyment of theater in the sensory immediacy of the actor's presentation.

NOTES

1. See Colin Mackerras, *The Rise of the Peking Opera 1770–1870* (Clarendon Press, Oxford, 1972), pp. 145–153, for a balanced account.

2. See Mei Lanfang, *Wutai shenghuo sishi nian* (Pingming chubanshe, Shanghai, 1952), vol. 1, pp. 62–69; an authoritative account of the school's history.

3. The information given here is from personal notes made in Hong Kong in 1952 from accounts provided by a former administrative member of the school.

4. The *si da dan* or "four great performers of leading women's roles" are Mei Lanfang, Cheng Yanqiu, Xun Huisheng, and Shang Xiaoyun.

5. Mei Lanfang, *Wutai shenghuo*, vol. 1, p. 40.

6. Ibid., pp. 36–42.

7. See Colin Mackerras, "The Growth of the Chinese Regional Drama in the Ming and Ch'ing," *Journal of Oriental Studies* 9, no. 1 (January, 1971): 84–90, for an excellent account of the complex history of this form.

8. *Qi Rushan quanji* (Qi Rushan xiansheng yizhu bianyin weiyuanhui, Taibei, 1964), vol. 1, pp. 1–6.

9. Ibid., vol. 2, pp. 52–66.

10. See *Wudao* 4, 5, 6 (1962): 42–43, 40–41, 33–39, a series of three articles on the history of the dance with illustrations showing development of sleeve movements.

11. Liu Wu-chi, *An Introduction to Chinese Literature* (Indiana University Press, Bloomington, 1966), pp. 159–194.

12. *Qinding, Daqing huidian tu*, chaps. 56–66. Compiled in 1694; revised and augmented 1727; revised by imperial order in 1771 and published in 100 vols.; later edition published in 1818 in 80 vols., with accompanying sets of plates in 32 vols. I am indebted to the articles published in *Dagong bao*, May 25, June 1, June 22, August 3, 1935, by Xu Dishan, "Sanbai nian lai Zhongguo di nüzhuang" for some of the information on women's costume.

13. See Mackerras, *The Rise of the Peking Opera*, pp. 91–98 for an account of the life and career of this actor.

14. See Zhang Xiaoxia, *Lianpu daquan* (Xiqu yanjiushe, Beiping, 1937).

15. Michel Saint-Denis, *Theatre: The Rediscovery of Style* (Theatre Arts Books, New York, 1976), pp. 55–57.

16. John Willett, trans. and ed., *Brecht on Theatre* (Hill and Wang, New York, 1966), pp. 91–96.

17. *The Illustrated Journal Guoju shubao*, published in Beijing, contained a series of interesting photographs of old regional stages in its issues, dated October 28, 1932–August 10, 1934.

18. Saint-Denis, *Theatre*, p. 55.

SELECTED READINGS

Famous Chinese Plays. Translated from Chinese to English by L. C. Arlington and Harold Acton. Russell and Russell, New York, 1963. A translation of thirty-three Beijing operas, with an introduction on stage conventions and other explanatory matters.

Mackerras, Colin P. *The Rise of the Peking Opera 1770–1870: Social Aspects of the Theatre in Manchu China*. Clarendon Press, Oxford, 1972. A definitive historical study in English treated in scholarly depth.

Mei Lanfang. *Wutai shenghuo sishi nian*. Edited by Xu Jichuan. 2 vols. Pingming chubanshe, Shanghai, 1952 and 1954. An autobiographical account of Mei's professional life as related to Xu Jichuan who compiled the text. Incomplete as these two volumes are—they do not deal with Mei's life beyond the early twenties—they provide valuable insights on the life and training of China's most celebrated actor and contain a great deal of practical information on the *jingxi* theater and its customs and methods.

Qi Rushan. *Qi Rushan quanji* [*The complete works of Qi Rushan*]. 8 vols. Qi Rushan Xiansheng yizhu bianyin weiyuanhui, Taibei, 1964.

Qi Rushan. *Mei Lanfang yishu zhi yiban* [*A speck of Mei Lanfang's art*]. Guoji xuehui, Beiping, 1935. Contains clear illustrations of the hand gestures of Mei Lanfang. Published in the collected works, but the printing is much inferior.

Qi Rushan, Zhang Daxia. *Chinese Opera Costumes*. National Taiwan Arts Center, Taiwan, 1961. A revised and expanded compilation of Qi's former studies of stage dress. There is an English-Chinese text and the book is illustrated with clear, full-page color drawings of individual garments.

Schönfelder, Gerd. *Die Musik der Peking-Oper.* Deutscher Verlag für Musik, Leipzig, 1972. The most detailed musicological study of Beijing opera in a European language, this book covers especially "text-music correlation," rhythm, and melody. It includes a separate small volume of musical examples.

Scott, A. C. *Traditional Chinese Plays,* translated, described, and annotated by A. C. Scott. Vols. I, II, III. University of Wisconsin Press, Madison, 1967, 1969, 1975.

Zhang Xiaoxia. *Lianpu daquan* [*Complete makeup record*]. Xiqu yanjiushe, Beiping, 1937. The most comprehensive illustrated work on the painted face makeups.

Zhou Yibai. *Zhongguo xiju shi* [*History of Chinese drama*]. 3 vols. Zhonghua shuju, Shanghai, 1953. An authoritative history of the Chinese drama that is indispensable for research.

Zhou Yibai. *Zhongguo xiqu lunji* [*Collection of papers on Chinese drama*]. Zhongguo xiju chubanshe, Beijing, 1960. An informative collection of essays containing very useful source material.

Zung, Cecilia S. L. *Secrets of the Chinese Drama: A Complete Explanatory Guide to Actions and Symbols as Seen in the Performance of Chinese Dramas.* Benjamin Blom, New York, 1937, reissued 1964. This includes synopses of fifty popular dramas. It concerns Beijing opera, rather than Chinese opera in general.

CHAPTER VI

THEATER AND THE MASSES

Colin Mackerras

THEATER was a mass form of art in China long before the twentieth century; with fluctuations, it has become even more so since the overthrow of the Qing dynasty. It has also continued to be a highly political phenomenon. Indeed, as the twentieth century has progressed and the political situation become more of an issue to the Chinese masses, so theater has tended to gain in significance for them as a factor both reflecting and influencing their country's development.

What is striking is that drama has not required national stability in order to grow. On the contrary, some of the most vital years for theater have been precisely the most unstable and traumatic politically. It is as if the Chinese people have been able to give vent to political uncertainty and anguish through dramatic expression. On the other hand, there are also years of flowering that have fallen in relatively stable periods.

THE SPOKEN PLAY BEFORE THE WAR AGAINST JAPAN

The first cultural revolution of the Republic of China began in 1915. Perhaps its most symbolic event was the publication of the journal *Youth Magazine (Qingnian zazhi),* the first issue of which appeared on September 15 of that year in Shanghai under the editorship of Chen Duxiu, shortly to become one of the major leaders of the May Fourth Movement. *Youth Magazine* was soon renamed *New Youth (Xin qingnian).* It was perhaps the most influential of all the publications of progressive youth of that period. In June 1918 this journal devoted an entire issue to Ibsen, explaining the relationship of his dramatic works to society and politics of their time and setting him forward as an example for Chinese intellectuals and youth to follow in the writing of their plays. The association of this cultural revolution with drama and vice versa was clear right from the start.

When the May Fourth Movement actually began on May 4, 1919 with a large nationalist demonstration in Beijing over China's betrayal at the Paris Peace Conference, the outburst stimulated an increasing participation in amateur drama by students, intellectuals, and others. They saw such activities as an antiimperialist and patriotic expression.

In the wake of the May Fourth Movement, Chen Dabei, Ouyang Yuqian, and about a dozen other dramatists organized the Popular Drama Society in May 1921. They issued a manifesto in which they declared that "theater occupies an important place in modern society, it is a wheel which impels society forward, and it is also an X-ray which seeks out the basic faults of society." The manifesto appeared as an appendix to the first issue of the Society's monthly journal entitled *Theater (Xiju)*, which was the first periodical devoted entirely to theater in China. Altogether ten issues were published; contributors discussed the theoretical and artistic aspects of theater, including opposition to the old traditional drama. The influence that the journal exerted on young playwrights appears to have been considerable.

In the remainder of the 1920s a number of other literary or dramatic societies, and corresponding journals, came into existence. Possibly the best known among them was the *Creation Quarterly (Chuangzao jikan)*, published by the Creation Society beginning in May 1922. The first issue contained the text of the play *A Night in a Coffee Shop (Jiafei dian zhi yiye)* by Tian Han, possibly the most prominent of all the dramatists of the period. The play was an attack on the traditional system of family and marriage in China; an expression of yearning for the right to choose one's own spouse. This theme was an extremely popular one, not only with the youth of the May Fourth Movement itself, but with Tian Han as an individual and with the dramatists of the period in general.

The spoken plays tended to focus on contemporary issues and to be set in the present or recent past. On the other hand, playwrights continued to use traditional themes as well. For instance, Ouyang Yuqian wrote a play called *Yang Guifei* about the famous concubine of Emperor Minghuang of the Tang dynasty, in fact the same topic as the Qing drama *The Palace of Eternal Youth*, discussed in chapter IV (see plate 31). In most cases, however, the dramatist succeeded in presenting the theme in such a way as to insert commentary on the society of his own day, thus advocating some kind of reform by bringing out the oppression of women, the tyranny of the traditional family system, and so on. Among the most distinguished of the writers of these historical plays was Guo Moruo who attempted, with some success, to identify his own psychology with that of famous personalities of the distant past and thus to see a social lesson for his own day in their experiences and sufferings.

When the Chinese Communist Party (CCP) was set up in 1921, it was quick to see the value of drama to further its own cause. During the united front period of the CCP and Guomindang (GMD) from 1924 to 1927, it organized troupes that presented items on relevant revolutionary themes. For instance, in celebration of May Day 1926, thirty or forty CCP members and "revolutionary youth" put on a play called *Blood of February Seventh (Erqi xie)*[1] based on the "February Seventh" massacre of 1923 when troops of the warlord Wu Peifu put down the great Beijing–Hankou railway strike.

The warlord governments opposed not only strikes but, not surprisingly, also progressive plays and drama societies. When Chiang Kaishek and the GMD attempted their reunification of China in 1926–1928 they followed a basically similar policy, making the life of the progressive playwright a difficult one indeed. Nevertheless, the early years of the GMD government show a further plethora of societies, associations, spoken-play companies, and new dramas on social and contemporary themes. The associations varied in political coloring: some were rather conservative in their outlook; others were extremely radical and even overtly sympathetic to the CCP, which Chiang Kaishek was expressly trying to suppress. A good example of the latter type is the Shanghai Society of Arts and Drama, founded in the autumn of 1929, which Chiang Kaishek's police closed down on April 29 of the following year.

Despite GMD opposition to leftist theater, the early years of its government were a period in which literary activity as a whole flourished. The League of Leftwing Writers, established in March 1930, is famous in the annals of the history of modern Chinese literature, partly because one of its principal driving forces was Lu Xun, recognized by virtually all critics as among twentieth-century China's greatest prose writers. The dramatists followed suit. Various leftist drama societies coalesced into a body called the Association of Shanghai Drama Companies, and early in 1931 this body was reorganized into the Chinese League of Leftwing Dramatists, corresponding to the League of Leftwing Writers. In September of the same year the League adopted a radical six-point program; the first two points suffice to show its tone and ideas.

1. We must go deeply among the proletarian masses in the cities. We must lead the proletarian drama movement through three methods; namely, independent performances of our own League, aiding the performance of worker comrades, or amalgamating the performances of our own League and worker comrades. The patterns of performance that we adopt must be such that the intellectual level of the masses of workers can fully comprehend them. . . .

2. In order to seize the revolutionary petty bourgeois student masses and small townspeople, our League must use the above-mentioned three types of formulae, that is, independence, aid, amalgamation, to incite, organize, and lead their drama movement and employ all kinds of methods to secure freedom of public performance in the areas under white terror [i.e., GMD controlled areas].[2]

The manifesto goes on to discuss the extreme importance of the peasants in the white areas and calls for the establishment of leftist influence over them through drama. It does not explicitly mention the CCP, but it does call for opposition to imperialism and to the GMD. It is also important in that its conscious division of prospective audiences into workers, townspeople, petty bourgeois students, and peasants suggests a greater emphasis on the masses than had hitherto been the case among urban playwrights.

Although the League's major thrust remained urban despite its intention to involve the peasantry, the same charge cannot be leveled against the spoken plays that existed in the Chinese Soviet Republic set up in Jiangxi province on November 7, 1931, with Mao Zedong as its chairman. The Red Army developed the "reportage play" through which it made known to the people events happening in the Soviet and its agrarian revolution. It appears that the "reportage plays" also "filled an important role in arousing the Red Army fighters."[3]

Theater flourished in the Jiangxi Soviet. The first troupe there was named the August 1, in honor of Army Day; August 1, 1927, the date of the Nanchang uprising, is regarded as the birthday of the Red Army. The troupe's impact comes through in the reminiscences of one of its organizers: "It received many letters from the front and the rear inviting it to give public performances or requiring playscripts and material. When the central government [of the Soviet] convened conferences or important activities of various kinds, it would often be invited to come forward and perform."[4]

In due course the number of troupes in the Jiangxi Soviet expanded to about sixty. They travelled through the villages and along the front and, according to Edgar Snow, were in such demand that the village soviets had to put in requests well in advance of any proposed visit.[5]

By this time the Japanese had occupied Manchuria (1931) and set up the puppet state of Manchukoku (1932). It was partly as a result of these events that the Chinese became increasingly aware of both the need and the potential of theater not only as a political weapon but specifically as a tool to arouse patriotism against a foreign aggressor and enemy. The League of Leftwing Dramatists expanded its activities. In the mid-1930s we find the growth of "national defense theater." This movement was led by such famous dramatists as Hong Shen and Tian Han.

Despite the importance of the anti-Japanese drama movement, the most distinguished playwright of the 1930s was undoubtedly Cao Yu, born in 1910. His plays may indeed reflect social comment, but he was certainly not as radical in political sympathies as the members of the League of Leftwing Dramatists, let alone the writers of the Jiangxi Soviet.

Cao Yu's earliest play was *Thunderstorm (Leiyu)*. It was published in 1934 in the *Literary Quarterly (Wenxue jikan)*, first performed in 1935 by amateurs of the Fudan University of Shanghai, directed by Ouyang Yuqian and Hong Shen, and given its first professional performance the following year. The play was a great success and immediately made Cao Yu's reputation, not only among Chinese but also foreign critics. In 1936 he published his play *Sunrise (Richu)* and the following year *Wilderness (Yuanye)*. These two plays also proved successful, both in terms of the public enthusiasm and critical response they aroused.

Thunderstorm is a long play with an exceedingly involved plot. Through youthful follies and insensitivity the manager of a successful coal mine, a man called Zhou Puyuan, brings disaster and death to the members of his family and a lonely, remorseful old age to himself. The whole play takes place against the background of an impending thunderstorm and the heavy atmosphere that accompanies it. Into several themes relating to the family, including incest, Cao Yu succeeds in weaving that of the labor movement, for one of Zhou's sons is in fact leading the workers against the coal mine manager's interests.

In the playwright's mind it is less Zhou Puyuan's stupidity than the traditional family system that brings about the concatenation of suffering and the tragedies of the play's denouement. Cao Yu is attacking not individuals but the society that makes them behave as they do. The modern scholar Joseph S. M. Lau has summed up *Thunderstorm's* significance as follows:

> The play, despite its artistic flaws, touches upon two of the most sensitive issues involved in the May Fourth Movement: a socialist concern for the plight of the workers under capitalist exploitation, and an individual effort to assert personal freedom and happiness under the crippling weight of patriarchal society. In brief, *Thunderstorm* was so ruthless in its attacks upon traditional Chinese morals and the social system that the government felt impelled, on three occasions, to place it under a ban.[6]

Although it is a Chinese play and reflects Chinese problems, *Thunderstorm*—and indeed Cao Yu's plays in general—is heavily influenced by Western models and values. Like earlier spoken plays, this one uses the dramatic conventions, scenery, and acting of Western dramas, not the stylized mannerisms of the Chinese traditional opera. Joseph Lau has called Cao Yu "the reluctant disciple of Chekhov and O'Neill." At some length he draws parallels, and admittedly also contrasts, between *Thunderstorm* and Eugene O'Neill's *Desire Under the Elms* and in particular between the central female characters of the two plays.[7]

Cao Yu and his *Thunderstorm* represent the acme of the artistic flowering of the semi-Westernized China which at the same time struggled both against Western influence and the Chinese past. Cao Yu was in no sense revolutionary, and he appears to have been much clearer about what he opposed than what he supported. He knew that the system of the past could no longer be defended but was not sure what to put in its place.

Cao Yu's plays, like the May Fourth Movement and the national defense theater, were peculiarly urban phenomena, and the extent of influence of the CCP in the 1930s was still limited. On the whole, the "political" theater thus tended to concentrate in certain areas of the country. This situation changed with the Lugou Bridge incident of July 7, 1937. The bridge was just outside Beiping and the incident signalled the city's occupation by Japanese troops as well as the full scale invasion of China.

THEATER IN THE WAR OF RESISTANCE AGAINST JAPAN

Chalmers Johnson has argued that it was the "Japanese conquest of north and east China" that really "unified and politicized" the Chinese peasantry, thus making them truly nationalist and really involved in their nation's future.[8] He believes that up until that time they had been apathetic and somewhat slow to respond to the CCP. The war thus gave the CCP the chance it needed to use the peasants to come to power. Whether his arguments are correct concerning the fortunes of the CCP is not at issue here, and there is an alternative view. The war against Japan was, however, a vital turning point in the history of Chinese theater. As Tian Han puts it: "It was in this period that theater genuinely achieved 'massization,' that is to say, it really went down deep among the people."[9]

As the war broke out the Chinese people, and in particular their playwrights and actors, united to an extent never known before, against the Japanese. One of the first results of this was that a group of cinema and theater activists in Shanghai organized the Shanghai Theater World Salvation Association, which immediately formed thirteen drama companies with the specific aim of spreading anti-Japanese and patriotic propaganda. Two of them, the eleventh and twelfth, remained in Shanghai, and the others went throughout the country, to Hangzhou, Nanjing, Swatow, and various parts of the interior; the fifth and part of the first even visited the CCP capital Yan'an. Some, such as the third and fourth, included amateur actors; others were entirely professional. Hong Shen led the second troupe, and he was not the only well-known dramatist in the leadership of the thirteen.

Nanjing fell to the Japanese in December 1937, and Hankou replaced it as the national capital. Many theater groups, actors, and dramatists, including such famous people as Mei Lanfang, Zhou Xinfang, Ouyang Yuqian, and Tian Han, gathered there and late in December 1937 set up the All China Theater World Association to Resist the Enemy. Its ambit ranged from plays to various styles of clapper opera, as well as other regional styles including Beijing opera, and in addition storytelling forms and the witty cross-talk called *xiangsheng*. The Association's manifesto stressed two balancing themes of unity for resistance to Japan because of the varying political persuasions of the members: "Our unity is in order to resist the enemy" and "Only resistance to the enemy causes us to unite." "Today's China does not fear the enemy's penetration," it went on, "but that internal national unity will waver." Here we return to the propaganda function of theater which is stated in the manifesto very strongly: "To spread propaganda against the enemy among the broad masses of the people of the whole country, the most effective weapon is undoubtedly drama—all kinds, all varieties of drama."[10]

A key phrase in the manifesto is "go to the peasant villages." One vital feature that the thirteen Shanghai companies shared with the Association to Resist the Enemy was their members' wish to reach the peasant masses. Apart from the CCP troupes this had been rare before the Japanese invasion. It was the war that made the actors and dramatists of the cities willing to undergo the discomforts of the villages and the countryside in a patriotic endeavour. Certainly, "to the peasant villages" became much more than a slogan. They went in small groups of seven or eight or in large groups of over a hundred. Like the wandering companies of the past, they used temple stages or, perhaps more modern, "temporarily built stages in school halls, classrooms, and playgrounds."[11] Just as often, they simply performed in the streets.

In one way there was nothing new about "going to the peasant villages," as the reference to the wandering troupes makes clear. But the wartime companies included not only famous actors but also intellectuals and well-known dramatists. Such people would hardly ever have gone to the peasantry in former times. The significance was that the Japanese invasion had raised the social status of peasant theater drastically.

Another feature that Shanghai's thirteen troupes and Hankou's Association shared comes through in the list of sites of their performances: the plays were put on in the streets. Such dramas were appropriate both for the cities and the countryside, both for the areas under the control of the CCP and of the GMD. They were extensively performed by front service corps, various propaganda groups, and itinerant troupes. Actors believed street theater to be particularly effective. In the first place it was a real spectacle and thus aroused considerable enthusiasm. The actors would "carry banners reading 'such-and-such a performing team,' and these would flutter majestically above the streets, while the performers enthusiastically struck gongs and drums,"[12] thus creating a mass collective feeling against a common enemy. The actors naturally cultivated this atmosphere of identity of interests, so characteristic of popular drama, especially when it takes place in the open air. Li Yanhui claims that the actors would send people to mix with the people and "secretly lead the audience's emotions, so that the propaganda effectiveness was very great."[13]

Since it was "the cause" that made dramas of this kind such good theater, they were eminently suitable for amateurs. Following the spread of rural drama to meet the Japanese invasion we find a corresponding increase in spare-time acting, like its professional counterpart aimed at spreading propaganda against the enemy. The people of the red areas were particularly enthusiastic; peasants and children founded their own dramatic societies in the villages. However, they were by no means the only amateur groups. Even in occupied Shanghai such groups were active; there were at least fifty of them in the early war years, "based mainly on professions or schools as units." They were intensely enthusiastic and hardworking and would perform "guerrilla style," to avoid the eyes of the occupation force, all over the city.[14]

Despite such activities there were some who believed the involvement of the masses had still not gone nearly far enough and that more concrete amateur organizations were desirable in the villages. Writing in 1944 towards the end of the war, Tian Han referred to the rural tours of professional troupes as "a kind of spreading seeds work." "If we wish to cause new drama to take root and sprout in the villages," he went on, "then we must foster the young peasants of that region as drama cadres to form themselves into healthy peasant companies."[15] Tian's hopes were to be strikingly fulfilled in later years.

In view of the explicit purposes for which wartime theater troupes, both professional and amateur, were formed and the nature of the political situation, it is not surprising that dramatists or actors quickly composed new works to accord with the situation at hand, which were sometimes not very good. Tian Han comments that, in the first period of the war, the dramas "almost entirely emphasized the propaganda function and ignored the truth that propaganda must be united with truth."[16] The problem was that to adapt plays, and much more so traditional operas, very quickly to deal with an explicit war situation was not easy. In earlier times actors espousing a cause had used traditional dramas on themes of rebellion or the relevant topic; they had not written whole new pieces specifically about one particular enemy. It may not have been too difficult for an actor in a Taiping-controlled area to insert a few comments against the Manchus in a drama the central theme of which was a rebellion of many centuries earlier. But to compose operas or plays dealing entirely with the evils of the Japanese was a different matter. Since the main aim was to incite the people against the Japanese, artistic refinement naturally had to come somewhat later. As far as the sources reveal, however, the propaganda content did nothing to turn the masses against the actors or the playwrights.

One major reason for this was that the items were direct, to the point, and easy to understand. A particular piece noted as a favorite in several sources was *Put Down Your Whip (Fangxia nide bianzi)*, which portrayed the cruelties of the Japanese and the sufferings of the people in Manchuria. Known as a street drama, it was performed many times in poor villages and remote areas. According to one source, it "would provoke enormous indignation" and "the sound of weeping among both army and people as they watched the drama."[17]

One particular traditional song and dance type widely adapted to contemporary wartime patriotic and revolutionary themes was the *yangge* (see plate 32). This is a folk form very popular among the peasants of Shaanxi and neighboring provinces. It is based on dances that developed out of work rhythms. The CCP with its capital in Yan'an in the *yangge* heartland got its artists to develop the form by adding spoken sections and adapting stories; the songs and dances thus took on the character of opera. The themes revolved around the everyday lives of the masses and of the Red Army, as well as relations between the two. One illustrative example is a short comedy published in 1943 called *Brother and Sister Opening Wasteland (Xiong-mei kaihuang)*, in which a girl and her elder brother compete, amid much fun, to become model workers. The *yangge* exemplified one side of the theater in the areas controlled by the Communists during the war. The performances were small in scale and based on stories often written and acted by the same people, professional or amateur playwrights and actors inspired to perform by their enthusiasm for the cause of the war against Japan and the revolution (see plate 33).

Naturally, both the CCP and GMD governments took an active

interest in all these plays, dances, and operas and encouraged them substantially. They also did what they could to ensure that the content suited their interests. The CCP certainly did not permit pro-Japanese or counterrevolutionary *yangge* in Yan'an, and the GMD tried to prevent people from contact with Communist drama, usually unsuccessfully. The GMD also took its own concrete measures to influence what dramas were read or shown in the areas it controlled. For instance, in 1939, the Textbook Editing Committee of the GMD government's Ministry of Education drew up a plan to select certain traditional Beijing operas for the edification of the people. Much other similar work was done by a range of government committees to supervise theater, old or modern.

New dramas specifically about the war against Japan constituted a major part of the standard repertoire, but those on historical themes remained well loved also. As a matter of fact, quite apart from the normal traditional operas, there were many based on topics from the past written by dramatists consciously trying to teach the masses more about the history of their own country through drama, once again with the ultimate purpose of promoting patriotism or revolution. In the occupied areas, historical dramas carried the advantage that their propaganda was less obvious and thus less likely to come under Japanese notice.

Curiously enough, however, probably the best known example of the historical plays came not from the occupied but the red areas—the Beijing opera *Driven Up Mt. Liang (Bishang Liangshan)*. The reason it assumes historical significance is because it was one of the very few dramas to which Mao Zedong gave his explicit approval. This work premiered in December 1943 in Yan'an; Mao saw it soon after and on January 9, 1944 wrote a letter to the actors commending them for showing history as made by the people and for seizing dominance of the stage from lords and ladies and their children. "Now you have righted this reversal of history and restored historical truth," Mao wrote, "thus opening up a new life for the old opera."[18] The drama is adapted from a scene in *The Water Margin,* and its significance, as Mao makes clear in his letter, lies more in its revolutionary content than its patriotism.

Both *Driven Up Mt. Liang* and the *yangge* piece mentioned earlier were in a real sense results of a forum held in Yan'an in May 1942 to discuss literature and art and their function in the revolution and the war against Japan. Two contributions to the forum were particularly important in affecting profoundly all works written in the red areas. They survive under the title "Talks at the Yan'an Forum on Literature and Art," by Mao Zedong.

MAO'S IDEOLOGY ON THE ARTS

The ideas that Mao put forward at the Yan'an forum have come to occupy a dominant position in Chinese society. Even now after his death the "Talks" are regarded as a kind of "classic" on the arts and therefore merit detailed attention here.

In the "Talks" Mao takes for granted that he and his listeners are dialectical materialists. Such a person holds that matter takes primacy in deciding the nature of societies. Thus, the first question he will ask is: "Who owns property and the means of production, such as land and factories?" The religion or beliefs of the people and the system of government are secondary to and rest on the first question. The nature of ownership determines the classes to which people belong, and consequently what they think and the kind of art they enjoy. The progress of society results from conflict between classes, which alone brings about change.

A primary question Mao raises in the "Talks" relates to the nature of art itself. He says that "works of literature and art, as ideological forms, are products of the reflection in the human brain of the life of a given society."[19] It follows that they cannot but reflect societies and, more specifically, the particular classes within societies. Indeed, one of the most famous of all his sayings on the arts is: "In the world today all culture, all literature and art belong to definite classes and are geared to definite political lines."[20] However, the arts not only reflect society, they also influence it. It is clear that in artistic creation the desire to influence society has been central for Mao and his followers; this has been so at all times not only during the war against Japan but since then as well. At the introductory session to the forum, held on May 2, 1942, Mao stated that the purpose of the meeting was "precisely to ensure that literature and art fit well into the whole revolutionary machine as a component part." They must, he said, "operate as powerful weapons for uniting and educating the people and for attacking and destroying the enemy,"[21] by whom of course he meant the Japanese.

Since the arts are so closely tied to the particular society that produces them, both by reflecting and influencing it, they cannot help but be a form of propaganda either for one side of a struggle or another; they do this whatever the intention of the artist. It follows that there are no eternal values in the arts, no absolute standards. This means that the value of a particular piece of art may change depending upon its function in a particular society.

> We deny not only that there is an abstract and absolutely unchangeable political criterion, but also that there is an abstract and absolutely unchangeable artistic criterion; each class in every class society has its own political and artistic criteria. But all classes in all class societies invariably put the political criterion first and the artistic criterion second. The bourgeoisie always shuts out proletarian literature and art, however great their artistic merit. The proletariat must similarly distinguish among the literary and art works of past ages and determine its attitude towards them only after examining their attitude to the people and whether or not they had any progressive significance historically. Some works which politically are downright reactionary may have a certain artistic quality.[22]

Despite the clear denial of any absolute standard in art there are certainly criteria by which one can judge it, not only politically but also artistically. These also change according to the time and the society.

Curiously enough, only a few months before the Yan'an forum Mao had formally condemned what he called "stereotyped Party writing" in a speech he made at a cadres' meeting in Yan'an on February 8, 1942. He had thus set forward a number of specific criteria for writing, and they are applicable to drama as well as to ordinary prose. The first and most serious indictment against stereotyped writing "is that it fills endless pages with empty verbiage."[23] Mao is thus following the age-old principle that "brevity is the soul of wit"; one should never say more than is necessary.

His second criterion and criticism of stereotyped writing is that it "strikes a pose in order to intimidate people."[24] In other words, pretentiousness and the deliberate intention of making one's audience seem or feel inferior is poisonous and must be rejected.

The mention of audiences raises a point that is among the most important implications of materialism: namely, that artistic ability is not innate but develops through experience. According to this view, people are not born with talent or genius, but with a material brain that is able to develop talent through social life. It follows that everyone is equally able, at least potentially, to appreciate art. Variations are induced by society, not by birth. At the Yan'an forum Mao devoted a considerable amount of space to the question "For whom should artists create?" and answered, the masses of the people. Referring in concrete terms to the areas under the control of the CCP he said:

> Here the audience for works of literature and art consists of workers, peasants, soldiers and revolutionary cadres. There are students in the base areas, too, but they are different from students of the old type; they are either former or future cadres. The cadres of all types, fighters in the army, workers in the factories and peasants in the villages all want to read books and newspapers once they become literate, and those who are illiterate want to see plays and operas, look at drawings and paintings, sing songs and hear music.[25]

The major implication of Mao's doctrine is that the arts, and in particular those of the theater, should not be designed for elites. This may appear quite uncontroversial in the light of the war situation in China at the time, but in view of the history of the arts in China his statement was highly important. In traditional China most kinds of art were the preserve of one or several particular classes. The regional theater was among the few forms truly open to the ordinary people, and it took time, as we saw in chapter IV, to reach the educated. Many of the most beautiful pieces of art that we associate today with traditional China, such as landscape paintings and short, elegant poems, were in fact created for and appreciated by none but the educated classes.

Inherent also in Mao's doctrine on the target of artistic expression is the necessity for artists to "popularize" their work. Once they have created acceptable works, it is their duty, as well as that of others, to ensure that the masses enjoy the opportunity to appreciate and learn from them.

The other side of the coin is the question of who creates art. If talent is not innate but develops from social experience, then all people are themselves potentially able not only to appreciate but also to create; that is, everybody can become an artist if the right social conditions apply. It is largely because of this doctrine that Mao has tended to lay heavy emphasis on amateurs. Of course, he does not deny the value of experts, specialists, or professionals, but they should be willing to take spare-time practitioners seriously and even learn from them.

Our specialists are not only for the cadres, but also, and indeed chiefly, for the masses. . . . Our specialists in drama should pay attention to the small troupes in the army and the villages. Our specialists in music should pay attention to the songs of the masses. . . . All these comrades should make close contact with comrades engaged in the work of popularizing literature and art among the masses. On the one hand, they should help and guide the popularizers, and on the other, they should learn from these comrades and, through them, draw nourishment from the masses to replenish and enrich themselves.[26]

The stress laid on the amateur artists was, as we have seen, a particular feature of the wartime Chinese drama, in all three areas, those under the CCP, GMD, and the Japanese. Amateur artists were to become even more vital in the period after 1949.

Since nothing is innate but based entirely on what happens in societies, artists cannot simply create material in a vacuum or out of their own minds; they require a source. For Mao, this source must be "the life of the people," which he describes as "a mine of the raw materials for literature and art, materials in their natural form, materials that are crude, but most vital, rich and fundamental."

It is legitimate, of course, even necessary, to draw on "the life of the people" either of the past or of foreign countries. "We must on no account reject the legacies of the ancients and the foreigners or refuse to learn from them, even though they are the works of the feudal or bourgeois classes."[27] Earlier in the war, Mao had developed his ideas on tradition in the arts as part of a discussion, in January 1940, of the kind of political system he was building in China. There he drew attention to the "splendid old culture" that China had produced over many centuries. Her people of today should study it critically, he argued, and "reject its feudal dross and assimilate its democratic essence."[28] The same argument applies to the subject of foreign arts.

Mao's overall doctrine on the arts is, then, highly practical and utilitarian. He was dealing with a numerically gigantic people steeped in tradition, whom he planned to haul towards progress. He was concerned with specific problems, a concrete and very powerful set of enemies. His hostility to the "ivory tower" and emphasis on the mass line and the creativity of the ordinary person if properly led, were highly appropriate from a political point of view. It is possible to argue that the CCP's greater awareness and more effective use of the theater as a political weapon was one factor leading to their victory over the GMD.[29] The artistic standpoint is a separate problem and beyond the scope of this chapter to judge. The arts are about emotions; attitudes towards them are consequently among the most contentious of all subjects and have aroused heated debates since the most ancient times.

AMATEUR THEATER IN THE PEOPLE'S REPUBLIC

Within eight years of Mao's exposition of his ideas on literature and art at the Yan'an forum, the CCP that he led had not only taken part in the successful defeat of the Japanese but also had overwhelmed its formal, if temporary, ally against Japan, the GMD, and established the People's Republic of China (PRC).

The new government quickly made known its policies on the development of the arts, and in particular the theater. It was immediately obvious that the idea of the theater as a mass form of art would continue and be intensified. Tian Han's hope to set up a nationwide organization in the countryside to espouse the cause of the rural spare-time theater soon became not only government policy but also reality. The short items of the amateurs, easy and cheap to perform and representing many drama forms, were a vital part of the Chinese theater scene and the concomitant slogan "small in scale, rich in variety" *(xiaoxing duoyang)* a widely familiar one. From June 18 to 29, 1951, the Ministry of Culture of the Central Government convened a conference on work in the arts and formulated a plan in regard to amateurs. Its policy was simply "to consolidate and develop mass spare-time artistic activity in the rural villages and the factories." Organizations in charge of culture and education at every level were directed to assume responsibility for providing appropriate performing material. "Every drama company and cultural work group and team should build up a constant and firm supportive relationship with one or more mass amateur art organizations."[30] Government organs were thus to be heavily involved in what the amateurs did; professionals, in the form of nearby drama companies, were expected to offer help on a formal and even organized basis.

By the time the conference was held from which this policy was generated the number of amateur companies had already begun to expand. There were already 3,000 rural amateur troupes in the province of Shandong alone. Numbers grew over the following years. In 1960, for instance, there were 39,000 worker and over 244,000 peasant spare-time companies throughout the whole country, with a total of, probably, in the realm of 8 million members. In a private inter-view in mid-1973, Li Xifan, the cadre then responsible for the litera-ture and arts section of *People's Daily*, indicated that the current total number of amateur actors in China was "several tens of millions."

The reader will recall that an important step towards such numbers was taken when the Chinese people used theater as a vehicle for war-time propaganda. They did not forget the lesson. One of the first crises they were forced to face was the Korean war, which Chinese troops entered in October 1950. Of course, it did not actually involve the occupation of China by foreign forces, but the people, especially those of the northeastern region near Korea, were convinced they faced that danger and prepared for it. Amateur companies played an important political and propaganda role, as suggested in the fol-lowing:

> Through the countryside of Hopei [Hebei] Province, 2,000 locally or-ganized amateur troupes are travelling, from village to village to give performances for the peasants in the long winter evenings. Around the theme of "protect the Homeland," their plays are woven out of the stuff of their own experiences. These true life stories impress the audi-ences profoundly and often, at the end of the show, the onlookers themselves join the players in shouting slogans. Many enroll as volun-teers for Korea on the spot.[31]

In this situation are a number of features reminiscent of the Yan'an period—the appeal to realistic experiences of the audience and to patriotism, the stirring of enthusiasm for the cause. The observation in the last sentence aims to show success but is not implausible even if taken literally. Certainly, it was typical of reports on the amateur per-formances at the time to claim that they had resulted in further recruits.

Encouragement of amateur theater has remained an important plank of cultural policy in the PRC in virtually all periods. The years of the spare-time performers' highest social status were probably those of the Cultural Revolution decade (1966–1976) when the doc-trine of the mass line reached its height. Amateur theater was then more vital and varied than professional. The post-Mao attitude was set by Hua Guofeng in his February 26, 1978 report to the First Ses-sion of the Fifth National People's Congress, when he said: "We should be active in organizing cultural centres, film projection teams and various forms of spare-time cultural activity for the masses."[32]

The central aim of amateur theater overall has been ideological, that is, to promote enthusiasm for the current social and political order. One could cite the case of a woman in Hubei soon after 1949 who, when asked why she wanted to spend her leisure on stage, replied: "What do you young people know? I am already fifty, but every day I live, I want to propagate the benefits of Chairman Mao and the CCP."[33] During the Great Leap Forward (GLF), amateur performers at a festival in Sichuan received praise because their work was "tightly integrated with the Party's policy that literature and art should serve proletarian politics, the development of production and the workers, peasants, and soldiers."[34] Again, in 1973, after the Cultural Revolution, a spare-time performing team from the People's Liberation Army (PLA) noted its duty in the arts as "putting Chairman Mao's revolutionary line into practice," "reflecting the ideals and aspirations of the masses, saying what they want to say and forging the heroic images in their minds."[35] In terms of content this ideological objective has resulted in a heavy emphasis on directly political and contemporary material. However, it should be added that the signs since the end of the 1970s point towards widespread boredom with too much propaganda and a greater interest in pure entertainment.

The political notion of integrating amateur performance with "the development of production," noted as a feature of the GLF, finds expression in the 1980s in the promotion of the "four modernizations" of industry, agriculture, science and technology, and national defense. One correspondent of a major daily for workers, explicitly writing with official approval, sums up the achievements of a workers' cultural club in an electrical machinery plant in Harbin. He observed that whereas previously many workers had frittered away their leisure time on cards and other valueless activities, sometimes even including brawling, they now wrote plays, acted, or watched healthy films. "One cannot talk of serving the construction of the four modernizations well," he opined, unless such healthy activity is extended. "This is not a small matter," he concluded, "and it is worth our giving earnest attention to resolving it."[36]

Within the broad policy of endorsement and encouragement there have been some variations in official attitudes towards amateur theater. Most of them boil down to the general problem of professionalization, that is, the tendency of spare-time artists to become like professionals. The model of amateur theater in China is enshrined in the slogan "small in scale, rich in variety," but professionalization means longer and bigger dramas, greater concentration on fewer forms and themes, more time and effort devoted to theater, more time off normal work, higher standards, more amateurs actually joining the ranks of professionals.

During most periods of the PRC, authorities have looked askance at professionalization and all that it entails.[37] Since about 1980, however, there has been a growing tendency for amateurs to ask for more time off work for their theatrical activities and for more of them to become professionals. Not only do the audiences demand higher standards of excellence from them, but the amateurs expect the opportunities to lift their levels effectively. One author wrote to a major literary journal complaining vigorously that amateur writers were not given enough time to write and were even criticized by their workplace leadership for their attempts, however industrious they were in their normal jobs. He was also angry that amateurs found so much difficulty in securing publication outlets for their works.[38]

PROFESSIONALS AND THE MASSES
IN THE PEOPLE'S REPUBLIC

Those amateurs who turn professional claim that by so doing they are serving the masses better. It has in fact been one of the most significant components of the CCP's mass theater policy to send urban professional companies on tour to factories and other units within their own city, as well as to small cities and, above all, to the peasant villages. In effect the CCP retained yet another practice that characterized the war against Japan.

Examples of rural tours by professionals can be found in virtually all periods of PRC history. At least until 1976 the general trend, however, was quite clearly to demand more and longer visits to rural areas ever more remote. Two major turning points pushing companies in this direction were the GLF in 1958 and the Cultural Revolution. The initial slogan "sending to the door" shows clearly that the aim was to prove that professionals were prepared to go to their audiences and not to expect the reverse. It implies shows designed to accord with audience demands in all respects; it also suggests considerable quantity, for if only a few doors were reached then the touring company might just as well have stayed at home.

Early attempts were only partly successful. In 1954 sixty-eight state operated opera troupes gave some 5,200 performances while on tour to a total of just under 10 million spectators; the comparable figures for the spoken play groups was a thousand performances with a million people in the audiences. These numbers indicate that the shows given were well patronized, especially the operas, and criticism came forward that the "number of performances was too small," and had "fallen short of realistic demand."[39]

The manner as well as the quantity also fell short of perfection. "Some companies had nothing in mind but completing their performance duties; they did no necessary investigation and research on the needs and loves of their audiences."[40] The troupes appear thus to have been a little lacking in enthusiasm. The days of foreign occupation to force home the necessity of going to the countryside were of course long gone and city companies sometimes were not too keen on the discomforts involved. They also feared a loss of income.

The Cultural Bureau of Jiangsu province undertook experiments to solve the problems and the results were widely broadcast. From December 1954 to the following March thirty troupes went all over the province giving 2,049 performances to nearly 2 million people. They claimed to have pleased their audiences well by two main methods: first, they fitted the content of the dramas to the current work of the audiences; second, they were careful to choose appropriate times and places, suitable not for themselves but for their audiences. Most of the troupes claimed to have earned more on tour than at home. The exceptions were attributed to "excessive entertaining of the peasants to drama free of charge."[41] Despite this rather rosy picture, financial loss remained a familiar objection to rural touring until the Cultural Revolution.

Following the Hundred Flowers Movement (1956–1957) and the succeeding Anti-Rightist Campaign (1957) the government's urge to send troupes to the countryside gained added importance. This was part of a general leftward trend in the Chinese political culture that characterized the GLF. The Ministry of Culture convened a conference on drama work in Beijing from December 5 to 14, 1957, and made very clear that there was much to be desired in the rural activity of the professional groups up to that point. The deputy Minister of Culture, Liu Zhiming, gave a speech at the conference outlining future policy. Among his main points were the following:

1. For urban troupes to go to the countryside and perform for the peasants could consolidate and strengthen the "worker-peasant alliance" and at the same time carry on socialist education among the peasantry.

2. It would encourage production activism among the peasantry and speed up socialist construction in the new peasant villages.

3. Through artistic instruction it would be able to give impetus to the development of amateur mass cultural life in the peasant villages.[42]

Liu Zhiming's points sum up nicely what have remained in essence the central aims and concepts of the movement, described since then by the slogan "down to the countryside, up to the mountains" (see plate 34). Like the amateur theatricals, this is primarily an ideological exercise through which the government hopes to spread its ideology and attitudes toward life among the people. The belief that ideological incentives will actually help to increase production comes through strongly; it is a doctrine very characteristic of the GLF and the Cultural Revolution, though not of all periods of the PRC.

Liu Zhiming's point about stimulating artistic creation in the villages exemplifies an important feature of the rural tours; the help amateurs and professionals give each other. The "integration" of the two types is a common theme for the GLF period and even more so in the Cultural Revolution. The workers or peasants help by providing the opportunity for ideological instruction and by giving ideas, often in the form of actual dramas they have written which the professionals can then act out. The visitors' assistance lies in instructing amateurs and giving inspiration through their art.

At about the time of the GLF we find the birth of an institution exemplifying Liu Zhiming's points: the caravan troupes (see plate 35). They originated in Inner Mongolia, where the large areas and relatively sparse population made it very difficult for the average person to enjoy access to drama performances. The caravan troupes, although centered on the cities, made it their job to visit all areas, however remote, of Inner Mongolia. Later the caravan troupes spread to all parts of China.

The Cultural Revolution added a great deal to the discussion about the sending of urban companies to factories and the countryside. The Red Guards complained that the drama companies had been too city bound and had not gone out to the masses enough. In particular they accused Liu Shaoqi "and others of his ilk of concocting the theory 'that performers are special,' in order to oppose and obstruct literature and art workers from the road of going to integrate with the workers, peasants and soldiers."[43] According to this theory it was quite reasonable for actors, as people with special talents, to have a privileged life and it was unnecessary for them to eat, live, or labor with the peasants. It may be that the years following the GLF saw a fall off in the rustication of urban troupes, but in view of the earlier material it is difficult to accept accusations of general sabotage.

The Fifth Plenary Session of the CCP's Eleventh Central Committee, held in February 1980, posthumously rehabilitated Liu Shaoqi and cleared him of all accusations made against him. In June 1981 the Sixth Plenary Session formally denounced both the GLF and the Cultural Revolution. Yet the notion that professional troupes should visit the countryside to serve the peasant masses has remained strong.

Early in 1982 *People's Theater* ran a series of articles on the subject. The editorial note spelled out the ideal when it claimed that "quite a few troupes had persisted up to now in the splendid tradition of going up to the mountains and down to the countryside." However, the main thrust of the articles was that urban troupes had come to ignore the legitimate theatrical needs of the peasantry and that this trend should be corrected. One of the authors, Gao Hanming, had been to Xinghua County, a very famous grain-producing area in Jiangsu, and hence a rich area. There he had found that in the county town troupes performed constantly, up to four shows a day, but in the nearby communes the peasants were starved for shows. "Because communications are inconvenient and the condition of theaters is not so good, troupes of county or city level and above do not want to go down." So while the mass line remains official policy, it is no nearer genuine implementation in the early 1980s than in the 1950s.[44]

The growing social status of the expert and technician in Chinese society, which has gone hand in hand with the policies of economic modernization, is unlikely to encourage the professionals to increase the number of their village visits. They will believe that they can make more money more conveniently and in greater comfort in the cities, performing for larger and more sophisticated audiences. Under these circumstances the peasants are bound to take a fairly low priority, especially those in remote areas. Even now, despite the enormous progress of recent decades, there are limitations on theater for the masses.

IDEOLOGY AND POLICY 1963–1982

The doctrine of the mass line reached its height, at least in terms of emphasis by Party authorities, during the Cultural Revolution (1966–

1976). It was then also that a form of drama was developed that, more consciously and minutely than at any other period, implemented the doctrines enshrined in Mao's "Talks at the Yan'an Forum."

From 1963 onward, Mao's wife Jiang Qing began to assert domination in the theater. She and her followers called for the immediate suspension of "ghost plays," that is, traditional dramas, and advocated only modern works on contemporary themes. In June and July 1964 the Festival of Beijing Operas on Contemporary Themes took place in Beijing and, from that time on, virtually no traditional operas were shown in public until 1977. Mao's doctrine of "assimilating the democratic essence" of the old feudal culture was applied to this situation by the retention of a limited number of characteristics of the traditional opera, such as acrobatics and sword fighting, but the themes, costumes, scenery, and characterization were all made revolutionary and modern.

In February 1966, Jiang Qing convened a Forum on Literature and Art in the Armed Forces in Shanghai. There she explained the concept of "model" operas. They must illustrate the class struggle and, on the basis of material taken from the life of the people, must create heroic proletarian images unequivocally on the side of the masses of workers, peasants, and soldiers and hostile to the bourgeoisie.

To display the model heroes fully, a system of priorities called the "three prominences" *(san tuchu)* was developed. These were:

Among all characters give prominence to positive characters.
Among positive characters give prominence to heroic characters.
Among heroic characters give prominence to the main heroic character.[45]

In October 1969, the first of the model operas revised according to Jiang Qing's dictates was published: *Taking Tiger Mountain by Strategy (Zhiqu Weihu shan)*. Others followed in later months and years. Two were revolutionary ballets: *The Red Detachment of Women (Hongse niangzi jun)* and *The White-haired Girl (Baimao nü)*. After 1972 especially, local variants of these dramas developed, all adhering to the main revolutionary principles.

Foreign theater or music was not performed at all. Any theatrical shows that broke away from the model opera principles were completely forbidden. A representative case in point is the Shanxi Opera *Going Up Peach Peak Three Times (Sanshang Taofeng)*, a story of rural China set in 1959, the year after the communes were established. Although based on a plot current before the Cultural Revolution, it was first performed in its present form at the North China Theatrical Festival held in Beijing early in 1974 (see plate 36). After a brief period of praise from the press it came under the savage attack of "Chu Lan," literally meaning "first wave,"[46] the pen name of a group of people under Jiang Qing's influence who published several important tracts on literature and art in the Chinese press. A serious media campaign began denouncing this opera as an attempt to bring back a number of cadres and leaders who had fallen during the Cultural Revolution, and as an attempt to restore the position of the traditional theater. The reasoning of the campaign was both complicated and involved but is interesting mainly in its exclusively ideological and political thrust. Numerous allusions to classical novels were made, not to raise an aesthetic or artistic argument, totally absent in the campaign, but as a weapon to show further the trickery of those who dared to produce this drama.

The fall of Jiang Qing and three other radicals, the "Gang of Four," on October 6, 1976, less than a month after the death of their protagonist Mao Zedong, brought about quick and deep changes in the Chinese theater. The first was much greater stress on the idea of "letting a hundred flowers blossom and a hundred schools of thought contend." The Chinese press has pushed this policy constantly, describing it as "a significant development to Marxism-Leninism by Chairman Mao in the realms of literature, art and science," and "an effective tool for strengthening the leading position of the proletariat, and implementing an all-round proletarian dictatorship."[47]

The Chinese have aimed at greater variety. Hua Guofeng made this point a central theme in several official statements on theater. In particular, it comes through loud and clear in his "report on the work of the government," delivered to the Fifth National People's Congress on February 26, 1978:

> The "gang of four" vehemently opposed Chairman Mao's policies of letting a hundred flowers blossom and a hundred schools of thought contend and of making the past serve the present and things foreign serve China. It wildly pushed fascist cultural autocracy and a policy of prohibition. It put into cold storage all the progressive films imported from abroad. It prohibited the performances of good historical plays and traditional operas. It banned large numbers of local operas, songs and dances of the nationalities, modern plays and excellent Chinese and foreign music. . . . Cultural poverty and insipidity was the result

of the gang's perversion and wrongdoing, and this aroused strong dissatisfaction among the people.[48]

It is obvious from Hua's comments that part of the new approach is a return to an appreciation for foreign cultures. The campaign against Western music of 1974, in which Chu Lan played so important a part,[49] is now ridiculed as absurd. Many items and kinds of art forbidden or suppressed under the Gang of Four are allowed or encouraged again. They include not only Western music but also traditional Chinese opera, modern spoken plays, and others.

Of those changes in attitude that relate not so much to the arts in general but more specifically to the theater, the most important lies in the portrayal of heroes and other characters in the dramas. Chinese policymakers and theater workers now regard the "three prominences" as having led to excessive formularization in the portrayal of operatic characters. They also imply a disdain for and lack of faith in the masses because of the emphasis they lay on heroes. "If this is not a declaration of the idealist viewpoint that 'heroes create history' then what is it?" demands one writer.[50] It is of course a central article of faith among materialists that it is the masses and social forces, not individual leaders, that make history. There is a certain irony in finding the Cultural Revolution itself derided as scornful of the masses.

Formerly, it was in the model operas that the theory of the "three prominences" was most fully enshrined. After October 1976, these lost their dominant place on the stage. Insofar as they remained, they did so in their pre-Cultural Revolution form. Since Jiang Qing had them all revised during and after the Cultural Revolution, she can now claim no glory at all for the versions currently on the stage. Again, the revisions were made in accordance with the "three prominences," so the Chinese can rightly claim that the survival of the models implies no acceptance of that theory.

Credit for the model operas goes not to the fallen Jiang Qing, as it did before October 1976, but to Mao Zedong and, above all, Zhou Enlai. He is "the great instructor, organizer and participant" in the revolution in the arts, who "took hold of typical examples, made investigations and attended rehearsals"[51] of the model revolutionary operas when they were being created.

Zhou Enlai has come into his own not only for his part in the creation of the models but also as a thinker on the arts in general. Whereas formerly very few authoritative statements come from anyone but Mao, now Zhou Enlai is also quoted as a reliable source of correct attitudes. In particular, in February 1979, *People's Daily* published in full a speech he made to a forum of writers and artists on June 19, 1961. It deals, among other matters, specifically with theater and emphasizes the need for variety but as a matter of fact does not contain many original ideas.

Its date is noteworthy, however: 1961 was the height of the "moderate" period that followed the GLF (1958–1960) and preceded the Cultural Revolution. The publication of Zhou's speech early in 1979 is symptomatic of a general trend in China that has gathered momentum since Mao's death: to dismantle steadily the Cultural Revolution and all its ideas. The era of Deng Xiaoping holds no brief for the radical ideas of that largest of rectification campaigns in any area of ideology, and especially not as it applied to the theater.

Consistent with the negation of the Cultural Revolution is the revival of interest in the seventeen years between liberation in 1949 and 1966. The post-Mao cultural authorities argue that, when the Gang of Four was in control, nobody said anything positive about the theater creations of the years 1949–1966. The Gang simple described that period as under the "dictatorship of a sinister line," meaning that bourgeois writers and specialists had total control of theater and the arts, and passed it off as valueless. The merest glance at the documents of the Cultural Revolution on the arts bears out the contention that they damned totally and never praised the theater workers, writers, and actors of the years 1949–1966. Now, however, the line has changed to the other extreme. It is difficult to find serious criticism or something other than praise for theatrical work of the pre-Cultural Revolution period; it is the decade of the Gang of Four that produced nothing worthwhile. Models worth emulation come unfailingly from before 1966, negative examples from the black years 1966–1976.

Since the Fifth Plenum of the Eleventh CCP Central Committee of February 1980, which rehabilitated Liu Shaoqi, the positive features of the pre-1966 period also include the former President of the PRC. It appears that Jiang Qing, Lin Biao, and the others regarded Liu Shaoqi as the "general backstage of the sinister line in literature and art," meaning that he instigated art workers not to obey, or even to oppose, Chairman Mao's directives on literature and art. This verdict has now been described as "completely untenable" and "total slander, fomenting discord."[52] Numerous other crimes the Gang and its followers heaped on Liu's head turn out to have been distortions and lies. On the contrary, Liu's line on the arts was correct, as on other matters. Falsehood attached rather to his enemies, the Gang and its followers.

As Liu Shaoqi has returned to favor the ideas of Mao's late years have come increasingly under criticism. Just before the fortieth anniversary, in May 1982, of Mao's "Talks at the Yan'an Forum," they were critically reevaluated. Fortunately for them, 1942 was well before Mao began to fall into error. On the other hand, the immense influence of the "Talks" during the Cultural Revolution renders them suspect. The first of the "incorrect formulations" is that "literature and art are subordinate to politics." Since this is one of the most important doctrines inherent in the "Talks," its negation represents a fundamental change in direction in China's policy towards the arts. Curiously enough, the new approach came simultaneously with an attack on "bourgeois liberalization," a doctrine which itself splits the arts from politics. It appears that the Chinese authorities tightened the political screws on artists just as they declared for the first time that nonpolitical art was a possibility. The inherent inconsistency points toward a doubt that the authorities will allow the scope of supposedly nonpolitical art or theater to extend very far.

Despite this drastic reversal, Mao's "Talks" as a whole were reaffirmed as "the guiding ideology for Chinese literature and art today." Their main "correct" ideas include the following.

> Literature and art are reflections of man's social life, which is the only source of literary and artistic creation. Writers of the proletariat and the people should reflect life from the standpoint of the proletariat and the people, and should prove their standpoint in deeds, not in words. They should go and live among the people and, first of all, go among the workers, peasants and soldiers.[53]

This suggests that the masses continue to be the fundamental source of inspiration for the arts. But the interpretation shifts the focus of creation from the masses to presumably professional writers or at least appears to confirm that there is indeed a trend towards higher status for professionals and greater professionalization for amateurs.

THE REPERTOIRE

Jiang Qing's theories undoubtedly exercised an extremely restrictive influence; never was China's theatrical diet as narrow as during the years of her greatest power, 1966 to 1976. The "models" were extremely few in number. One of them was *Taking Tiger Mountain by Strategy*.

Based on a novel, this work was adapted into a Beijing opera in 1958 by the Shanghai Beijing Opera Company. In 1963 Jiang Qing came to know of it and had it revised for the 1964 Festival of Beijing Operas. It was subsequently revised again several times before achieving model status in October 1969.

The opera is set in Manchuria in the winter of 1946 during the War of Liberation between the CCP and the GMD. The main hero is Yang Zirong, a scout platoon leader of the PLA who, together with PLA regimental chief of staff Shao Jianbo, determines to defeat the local GMD leader Vulture. The PLA would thus liberate the entire area and implement Mao's directive to "build stable base areas in the northeast." By getting himself into the confidence of the enemy, Yang arranges for a CCP assault on Tiger Mountain, the enemy headquarters, while Vulture is celebrating his fiftieth birthday (see plate 37). The attack ends in victory, and Vulture is captured alive.

The support of the masses for the CCP is portrayed as the critical element in the victory. The whole of scene 7, "Arousing the Masses," shows Shao Jianbo winning over the local people who have suffered greatly through Vulture's cruelty.

The character of Yang Zirong is carefully worked out. According to those responsible for the revised script, all his actions and gestures show him as "a fearless proletarian revolutionary hero, with largeness of mind and a thoroughgoing proleterian revolutionary spirit, one who in all circumstances gives prominence to proletarian politics."[54] He is totally loyal to Mao and Mao Zedong thought.

The revisions of the original 1963 version include some major changes in Yang's characterization. One is to portray him with a deeper relationship to and class feelings for the masses. Another is to underline his ideology by making him refer often to Mao Zedong thought and the revolution. A third is to eliminate his flirtations with Vulture's foster-daughter and his ribald stories in the GMD headquarters.

Taking Tiger Mountain by Strategy is exciting and fast-moving on the stage. There is certainly dramatic tension. On the other hand, it lacks love interest of any kind, tragedy, or real humor. Yang's character is too contrived to be convincing. There is hardly a line in the opera without conscious ideological content: politics carried to the final degree.

The change of policy that followed the fall of the Gang of Four brought about revival in the Chinese theater, both in terms of forms and specific items. Between 1966 and 1976 there were very few spoken dramas *(huaju)* and sung dramas *(geju)* performed in China. Both are now restored to favor. One illustrative example is *The White-haired Girl*, originally a *geju*, changed by Jiang Qing into a ballet, but in February 1977 repremiered as a *geju*. Another form to return after a ten-year break is the dance-drama *(wuju)*, a Westernized form of dance with accompaniment from an orchestra containing both Western and Chinese instruments. A representative piece is *Tales of the Silk Road (Silu huayu)*.

The most interesting forms to come back have been those of the Chinese regional theater, the origins of which are discussed in chapters III and IV. In the 1950s and early 1960s the Chinese claimed that there were over three hundred forms of regional drama in their country. During the Cultural Revolution virtually all of them, except the Beijing opera, disappeared. An attempt to revive them in 1972 made only limited headway and was in any case totally confined to modern opera and revolutionary themes. Just as with Beijing opera, many of the original essential characteristics of the regional dramas were omitted or suppressed. However, after 1976, and especially in 1978, many articles appeared in the press describing the recovery of the main regional forms and including reference to their special features. The following commentary on the best-known and most widespread form of regional theater in the southwest of China brings out this point:

> The musical patterns and the rich tunes and styles, with their great variety, the drums and gongs and the "helping chorus" of the Sichuan Opera, which are so affecting to the people, the entire art of the Sichuan Opera, formed into a single unit through the three parts "helping," "striking," "singing," have a deep flavor of life and a strong power of attraction. They are causing the broad masses of the people who love Sichuan Opera intense fascination.[55]

The "helping chorus" involves the repetition and explanation of phrases sung by a major character through the agency of a small chorus in a manner slightly similar to ancient Greek drama. In one type of Sichuan opera all instruments in the orchestra are percussion, hence the reference to "striking." But most important of all is the allusion to the "deep flavor of life," a clear indication that the form's popularity is due to its being a genuinely native and local style of mass opera.

Turning from form to content and particular works we find that, here again, the period before 1966 is particularly well represented, especially in the early years after the fall of the Gang. One interesting revival is the Beijing opera *Driven Up Mt. Liang,* the historical opera approved by Mao. It was restaged in May 1977 to commemorate the thirty-fifth anniversary of Mao Zedong's "Talks at the Yan'an Forum."

During 1978, the number of traditional operas shown multiplied greatly. In September and October 1978, for example, it was possible to see dramas on all kinds of historical themes, patriotic wars, peasant rebellion, the wronged woman winning her case through the agency of the upright judge, love stories, and even myths. In some cases the progressive content had become so faint as to stretch imagination. In all cases the theaters were full.

Of course, modern plays and operas on contemporary topics were numerous among those works that had been popular before 1966, suppressed by the Gang, and then returned after October 1976. They included the spoken drama *Lei Feng,* about a young selfless soldier, Lei Feng, and the sung drama *Sister Jiang (Jiangjie),* based on a story of the last stages of the War of Liberation against the Guomindang in Sichuan.

Another category of modern items was late Cultural Revolution compositions quickly banned by the Gang. By far the most important in this category is the Shanxi Opera *Going Up Peach Peak Three Times,* in 1974 the target of a bitter campaign.

In 1978, the Chinese leadership made a spectacular about turn on the quality of this drama. It accused the Gang of Four of fraudulently using *Going Up Peach Peak* to mount a deliberate campaign to undermine Zhou Enlai's authority and strengthen their own political power.

> On every front they struck out. They calculated how they could manu-
> facture incidents; they made trouble and carried out sabotage in every
> way possible. [In these ways they planned] to discredit all the wise
> Party measures which Premier Zhou was implementing as "the black
> line and reversal," "a countercurrent to negate the Great Cultural Rev-
> olution."[56]

Just like those of Chu Lan and their followers, these arguments are essentially political. One can claim that to combat a political denunci-ation of a drama, it is necessary to debate on a political level. Yet the fact is that the new leaders are using a tactic very similar to that they denounce, by implication, in the Gang of Four: they are using the supposed political content of drama to undermine the influence of their adversaries.

We move next to the subject of dramas newly written since the smashing of the Gang of Four. One work that has aroused unusual interest, expecially from a political point of view, is *Where Silence Reigns (Yu wusheng chu)*. It is set against the background of the famous Tiananmen Square incident of April 5, 1976, when clashes between police and a large crowd assembled to pay tribute to Zhou Enlai resulted in violence and many arrests. The Gang of Four instantly jumped in to declare the incident counterrevolutionary, and to mount a large-scale campaign against Deng Xiaoping. Those who took part in the incident knew the Gang's judgment on it was false and unfair. They nursed their silence while the Gang remained in power, but after Deng Xiaoping was rehabilitated in July 1977 it was only a matter of time before the Tiananmen incident itself would be reinterpreted. In the event, the New China News Agency announced on November 15, 1978, that the Beijing Municipal CCP Committee had declared it a "completely revolutionary action." There are only six characters in the play, at the end of which one of them is thrown into prison as a counterrevolutionary for his part in the Tiananmen incident. The audience knows that this injustice will be righted, so the tragic ending is no more than apparent.

The author of the play is Zong Fuxian, a young worker in the Shanghai Heat Treatment Plant. Like its creator, its first performers were amateurs who premiered it late in September 1978 in Shanghai. Meanwhile, the script was published in Shanghai's *Wenhui bao* on October 28, 29, and 30.[57] Audiences and producers were enthusiastic about it, and no sooner had the Beijing CCP Committee cleared the incident than the play was premiered in the capital on November 16.

There could hardly be a play more directly linked to current political development than *Where Silence Reigns*. Unlike *Going Up Peach Peak Three Times*, this play is going through no "reversal of verdict." It is the incident surrounding it that is the subject of such a change. But just as, in the final analysis, *Going Up Peach Peak Three Times* is about personalities in the highest echelons of leadership, so too *Where Silence Reigns* concerns figures who dominate, but do not actually appear. In this case they are of course Zhou Enlai and Deng Xiaoping, on the positive side, the Gang of Four on the negative.

Hua Guofeng did very nicely out of the Tiananmen incident, being confirmed as premier two days after it happened, and easily could have been somewhat nervous about the incident's great popularity. His subsequent demotion in September 1980 confirms the validity of such anxiety.

In *Where Silence Reigns* Zhou Enlai and Deng Xiaoping do not need to be on the stage to make their presence felt. But in fact one of the most striking features of the dramas written since October 1976 is their portrayal of former revolutionary leaders as flesh-and-blood characters, especially Mao Zedong, Zhou Enlai, and Zhu De. It is the first time this has happened in China. For actors with physical resemblances to the best-known revolutionary leaders it has become part of the trade to vie for the honor of acting out their roles and imitating their mannerisms and peculiarities.

Not surprisingly the particular dramas written so far have centered around the preliberation period when the three main heroes were still in their prime. A good illustrative example is *The Xi'an Incident (Xi'an shibian)*, a nine-scene spoken play which focuses on the end of 1936 when Zhou Enlai "with great tact and resourcefulness managed to find a peaceful solution" to the problem of Chiang Kaishek's arrest outside Xi'an by one of his own generals aiming to compel him to resist Japan.[58] This particular play was premiered on Beijing television on January 8, 1979, the third anniversary of Zhou Enlai's death. Not only Zhou Enlai but also Mao Zedong and Zhu De have parts in this play (see plate 38).

Not all the new items written since 1976 center on CCP history or on the state of society since the departure of Mao and the Gang. They include also some in modern forms on themes from distant history. A representative piece is the dance-drama *Tales of the Silk Road*, which has attracted a good deal of commentary and attention in China.

The story is set in the Tang dynasty (618–907), mostly on the Silk Route. Yingniang, the daughter of a painter, is kidnapped by bandits, sold into slavery as an actress, and then saved by her father and a Persian merchant called Enus. Her father entrusts her to Enus to prevent her falling into the hands of an evil official, and she goes to Persia (see plate 39). In the end she returns home and exposes the machinations of the official, but not before the latter has succeeded in bringing about her father's death.

The emphasis, even glorification of the past is a particularly striking feature of this dance-drama. Although it is contemporary, its creators have specifically attempted to recreate some aspects of the art of the Tang dynasty.

> The choreographers started from postures of musicians and dancers—both Chinese and Persian—shown in the Dunhuang murals, and went on to design the dances. They did considerable historical research to get them as authentic as possible. Figures in the murals of dancers or musicians playing the *pipa*, . . . were the inspiration for a dance by Yingniang in Scene Two. Reflecting the character of Yingniang as a bold and intelligent young woman of political integrity, this dance like a musical theme runs through the entire drama.[59]

Dunhuang is a famous city in Gansu province where an extraordinarily rich collection of manuscripts, murals, and other artifacts has been uncovered, beginning in July 1899. The finds have been of truly monumental importance for the world's knowledge of medieval Chinese history, especially the Tang period. It is perhaps not an accident that the dance-drama should originate from Gansu, which is justly proud of Dunhuang. The Gansu Song and Dance Ensemble has performed the piece in many parts of China itself, as well as outside the country.

The comment in the quotation that Yingniang is a "woman of political integrity" shows that the dance-drama is intended to be political, despite its setting in the remote past. It is the official who is the main negative character. Yet one scene of the drama takes place in a Persian palace with appropriately luxurious scenery. A merchant is hardly an expected major positive character for a proletarian dance-drama.

There is clearly a foreign policy significance in the item. It emphasizes China's openness and friendliness to foreigners and foreign powers, then and now. On the other hand, it is still rather unusual to find Chinese dramas that include even one scene set outside China itself.

The attempt to reach the masses through dramas set either in the past or present has been a vital and developing theme in the drama policy and reality of the PRC. The overwhelming aim has been to propagate socialism, patriotism, and acceptance of the government line, in other words to unify the people more thoroughly behind the new revolutionary order and hence ensure its survival and consolidation.

Alan Liu has put forward an interesting hypothesis connecting communications in general with national integration in China. He argues that "China in 1970 is, in terms of national identity, a more integrated nation than China before 1949."[60] There is greater cohesion and unity both political and cultural than there used to be. He states that the most important part of the media system is "its function in the national integration of China,"[61] so it is the media that can claim much of the credit for the country's improved situation.

Theater has functioned as a vital part of China's mass communications, although Liu does not include it among the media; he refers only to radio, the press, books, and films. It may be argued, however, that theater is just as important as any of the media he lists. This is because even now theater remains a dominant method not so much for controlling what the people know, for which clearly radio is much more important, but for influencing how they feel.

At the December 1957 conference of the Ministry of Culture, Liu Zhiming referred to socialist education through theater. What he meant was that it was a medium for the development of the people's attitudes towards life, government, labor, sacrifice, service, and so on, in the direction of socialism. We return again to the question of images, of what qualities the people see as good or bad, the kind of person they admire or dislike. In a country such as China, where quick and radical social change has recently taken place, popular attitudes or value systems are particularly important; for if attitudinal change fails to keep pace with industrial, economic, and technological change, then old ways return.

National integration necessitates narrowing some important social gulfs, such as those between the people of the countryside and those of the cities and between the Han and the national minorities. Clearly cultural differences remain between the rural and urban areas, and even more between Han and non-Han. But a unified country requires some degree of unity in its culture; political and cultural integration reinforce each other, resulting in greater unity, just as the converse can mean fragmentation.

It is in these respects that the way the PRC has used theater is a very important part of its national integration. Theater even now is a more familiar vehicle of communication to the peasantry than are the newer forms of newspapers and radio, because it is part of their traditional culture. Above all, theater appeals to the people's emotions much more directly than radio or newspapers. Moreover, it is significant that drama forms a substantial part of the content of both film and radio, as well as television. Theater as propaganda played an important and broadly successful role in unifying the Chinese against the enemy during the war against Japan. Similarly, it has continued as a vital, and also broadly successful, mechanism in securing integration since 1949.

NOTES

1. Zhang Jichun, "Taiyuan huaju huodong de huiyi," in Tian Han et al., eds., *Zhongguo huaju yundong wushi nian shiliao ji, diyi ji* (Zhongguo xiju chubanshe, Beijing, 1958), p. 214.

2. See the Program in Tian Han et al., eds., *Zhongguo huaju,* pp. 305–307.

3. Ting Yi, *A Short History of Modern Chinese Literature* (Foreign Languages Press, Peking, 1959), p. 220.

4. Zhao Pinsan, "Guanyu zhongyang geming genjudi huaju gongzuo de huiyi," in Tian Han et al., eds., *Zhongguo huaju,* p. 187.

5. Edgar Snow, *Red Star Over China* (Penguin, Harmondsworth, 1972 ed.), p. 144.

6. Joseph S. M. Lau, *Ts'ao Yü, The Reluctant Disciple of Chekhov and O'Neill: A Study in Literary Influence* (Hong Kong University Press, Hong Kong, 1970), p. 6.

7. Ibid., pp. 15–27.

8. Chalmers Johnson, *Peasant Nationalism and Communist Power: The Emergence of Revolutionary China 1937-1945* (Stanford University Press, Stanford, 1962), p. xi.

9. Tian Han, *Zhongguo xiju yundong* (Shangwu yinshuguan, Chongqing, 1944), p. 17.

10. The manifesto is printed in full in Tian Han, Ouyang Yuqian et al., eds., *Zhongguo huaju,* pp. 310–312.

11. Hong Shen, *Kangdi shinian lai Zhongguo de xiju yundong yu jiaoyu,* Zhonghua jiaoyu jie congkan (Zhonghua shuju, Shanghai, 1948), p. 10.

12. Lin Fei, "Yanju yu guanzhong," in Ma Ling, ed., *Guofang xiju* (Swatow, 1938), p. 5.

13. Li Yanhui, *Xiandai Zhongguo xiju jianshi* (Qingnian shuju, Singapore, 1959), p. 51.

14. Gu Zhongyi, "Shinian lai de Shanghai huaju yundong," supplement in Hong Shen, *Kangdi,* p. 150.

15. Tian Han, *Zhongguo xiju yundong,* pp. 93–94.

16. Ibid., p. 9.

17. Li Huiying, *Zhongguo xiandai wenxue shi,* Daxue congshu (Dongya shuju, Hong Kong, 1970), p. 225.

18. The Chinese original of the letter can be found, among other places, in Huang Yuchuan, ed., *Mao Zedong shengping ziliao jianbian yibajiusan nian—yijiuliujiu nian* (Union Research Institute, Hong Kong, 1970), p. 221. I have followed the official translation in "Hail the Great Victory of the Revolution in Peking Opera," *Chinese Literature* 8 (August, 1967): 125–126.

19. "Talks at the Yenan [Yan'an] Forum on Literature and Art." *Selected Works of Mao Tse-tung Volume III* (Foreign Languages Press, Peking, 1965), p. 81. I have everywhere followed this official translation. Bonnie S. McDougall has translated a much earlier version in *Mao Zedong's "Talks at the Yan'an Conference on Literature and Art": A Translation of the 1943 Text with Commentary,* Michigan Papers in Chinese Studies No. 39 (Center for Chinese Studies, The University of Michigan, Ann Arbor, 1980), pp. 57–86. In none of the passages quoted is there substantial difference between the two versions.

20. "Talks," p. 86.

21. Ibid., p. 70.

22. Ibid., p. 89.

23. "Oppose Stereotyped Party Writing," *Selected Works of Mao Tse-tung Volume III,* p. 56.

24. Ibid., p. 57.

25. "Talks," pp. 71–72.

26. Ibid., p. 84.

27. Ibid., p. 81.

28. "On New Democracy," *Selected Works of Mao Tse-tung Volume II* (Foreign Languages Press, Peking, 1965), p. 381.

29. See also the similar view put forward by David Holm in "Hua Guofeng and the Village Drama Movement in the North-west Shanxi Base Area, 1943–45," *The China Quarterly* 84 (December, 1980):669–693, especially p. 669.

30. See Du Lijun, "Guanyu nongcun jutuan de jige wenti," *Xin Zhonghua banyue kan* 14, no. 19 (October 1, 1951):33.

31. "Art Fights for Korea," *People's China* 3, no. 1 (January 1, 1951):26.

32. "Unite and Strive to Build a Modern, Powerful Socialist Country!" *Peking Review* XXI, 10 (March 10, 1978):29.

33. *Changjiang ribao* (Hankou), July 15, 1951.

34. Zhu Dannan, "Xiang yeyu xuexi, liangtiao tui zoulu, zhengqu qunzhong wenyi de gengda fanrong," *Sichuan xiqu* 2 (February 10, 1959):5.

35. *Renmin ribao,* March 25, 1973.

36. *Gongren ribao,* March 19, 1980.

37. I have considered this problem in *Amateur Theatre in China 1949–1966* (Australian National University Press, Canberra, 1973), pp. 29–34 and in "Chinese Opera after the Cultural Revolution (1970–72)," *The China Quarterly* 55 (July/September, 1973):506.

38. Zhang Lu, "Yeyu zuozhe de kuzhong," *Wenyi bao* 2 (February 12, 1980):31.

39. Li Lun, "Gengduode, geng youxiaode wei gongnongbing yanchu," *Xiju bao* 13 (January 22, 1955):25.

40. Ibid., p. 26.

41. "Jiangsu sheng Wenhua ju zuzhi difang xijutuan zhi nongcun xunhui yanchu gongzuo zongjie," *Xiju bao* 24 (December 9, 1955):7.

42. "Yishu biaoyan tuanti xianxiang shangshan," *Xiju bao* 60 (December 26, 1957):8.

43. *Renmin ribao,* November 23, 1968.

44. *Renmin xiju* 2 (February 18, 1982):3.

45. See, for instance, *Renmin ribao,* June 25, 1972.

46. *Renmin ribao,* February 28, 1974. The campaign against the opera is discussed in Colin Mackerras, "Opera and the Campaign to Criticize Lin Piao and Confucius," *Papers on Far Eastern History* 11 (March, 1975):182–195.

47. "Geming wenyi shi dang de shiye, bushi hangbang de shiye," *Hongqi* 308 (April 3, 1977):41, 42. Numerous similar passages could be cited.

48. *Peking Review* XXI, 10 (March 10, 1978):31.

49. See, for instance, the article "Deepen the Criticism of the Bourgeois Theory of Human Nature," *Peking Review* XVII, 23 (June 7, 1974):18–22, where Beethoven and Debussy, among others, are denounced.

50. *Renmin xiju* 12 (April 25, 1977):59.

51. *Ta Kung Pao* (English version) 572 (June 2, 1977):6.

52. *Renmin ribao,* May 14, 1980.

53. Xin Xiangrong, "Guiding Ideology for Literature and Art," *Beijing Review* XXV, 18 (May 3, 1982):3.

54. "Strive to Create the Brilliant Images of Proletarian Heroes," *Chinese Literature* 1 (1970):62.

55. *Renmin ribao,* February 8, 1978.

56. *Renmin xiju*'s Editorial Department, "'Sanshang Taofeng' shijian shi yida zhengzhi yinmou," *Renmin xiju* 29 (September 18, 1978):20.

57. *Guangming ribao,* November 5, 1978.

58. *Beijing Review* XXII, 5 (February 2, 1979):29.

59. Wang Xi and Liu Qingxia, "Along the Silk Road Dance Drama," *China Reconstructs* 29, 3 (March, 1980):24.

60. *Communications and National Integration in Communist China,* Michigan Studies on China, No. 2 (University of California Press, Berkeley, 1975 ed.), p. 177.

61. Ibid., p. 2.

SELECTED READINGS

Chinese Literature. Foreign Languages Press, Beijing, 1951– . Initially a quarterly, then bimonthly, now a monthly periodical in English dealing with literature and the arts in China. It includes drama scripts, reviews, and commentary on how theater affects society as well as material on the ideological aspects, always from the current point of view. It also includes news items relating to theater.

Hong Shen. *Kangzhan shinian lai Zhongguo de xiju yundong yu jiaoyu* [*The Chinese theater movement and education in the decade since the war of resistance*]. Zhonghua jiaoyu jie congkan [Series of Chinese Education World], Zhonghua shuju, Shanghai, 1948. Highly informative on the social rather than literary side of the drama during the decade beginning with the outbreak of the war. Contains a supplement by Gu Zhongyi on "the spoken play movement in Shanghai" over the same period.

Howard, Roger. *Contemporary Chinese Theatre.* Heinemann, London, 1978. Covers the various types of theater in the PRC. The focus is heavily on the Cultural Revolution, but there is a chapter on "the plays of 1949–65."

Kuan Han-ching, A Play by Tien Han. Foreign Languages Press, Peking, 1961. The English edition of the play based on the life of the great Yuan dynasty dramatist, Guan Hanqing.

Mackerras, Colin. *Amateur Theatre in China 1949-1966.* Contemporary China Papers No. 5, Australian National University Press, Canberra, 1973.

Mackerras, Colin. *The Chinese Theatre in Modern Times, from 1840 to the Present Day.* Thames and Hudson, London, 1975.

Mackerras, Colin. *The Performing Arts in Contemporary China.* Routledge and Kegan Paul, London, 1981. Focuses mainly on the period since the death of Mao in 1976.

Mao Tse-tung [Zedong]. *On Literature and Art.* Foreign Languages Press, Peking, 1967. A collection of Mao's principal works on the subject named, especially the "Talks at the Yan'an Forum."

Meserve, Walter J. and Meserve, Ruth I., eds. *Modern Drama from Communist China.* New York University Press, New York, 1970. A collection of nine dramas, reprinted from PRC publications, with an introduction.

Mowry, Hua-yuan Li. *Yang-pan Hsi: New Theater in China.* Center for Chinese Studies, University of California, Berkeley, 1973. A highly scholarly terminological study of the "model" dramas. It includes synopses of the "models" and character lists.

Renmin xiju [*People's theater*]. Renmin wenxue chubanshe, Beijing. This began publication as a bimonthly in March 1976 and became a monthly in July. It contains playscripts and articles of all kinds on theater—ideological, social, political, artistic, and literary. It is the most indispensable of all sources for post-1976 Chinese theater.

Snow, Lois Wheeler, *China on Stage: An American Actress in the People's Republic.* Random House, New York, 1972. By the widow of one of the foremost American journalists on the PRC, this book contains translations of four of the "model" dramas of the Cultural Revolution. There is also extensive commentary on the dramas and the theory behind them from a very sympathetic point of view.

Sunrise, Tsao Yu: A Play in Four Acts. Translated from Chinese to English by A. C. Barnes. Foreign Languages Press, Peking, 1960. This translation of Cao Yu's second play is based on a Chinese edition of 1957.

The White-haired Girl: An Opera in Five Acts by Ho Ching-chih and Ting Yi. Translated from Chinese to English by Yang Hsien-yi and Gladys Yang. Foreign Languages Press, Peking, 1954. An early and famous opera written in the CCP-held areas and based on the principles of Mao Zedong's "Talks at the Yan'an Forum on Literature and Art."

The Wilderness. Translated from Chinese to English by Christopher C. Rand and Joseph S. M. Lau. Hong Kong University Press, Hong Kong; Indiana University Press, Bloomington, 1980. A translation with extensive explanation of one of Cao Yu's well-known plays.

Thunderstorm. Translated from Chinese to English by Wang Tso-liang and A. C. Barnes. Foreign Languages Press, Peking, 1958. A slightly incomplete translation of Cao Yu's most famous play.

Ting Yi. *A Short History of Modern Chinese Literature.* Foreign Languages Press, Peking, 1959. This is a translation by several people of a work originally in Chinese. It deals from a strongly leftist view with literary, ideological, and social aspects of various forms of literature, including drama, from the May Fourth Movement to liberation.

Xiju bao [Theater journal]. Yishu chubanshe, Beijing, 1954–1966. A monthly periodical from 1954 to 1956 and again from 1960 to 1966, a twice monthly from 1957 to 1959, this journal was suspended at the beginning of the Cultural Revolution and has never been revived. It deals with all kinds of theater on a journalistic basis, but covers all aspects—social problems, reviews, descriptions, and so on. It does not include texts of dramas. Essential reference material for all work on the Chinese theater between liberation and the Cultural Revolution.

CHAPTER VII

TRADITIONAL THEATER IN CONTEMPORARY CHINA

Elizabeth Wichmann

IT IS CLEAR from the preceding chapters that ideological and political concerns have affected theatrical development throughout Chinese history, becoming even more influential in the twentieth century. Since 1976, changes in official policy toward theater have led to a great increase in the range and variety of theatrical activity in China. Although spoken drama, sung drama, and dance-drama—forms based upon Western models and therefore new to this century—have returned to favor, this variety is provided primarily by a broad spectrum of increasingly active forms of traditional theater. These forms all share certain aesthetic principles and values which constitute their link to Chinese theatrical tradition but also limit their appeal to new audiences. In the present-day competition for audiences among various forms of entertainment, the development of traditional theater will depend upon the way in which its basic aesthetic features can be adapted to altered social conditions.

AESTHETIC FEATURES OF CONTEMPORARY THEATER

Beijing opera, described in detail in chapter V, has been the nationally dominant form of theater in China for at least one hundred years. However, it is only one among more than 360 indigenous, or traditional, forms of Chinese theater currently being staged.[1] The majority of these forms are regional in nature, differing from one another in dialect, musical system and its adaptation to that dialect, musical accompaniment, play content, and numerous performance features including staging, acting, and movement practices. It is nonetheless possible to say that these forms are basically similar in certain major ways, and immediately recognizable as quite distinct from the new, Western-influenced forms that developed in the twentieth century. Practitioners of these traditional theater forms invariably ascribe this readily perceivable distinction to three basic aesthetic principles shared by all traditional forms: synthesis, convention, and stylization.[2]

Song, music, dance and pantomime, story, and speech are all present in every traditional theater form; many make use of acrobatics to varying extents as well. The presence of these elements is not the primary characterizing feature, however. It is their synthesis *(zonghe xing)*, rather than presentation in sequence, that is characteristic of traditional theater.

Song in performance is inextricable from its musical accompaniment and from the choreographed movement of the singer; pantomime is interwoven on the stage with percussion accompaniment, as is speech. While the story may be told aurally in some passages and visually in others, if the focus at a given moment is aural, as on a singer relating a sad separation from a loved one, that song is performed within the complementary visual fabric presented by the unceasing, gentle synchronized movements of eyes, hands, torso, feet, and often the body through space. And if the focus is visual, as upon a brave warrior ascending a steep mountain, that pantomime is within a texture of percussive sound provided by the orchestra. The same sort of percussive sound, but with different applications, forms a similar aural punctuation to speech; and the speech is performed within a visual fabric of movement punctuation as well. Extended speech or song without choreographed movement or accompanying sound rarely occur in traditional theater, nor does extended movement, dance, or pantomime without musical or percussive accompaniment.

The term convention *(chengshi xing)* refers to practices that have a specific meaning ascribed by tradition, and hence serve to signal that meaning to the audience. Traditional theater forms utilize a great many conventions, some of which are immediately understandable to an uninitiated audience, while others require preknowledge for comprehension.

Movement conventions most frequently fall in the former category, especially pantomimic actions such as opening and closing of doors and windows, mounting and descending stairs, tending fowl, sewing, and movement over rough terrain and in conditions of darkness, heat, cold, rain, and wind—these actions are directly communicative and require no informed expertise on the part of the spectator. Other movement conventions are more formal, such as the act of walking in a large circle, which connotes travelling a great distance, and the straightening of costume and headdress parts upon entrance to signal the presence of an important character who is about to speak. The conventional movements of certain costume parts, such as water sleeves and pheasant feathers, may also have either dramatic or formal meanings.

The simple staging of traditional theater achieves its highly plastic nature through the use of conventions. The table and chairs, through their placement and use, serve as conventions for a city wall, a mountain, a bed, a throne, or simply a table and one or two chairs. Conventional use of stage properties frequently signals the presence and use of larger objects not visually present on the stage; a whip signals the presence of a horse, an oar that of a boat, and large blue banners swung in wide arcs close to the stage floor that of rushing water.

Perhaps the single most important convention is that of role types, which serve as both a convention in themselves and as a focus for headdress, costume, and makeup conventions. The role types of Beijing opera are fairly representative of those of traditional theater as a whole, though some theater forms may blend role types, or feature certain ones more predominantly than others. Each of the four principal role types, and even more specifically their numerous subcategories, are indicative of a particular age, sex, and social status or class. The conventional use of design and color in the headdresses, costumes, and makeups of each role type serves to directly state these characteristics. The makeup conventions for *jing,* or painted face roles, are even more specific, signalling the personality and temperament of the wearer as well.

Stylization *(xiangzheng shoufa)* is probably the aesthetic principle closest to the heart of traditional theater. It refers to the divergence between the behaviors of daily life and their presentation on the stage —the nonrealistic representation of those behaviors in performance, within a particular style. All forms of traditional Chinese theater are stylized. However, whereas conventions are for the most part shared among all the forms, having the same meanings in each, it is primarily through differences in the manner of stylization that the various forms of traditional theater can be distinguished from one another.

Both physical and vocal aspects of traditional theater performance are stylized, and it is within the various role types and their subcategories that the specific stylizations occur. Physical stylization tends to be fairly similar for each role type throughout traditional theater forms, and hence more indicative of a particular role type than of a particular form of theater. The distinctive Beijing opera walking styles of the *dan* and *sheng,* described in chapter V, are readily recognizable in other traditional forms, as are the stylized hand and eye movements of the *huadan.* While some regional forms do not include certain role types—the *jing* being the type most frequently excluded—the posture, walk, and gesture style of every role type included in each form can definitely be recognized as belonging to that role type, throughout the various forms of traditional theater. Vocal stylization, however, is in many instances markedly different from one theater form to another, being simultaneously indicative of a particular role type and of the particular form of theater. In Beijing opera the young female speaks and sings in a clear, piercing falsetto, produced in the forehead and front of the face. Other forms utilize quite different vocal range and production for young female roles, including extremely high natural register production, midrange chest-supported nasal production, and a type of vocal production nearly resembling the yodel, in which the performer must have a very wide vocal range. Through their combined imagery, the vocal and physical stylizations of each role type convey the primarily Confucian values and resulting behavior patterns traditionally deemed appropriate by society for each type of role thus portrayed.

Musical stylization is even more important than vocal stylization in distinguishing among the forms of traditional theater. It occurs within two basic patterns. Beijing opera's *pihuang* style, with its characteristic accompanying musical instruments, two predominant modes, prescribed metrical arrangements, and characteristic melodic patterns is an excellent example of the major pattern for theater music in contemporary China. The music of many traditional theater forms is devised according to this pattern, each utilizing a particular musical style and its accompanying instruments, associated modes, and metrical arrangements, and having its own unique characteristic melodic patterns produced by the combination of that musical style and the dialect used by that form. Some traditional theater forms use the older pattern characteristic of *kunqu,* in which entire tunes within specific modes predate given plays, for which lyrics are then composed. But whichever pattern is used, the musical style of each form, when coupled with its dialect, produces a musical stylization unique to that form.[3]

Finally, the overall aesthetic aim of all traditional theater forms is rooted in stylization. Traditional theater in contemporary China is a performer-oriented theater; the script serves primarily as a vehicle for performance. Every major performer in each performance must present a constant stream of expression; all internal aspects of the character being portrayed must be made external. Generally speaking, speech furthers the plot, while movement elaborates upon it and song deepens it by expressing emotion. A case can be made for the social origins of this phenomenon; Chinese society is basically one in which direct expressions of emotion are frowned upon. Speech is used in the theater for interaction, much as it is in daily life, although stylistically in a somewhat different manner, while movement and song are used to express subjective experience and inner feelings to the audience. The strength of the performance is therefore in music and movement; while a Western-style spoken drama may use ten thousand words in its script, the longest traditional plays contain only half that number, and most average about twenty-five hundred words.[4] The combined aim of the physical, vocal, and musical stylizations of traditional theater is to convey the essence and spirit of life, rather than to present its realistic likeness.

In post-1976 China, all traditional theater forms pursue this aim, utilizing playscripts that fall within three basic categories.[5] The first type, called "traditional plays" *(chuantong xi),* are plays that were already in performance before 1949 and were therefore usually devised or written without the intention of conveying particular ideological viewpoints. Some of them have been altered somewhat to remove or replace objectionable attitudes and situations, particularly those with erotic content, and are therefore termed "revised traditional plays."[6] All such plays fully utilize and in fact exemplify the aesthetic principles and performance techniques of traditional theater.

The second category is called "newly written historical plays" *(xin biande lishi ju).* The term "historical" is used loosely here—while some of these plays do concern historical figures, many have mythological heroes such as the Monkey King Sun Wukong and the legendary Judge Bao. These plays are written to consciously embody ideological viewpoints and attitudes and are distinguishable from traditional playscripts on that basis. While none were produced between 1966 and 1976, they are currently the major focus for contemporary playwrights. In terms of performance, the important characteristic of newly written historical plays is that they are set in the past and can therefore use the entire body of traditional performance techniques, including the costumes and stage properties and the full repertoire of conventional and stylized movement which they facilitate. To an audience unfamiliar with the texts of traditional plays, newly written historical plays and traditional plays therefore appear essentially identical in performance.

The third category of plays is made up of those termed "contemporary plays" *(xiandai xi)*. Like newly written historical plays, contemporary plays consciously embody ideological viewpoints. However, their plots, themes, and characters are all of the twentieth century. The performance of contemporary plays cannot therefore rely entirely upon traditional aesthetic principles and performance techniques. Much of the traditional conventional and stylized movement is simply not practicable without the traditional costumes and stage properties; such movement problems are compounded by the addition of realistic scenery, since conventionalized movements intended to convey the physical environment on a bare stage become superfluous. Perhaps even more fundamental is the problem presented by role types; developed to portray Confucian values and their resulting behavior patterns at different levels of social status, the role types are often inappropriate for the portrayal of postliberation characters. The performance of contemporary plays therefore requires the creative development of new performance techniques. Though there were of course ideological reasons for there being so few model revolutionary contemporary Beijing operas developed during the Cultural Revolution, these performance considerations were certainly a major contributing factor as well. And while a number of contemporary plays were written to criticize the Gang of Four between 1977 and 1979, many more newly written historical plays have been composed since 1976 than have contemporary plays. However, cultural officials continue to express a need for and to give respect to plays written to express contemporary themes in a modern setting.[7]

The range of stylization in traditional theater forms combined with the very different subject matter of the three types of plays performed in traditional theater means that many specific aesthetic values are particular to just one form or type of play. However, three fundamental aesthetic values shared by all forms and plays of traditional theater are evident.

The first concerns posture and movement, both of various parts of the body in isolation, and of the entire body in or through space. Straight lines and angles are to be avoided; the aesthetic aim is the presentation of a three-dimensional network of circles, arcs, and curved lines.

In stasis, this means for instance that an outstretched arm will be held in an extended curve unbroken at either the shoulder or elbow by angles. In movement, this aesthetic applies to action as small as the gaze of an eye, and as large as the blocking of principal characters. In many role types, the actor's eyes are used to focus the attention of the audience, to lead it with the movement of a gaze. In such an instance, if the performer intends to indicate an object on the ground, the gaze of his or her eyes will begin away from the object, sweep up first, and then curve down to rest on the object. Conversely, if the gaze is to end in an indication of something above eye level, it will travel down as it moves toward that object, and then sweep up to light upon it. This same use of the arc is made in pointing gestures, which first curve away from the direction in which the hand will ultimately point; a pointing directly in front of the body will begin with a sweep into the body before curving out, a pointing to the left will begin with a sweep to the right, and vice versa. In movement through space, the performer similarly avoids straight lines and angles. A move from downstage center facing out to an upstage center chair is therefore made by circling to either the left or the right while gradually turning to face upstage, moving diagonally to the side of the chair, and then circling again in the opposite direction to return to the front face position, this time directly in front of the chair. The resulting s-shaped curve has been compared to the movement of a marionette puppet, necessary in order to keep the puppet's strings from entangling, and hypotheses have been drawn on this basis concerning the origins of theater movement in puppet theater.[8] Whatever the causal relationship, such curved movement patterns are a basic aesthetic of traditional theater.

A second aesthetic value concerns both movement and vocal production. Whether in dance, pantomime, acrobatics, song, or speech, the actor's performance must at all times appear effortless. Any hint of strain at hitting a high note, performing a complex series of somersaults and flips, or speaking an extended declamatory passage without apparent pause for breath is perceived as indicating that the performer's command of technique is insufficient. The appearance of strain or effort is uncomfortable for the audience and undercuts the aim of conveying the spirit and essence of life in performance. The rigorous training program described in chapter V remains critical to the development of stage artistry, for only such a program can bring about the control needed for apparently effortless performance of the physically strenuous and complex techniques of traditional theater.

The final fundamental aesthetic of traditional theater applies to all aspects of performance—everything on the stage, everything within the world of the play, must above all be beautiful. In terms of costume, this means that a beggar in a traditional or newly revised historical play will be dressed in a black silk robe covered with multicolored silk patches, rather than in actually dirty or tattered clothes. And in a contemporary play, the clothes of the poorest peasant are clean and neatly patched, while a soldier just in from days on maneuvers will at most be marked by a few strategically placed tears and conventionally suggested blood stains on an otherwise crisp and clean uniform. In terms of acting style, the absolute requirement for beauty means that the actress portraying a young woman who has just received heartbreaking news will on no account cry real tears, for the accompanying red eyes and runny nose are considered anything but beautiful. The act of crying will instead be presented in a stylized fashion, and if the actress is good, will be quite moving. In training schools and rehearsal halls, the criticism heard with much the greatest frequency, directed at speech, song, movement, and acting style alike, is that the particular sound or action being performed is incorrect because it is not beautiful. And the highest praise which can be given a performance is to say that it is beautiful.

Because they are all based upon these aesthetic principles and values, traditional theater forms are both fundamentally similar to one another and quite distinct from the newer forms of the twentieth century. The spoken drama *(huaju)*, sung drama *(geju)*, and dance-drama *(wuju)* of the twentieth century are based to varying extents upon the aesthetics of several Western models, and are therefore immediately distinguishable from the traditional forms. But since the Western forms of theater that serve as models are quite different from one another, twentieth-century forms are not usually viewed in China as being a discrete category in themselves. In fact, whereas the traditional forms are collectively referred to in contemporary China by the generic term *xiqu*, twentieth-century forms as a group are generally referred to only by the broad term *xiju*, or theater, a concept which naturally includes traditional forms as well. It is the extent to which aesthetic principles and values of the traditional theater are present in each of the newer twentieth-century forms, and the way in which they are blended with the aesthetics of the Western models, that most illuminates both the individual and Chinese natures of each of these newer forms.

Spoken drama is the most thoroughly Western-based form. As such, it utilizes certain aesthetics of Western realistic theater, including the demands for realism in the portrayal of its characters and in its staging techniques, as well as for an emphasis upon well-made plots in its scripts. Since it is further in nature from traditional theater, containing neither song nor dancelike movement, it reflects the least influence of the aesthetic principles and values of traditional theater; there is essentially no synthesis in the manner of traditional theater, and very little convention and stylization. To say there is no such influence, however, is to deny the sinicization of the Western models in their adaptation to Chinese content and to deny the force of those traditional aesthetic principles and values within the broad range of Chinese theatrical activity. Spoken drama, like traditional drama, holds beauty as a primary aesthetic value. In the creation of beauty within the context of spoken drama, conventions and stylizations have been adopted for the portrayal of actions and situations which, if performed thoroughly realistically, would jar with that aesthetic. Stylized conventional gestures of pain, anger, sadness, and heroism in the face of physical adversity may trouble the Western viewer when seen in the performance of Western-style spoken drama, but they are well within the Chinese theatrical tradition.

Sung drama and dance-drama present more obvious blends of Chinese and Western forms, techniques, and aesthetics. In the former, Western opera influence may be seen, as well as the influences of both traditional Chinese theater and folk music. In the latter, elements of Western ballet and modern dance blend with Chinese folk dance and traditional theater movement. In both, Western realistic staging techniques are combined with conventional staging elements of the traditional theater. The basic aesthetic values of apparent effortlessness and beauty are evident throughout.

PATTERNS AND PROBLEMS OF DEVELOPMENT

The strength and ubiquity of traditional theater aesthetics, substantially affecting even the Western-based forms of Chinese theater, are perhaps the reason that creation, in the Western sense of bringing into existence something that is more or less totally new, is not a major attribute of Chinese theater. The conscious creation of new forms of theater determined to break completely with the past, such as the romantic, realistic, expressionist, impressionist, and surrealist movements of the late nineteenth- and early twentieth-century Western theater, do not have Chinese parallels. Though the early history of spoken drama in China resembles somewhat the beginnings of its Western counterparts, it differs in a crucial aspect: the theater form being supported was an imported, already proven Western one rather than a new indigenous development. Creativity in Chinese theater has consisted rather in making creative changes and developments in and among already existing forms of theatrical expression.

Creativity within a traditional theater form is perhaps best exemplified in this century by the work of Mei Lanfang. Originally performing in *qingyi* roles, he later combined the techniques of *qingyi, huadan,* and *wudan* in various ways to produce young female characters overwhelming in both their theatricality and subtlety, featured in plays that gave the performer the opportunity to demonstrate his superlative command of acrobatic, song, speech, movement, and acting techniques. For these plays he commissioned scripts that are of exceptional literary quality for Beijing operas, as this form is not noted for its emphasis upon text, and developed new costumes and dances based upon historical models. On his death he left Beijing opera more highly developed and regarded than he found it, and in the course of his career he raised the stature of young female roles in that form to the importance of those of mature men.[9]

Such creative development and assimilation has in the past given rise to new forms of traditional theater as well. Wei Liangfu's work in developing Kunshan music, incorporating his knowledge of both northern and southern theatrical music, gave rise to the music of *kunqu,* which became the dominant national theatrical form and held that position for three hundred years, as described in chapter III. The creative combination of techniques from several regional traditional theater forms gave rise to *kunqu's* successor, Beijing opera, as documented in chapter IV.

The "model revolutionary contemporary Beijing opera" plays of the Cultural Revolution are the most recent example of creative experiment in traditional Chinese theater. While strictly speaking they are a new type of play rather than a new form of theater, their performance is appreciably different from that of traditional Beijing opera plays, using as they do a creative combination of Western staging techniques and orchestration, traditional musical style, traditional and spoken drama movement and speech, as well as musical and movement elements from regional traditional theater forms and folk performances.

It is clear from essays in the official press during the period 1978–1982 that the present official aims regarding theater are to preserve traditional forms, primarily in the production of traditional plays, and to creatively develop these forms in the production of newly written historical plays and contemporary plays. Forms that made their appearance in twentieth-century China are also given encouragement to develop creatively.[10]

Preservation is of course of critical importance. Traditional theater forms constitute a major portion of China's traditional cultural heritage. Additionally, creative development based upon these traditional forms absolutely requires their healthy survival. However, preservation alone would very likely result in museum piece theater, certainly a much lesser achievement than the continued existence of a living, developing body of national theater forms.[11]

While it is possible that superlative actors will arise, capable of creatively expanding the techniques of traditional theater forms in the manner of Mei Lanfang's contribution to Beijing opera, it is unrealistic to rely upon such a chance development. This is especially true in contemporary China; practice and training have had only five years of relative normality after the extended break caused by the Cultural Revolution, and practice and training are critical for the development of the technical expertise such a performer would require to contribute substantially in this manner. Furthermore, the type of theatrical production developed in the Cultural Revolution, with its emphasis on committee work and revision rather than on individual contribution, is still the primary working method, further reducing the likelihood of individual performers singlehandedly bringing about substantial artistic changes. It is much more likely for development within existing forms, as well as the development of new forms, to occur as a result of creative borrowing between forms and assimilation of folk and Western techniques.

The enormous range of theatrical forms and techniques in contemporary China, coupled with the variety of Western dramatic and theatrical elements becoming increasingly familiar in China, present a rich field for creative borrowing and assimilation. A literally innumerable array of musical, acting, movement and dance, and staging possibilities present themselves.

While the most ambitious and far-reaching example of this sort of creative development to date remains the model revolutionary contemporary plays of the Cultural Revolution, other examples are already evident. The dance-drama *Tales of the Silk Road (Silu huayu)*, discussed in chapter VI, is a good case in point. The drama combines Chinese and Western musical instruments and styles for accompaniment; blends ballet, modern, and folk dance movements, as well as movements created from postures in Tang dynasty murals in its dances; and has costumes based on those murals and modified by folk costumes and contemporary Chinese moral and aesthetic values concerning dress. In doing so, a production of great popularity was created, which has been in continuous performance in a number of Chinese cities since 1979. Furthermore, aspects of creative assimilation in this production have already found their way into other, traditional theater forms.

In a 1980–1981 production of the newly written historical play *Wang Xifeng Disrupts Ningguo Prefecture (Wang Xifeng danao Ningguofu)*, performed by the Jiangsu Provincial Beijing opera troupe, a costume based upon those created for *Tales of the Silk Road* was designed for one of the principal female opponents of the main character (see plate 40). New movement patterns in the style of traditional Beijing opera movement were developed to use that costume to full advantage in the Beijing opera form.[12]

Other developments include the many scenic devices of spoken drama that have been adapted for use in traditional theater, primarily in the production of newly written historical plays, although they do occur at times in traditional play productions as well. Lighting and sound effects, multiple-set realistic scenery, rear projections, and special effects such as smoke and flash pots, are among them (see plates 41–43). Such developments, however, do not generally concern actual performance technique.

Substantial creative development within traditional theater forms, with the major exception of the model revolutionary contemporary Beijing operas, remains scarce. The scarcity of contemporary plays is partly the result of the performance difficulties they pose for practitioners of traditional theater, as discussed above. Throughout the various forms and play types of traditional theater, it is due largely to the problem of authenticity and to the question of subject matter in scripts.

Each of the more than 360 forms of traditional theater is well defined, having its own characteristic musical style and method of stylization. Especially in light of the emphasis upon preservation of traditional theater forms, extensive creative development particularly in performance technique presents a critical problem; it runs the risk of exceeding the parameters of the particular form. To do so would be to lose the authenticity, the characteristic "flavor" of that form. Experiments in utilizing techniques from other traditional theater forms and from folk forms may be criticized as diluting the purity and integrity of the original form, as blurring those distinctions between it and the others that give it its uniqueness. Experiments in incorporating elements from the more Westernized twentieth-century forms may provoke the criticism that the resulting performance is merely spoken drama with singing tacked on; that the original form has lost an appreciable portion of its Chinese character—an extremely sensitive issue.[13]

The second primary difficulty involved in creatively developing theater forms is the question of subject matter and resulting scripts. Plots, themes, and characters are of the utmost relevance to the creative development of performance techniques, since the script provides the vehicle for performance. At the same time, it is the script that allows for the projection of value systems through images, a conscious and major concern of the Chinese authorities. It is not currently possible to produce a script solely from performance considerations; the ideological content remains of considerable importance. However, particularly in the area of contemporary plays, the specifically desired ideological content and the manner in which it is to be presented are uncertain. In terms of their scripts, contemporary plays during the Cultural Revolution and until the fall of the Gang of Four were used exclusively as ideological vehicles; the value system they projected was the highly and purely political one of those leftists in power at the time. The slow process of disengaging the category, "contemporary play," from the personal politics of Jiang Qing and her comrades, as well as from its definition as a literary form synonymous with pure propaganda, is still underway. Until this process is completed, the question of subject matter for contemporary plays will remain highly problematic, as to a lesser degree will that for newly written historical plays. Only the traditional plays are essentially free from the current problem presented by the relationship of politics to dramatic content, since they originated before the conscious inclusion of specific ideological content in playscripts. It is therefore not surprising that the majority of traditional theater productions currently use traditional playscripts, and that far fewer contemporary plays are being written and staged than are newly written historical plays.[14]

In addition to these uniquely Chinese problems, the influences of a more general problem facing world theater as a whole are also being felt in China; stage art is increasingly in competition with film and television for its audiences. In China, a major reason for this dichotomy and resulting competition is the difference between the overall nature of contemporary life and that of the period during which the traditional theater forms originally developed.

Qing dynasty China was a thoroughly rural and nonindustrial society, experiencing appreciable Western cultural influence only during its waning years. Contemporary China, on the other hand, while still having a population based primarily in the countryside, is marked by industrializing cities as well as a growth of industry in rural areas, by the current campaign for the Four Modernizations, and by increasing Western cultural influence on many fronts. The "speed of life" in contemporary China is considerably faster than it was when the traditional theater forms now extant arose.

Theater is by definition a reflection of life. It is produced and maintained in popularity by the society that it reflects. The performance-oriented theater forms developed to convey the essence of life in Qing dynasty society, with their lack of emphasis upon plot and extensive use of convention and stylization, are less action- and speech-oriented, more leisurely, and more indirect than is contemporary life. Television and film, much more realistic forms which are action- and speech-oriented, simply reflect contemporary life more accurately and immediately. In the case of foreign imports, they give their Chinese audiences a chance to see what life in other cultures and societies is like.[15]

Spoken drama is the theater form which at present most readily competes with the screen arts. Like them, it is basically realistic and oriented toward plot. Unlike the traditional theater forms, it can respond quickly to changes in ideological criteria for content—in fact, often more quickly than can film and television produced in China. It is therefore capable of being the newest performance art, in terms of both form and content, playing in a given town at a given time. And "new" is a critical drawing factor for an audience deprived of variety for more than ten years.

Sung dramas and dance-dramas are also relatively Western, and therefore realistic, in Chinese terms. At the same time, they contain elements of performance deemed inseparable from theater in China for centuries, elements that spoken drama lacks—music and choreographed movement. Their combination of these new and old elements currently draws for them a sizeable audience.

It is, then, traditional theater that faces the most immediate competitive threat from the screen arts. Contemporary plays are at present problematic. Traditional and newly written historical plays are unavoidably "old," are too thoroughly grounded in a past society to apply directly to the needs of the present day. Some forms of regional traditional theater, such as *yueju* of Zhejiang province, *pingju* of the northeast, and *huju* of Shanghai fare a bit better in this respect than do major national traditional forms such as Beijing opera and *kunqu*. Due primarily to the liveliness of regional dialect in their speech, they are closer to the lives of their audiences than are the national forms; they contain specific characteristics of their regions and are therefore more congruent with the tastes of audiences in their regions. None has as yet, however, risen to prominence outside of its own region. Whether or not any of them will be able to do so is in question; the very reasons for their regional popularity make them somewhat removed from the broad national audience.[16] In most forms of traditional theater, including the major national forms, experiments with realistic sets and scenic effects for newly written historical plays, and occasionally even for traditional plays, have perhaps temporarily lured audiences through their novel use of technology and their "realism." However, practitioners, officials, and audiences have already begun to question this practice, since it necessitates a warping of aesthetic principles and values.[17]

Though attendance remains high at traditional theater performances, theater officials see this as a relatively short-range phenomenon. They view it as being due primarily to the curiosity appeal of the old society and traditional performance techniques seen in the production of traditional and newly written historical plays, no matter what staging techniques are used, after the ten year hiatus produced by the Cultural Revolution. Since 1979, there has been a steady decrease in the length of time a traditional or newly written historical play can run and command sufficiently large attendance to make it worthwhile. Also, audience composition has been changing during the same period. While in 1978, various age groups were generally represented in audiences in the same proportions as in the society at large, spectators over the age of forty-five have since come increasingly to dominate audience membership.[18] The general decline in attendance at these plays and the mounting loss of younger members of the audience may stem from the distance between the type of Chinese society reflected by the traditional theater and the contemporary population, especially those too young to have acquired serious tastes for traditional theater prior to the Cultural Revolution. While no statistics are available to demonstrate that people who fail to attend traditional theater performances are in fact viewing twentieth-century forms or screen arts instead, there are some indications that this is in fact the case. Perhaps most telling is the marked preference among traditional theater performers under forty-five years of age for spoken drama, films, and television as recreational viewing on their nights off.[19]

Such a preference for more contemporary forms of performance should not be taken to signal a lack of interest on the part of these younger performers in their own performing art, however. This same group of performers also overwhelmingly indicated interest in and a desire to do further work with contemporary plays in their own traditional theater forms. Such a desire may in part be predicated on the personal, emotional investments made by these people in the model revolutionary contemporary plays of the Cultural Revolution—their elders were much less involved with these plays. However, there is a large element of practicality in such a view, as shown by the ongoing official support for contemporary plays. Dealing as they do with twentieth-century people and events and using a potentially much broader range of performance techniques, contemporary plays stand a much better chance of competing successfully with twentieth-century forms and the screen arts for audiences.

Contemporary plays offer the opportunity for the presentation of contemporary characters in plots and on themes directly applicable to the needs of the present day. Simultaneously, they present abundant possibilities for the blending of new, more realistic and action-oriented aesthetics and techniques with the centuries-old aesthetic principles, values, performance elements, and resulting techniques of traditional Chinese theater. While the creative and ideological problems presented by contemporary plays are undeniably formidable, they are probably the main hope for a living theater based in the indigenous Chinese theatrical tradition.

NOTES

1. The figure is from an interview with provincial-level theater officials in Jiangsu Province, October 28, 1980.

2. Most of the data and opinion in this chapter are based upon two years of field research in China, primarily in Nanjing, Jiangsu Province, but also in Beijing, Shanghai, and Lanzhou, Gansu Province, from August 1979 to August 1981. Only where data are specific to one interview or observation situation, rather than drawn from the notes and tapes of the total research period, is it noted below.

3. For a more detailed English language analysis of traditional Chinese theater music in the twentieth century, see Rulan Chao Pian, "Aria Structural Patterns in the Peking Opera," in J. I. Crump and William P. Malm, eds., *Chinese and Japanese Music-Dramas* (The University of Michigan Center for Chinese Studies, Michigan Papers in Chinese Studies No. 19, Ann Arbor, 1975), pp. 65–98.

4. The figures are from lectures given to students majoring in traditional play directing at the Jiangsu Provincial Traditional Theater School in the spring of 1980.

5. While the three categories of plays have been recognized as such since the establishment of the Drama Reform Committee in July of 1950, the current policy of "san zhe bing ju," or "simultaneously develop the three," is associated with Zhou Enlai's policies of the 1950s and early 1960s regarding theatrical development. For a fairly comprehensive history of theater in China since 1949 as viewed from the current perspective of cultural officials, see "Zai Zhongguo xijujia xiehui disanci huiyan daibiao dahui shang, Zhao Xun tongzhi zuo ju xie gongzuo baogao," *Renmin xiju* 12 (1979):8–16.

6. Mei Lanfang, "Zhongguo xiqu yishu de xin fangxiang," *Wenyi bao* 16 (1952): 10–14. An abbreviated version is also available in English as "Old Art with a New Future," *China Reconstructs* 4 (September–October, 1952):21–24.

7. Numerous examples of official support and encouragement of contemporary plays have been published since 1976. A representative piece is: Huo Dashou, "Jicheng gexin, wenbu qianjin—quan guo xiqu jumu gongzuo zuotanhui ceji," *Renmin xiju* 9 (1980):3–7. More recent expression can be seen in: "Wenhua bu zai Ning zhaokai xiqu xiandai xi zuotanhui—ba jutuan chengli xiqu xiandai xi yanjiu hui," *Renmin xiju* 1 (1981):57.

8. See Sun Kaidi, *Kuilei xi kaoyuan* (Shangza, Shanghai, 1952), for a well-supported thesis aiming to prove that puppetry was the origin of theater in China, and that theater therefore imitates the techniques of puppetry. See Sun Rongbai, *Jingju changshi jianghua* (Zhongguo xiqu chubanshe, Beijing, 1959), p. 7, for a description of s-shaped movement patterns in Beijing opera.

9. For more information on Mei Lanfang in English, see A. C. Scott, *Mei Lanfang, Leader of the Pear Garden* (Hong Kong University Press, Hong Kong, 1959); Wu Zuguang, Huang Zuolin, and Mei Shaowu, *Peking Opera and Mei Lanfang* (New World Press, Beijing, 1981); and William Dolby, *A History of Chinese Drama* (Paul Elek, London, 1976). In Chinese, see Mei Lanfang, *Wutai shenghuo sishi nian* (Zhongguo xiju chubanshe, Beijing, 1980); and Qi Rushan, *Qi Rushan quanji* (Qi Rushan xiansheng yizhu bianyin weiyuanhui, Taibei, 1964).

10. One of the most comprehensive analyses to date on the considerations involved in preserving and creatively developing traditional theater is: Liu Housheng, "Xiqu

bixu yongyuan tui chen chu xin," *Renmin xiju* 4 (1979):5–9. A shorter analysis from the same year by Zhu Hong is in *Guangming ribao,* October 16, 1979, p. 3. Throughout the year 1980, *Renmin xiju* carried at least one article per month on this topic, listed in each index under the section heading, "Tui chen chu xin," or "Weed Through the Old to Bring Forth the New." Representative articles on the development of spoken drama include those by Li Moran in *Guangming ribao,* June 11, 1979, p. 3, and Ding Haiping in *Guangming ribao,* June 2, 1980, p. 3.

11. A representative statement of support for the preservation of traditional Beijing opera plays, and a study of the problems involved in such preservation, can be found in: "Jingju yishu de jicheng, gexin yu fazhan—Shanghai jingju yishu gongzuozhe zuotanhui jiyao," *Renmin xiju* 11 (1979):23–27, 37.

12. Between the November 1980 and January 1981 runs of this production, comments by participant performers, officials, and members of the audience led to further adaptation in both the costume itself and the movements of the performer who wore it.

13. Practitioners frequently discuss such criticisms, and the problems posed by them, in working meetings. Mention of these criticisms and resulting problems can also be found in the official press, e.g.: "Jingju xiang he chu qu—jingju yishu zuotanhui fayan zhaiyao," *Renmin xiju* 1 (1980):2–13.

14. For an analysis of the considerations involved in creatively developing the literature of Beijing opera, see: Wang Zengqi, "Cong xiju wenxue de jiaodu kan jingju de weiji," *Renmin xiju* 10 (1980):22–24.

15. The issue of theater and its relationship to contemporary life is probably the major one being discussed by practitioners of traditional theater forms, especially Beijing opera and *kunqu,* at the present time. Representative publications on this topic include: "Jingju guanzhong ping jingju—jingju guanzhong daibiao zuotanhui fayan zhaiyao," *Renmin xiju* 2 (1980):2–6; Zhang Junqiu, et al., "Jingju yanyuan da jingju guanzhong," *Renmin xiju* 3 (1980):25–32; and Tong Zhiling, "Wei jingju zhengqu gengduo de guanzhong," *Renmin xiju* 6 (1980):4–6.

16. The possibility of major national forms assimilating characteristics of regional forms is a real one, however. For discussion of the relationship of regional traditional forms to major national ones, see *Renmin xiju* 11 (1979):23–27, 37; and 10 (1980): 22–24.

17. Reflections in the official press of the controversy over scenery in traditional theater can be found in: Luan Guanhua, "Xiqu bujing chuangzuo de jicheng yu gexin," *Renmin xiju* 10 (1979):40–41; "Ben kan duzhe dui jingju wenti de yixie yijian—duzhe lai xin zongshu," *Renmin xiju* 5 (1980):42–44; and Luan Guanhua, "Jie hou fuxing de jingxiang—guangan 'Shoudu wutai meishu sheji zhanlan,'" *Renmin xiju* 1 (1981):33–34.

18. The critical problem of attendance at traditional theater performance, particularly in the case of Beijing opera, is a major topic of discussion among practitioners and officials. It is also featured in the official press: see *Renmin xiju* 1 (1980):2–13; 2 (1980):2–6; 3 (1980):25–32; and 6 (1980):4–6.

19. This tendency is not shared by performers over forty-five, who overwhelmingly indicated their preference for viewing their own or other forms of traditional theater when time permits.

CONTRIBUTORS

William Dolby is lecturer in Chinese at the University of Edinburgh and has previously been lecturer in Chinese at the University of Malaya. He has published numerous articles and books on Chinese literature and performing arts, including *A History of Chinese Drama* and *Eight Chinese Plays,* at present the only Western anthology of translations of Chinese dramas through the ages. His translation of Li Xingfu's *Chalk Circle* has been broadcast a number of times.

John Y. H. Hu is professor of drama and comparative literature at National Taiwan University, from which he received his B.A. degree. Since earning his Ph.D. in drama and comparative literature from Indiana University in 1969, he has taught at Michigan State University, the University of Hawaii, and Melbourne University. Among his publications are *Ts'ao Yu* in English and *On the Plum Song: A Collection of Essays on Drama and Literature* in Chinese. He has translated into English and produced for Western audiences a number of traditional Chinese plays.

Colin Mackerras is chairman of the School of Modern Asian Studies at Griffith University in Australia. He holds degrees in Chinese language and history and in 1970 received his Ph.D. from Australian National University for his studies on Beijing opera. He taught at the Beijing Institute of Foreign Languages from 1964 to 1966, and at that time began collecting an extensive library on Chinese theater. He has returned to China many times since, including a five-month stay in 1982 to research the performing arts of the minority nationalities. Among his many publications on Chinese theater are *The Rise of the Peking Opera 1770-1870, Amateur Theatre in China 1949-66, The Chinese Theatre in Modern Times,* and *The Performing Arts in Contemporary China.*

A. C. Scott, professor emeritus of theater at the University of Wisconsin–Madison, made an intensive study of theater and dance styles during a long residence in China and Japan. At the University of Wisconsin–Madison he directed a pioneer program for theater students which incorporated an understanding of Asian performing arts as an essential element in the training curriculum. His publications include *The Classical Theatre of China, Traditional Chinese Plays* (vols. 1–3), and *Actors Are Madmen: Notebook of a Theatregoer in China.*

Elizabeth Wichmann is instructor of Asian theater at the University of Hawaii, where she received her Ph.D. in May 1983. Her dissertation on aural performance in Beijing opera was the culmination of two years of study in Nanjing with the Jiangsu Province Beijing Opera Company and the Jiangsu Province Traditional Theater School. In the course of her stay in China from 1979 to 1981, she became the first foreign woman to perform Beijing opera on the Chinese stage. She has had extensive performance experience in many forms of Asian theater and holds degrees in theater, speech and drama education, and Chinese language and civilization. She co-edited *Asian Theatre: A Study Guide and Annotated Bibliography* and is associate editor of the *Asian Theatre Journal.*

GLOSSARY OF CHINESE TERMS*

ban, the main beat of the bar

ban, hardwood clapper

bangzi, datewood clapper

Bangzi qiang, "clapper opera"

bianwen, form of balladry popular in the Tang

canggu, "grey hawk," role category in adjutant plays

canjun, "adjutant," role category in adjutant plays

canjun xi, "adjutant plays," pre-Yuan theater form

chaiyi, type of costume, upper garment for lower-class people

chengshi xing, "convention"

chou, male role category, clown, comic

chuanqi, "marvel tales" (Tang); form of southern drama (Yuan and Ming)

ci, a form of poetry in which the length of the lines is irregular

dan, female role category (in Yuan *zaju* and later forms)

daqu, ballad form of the Song and Jin

dizi, "side-blown flute," wind instrument

erhu, "two-stringed Chinese fiddle"

erhuang, one of the two main styles that form the Beijing opera

fujing, "clown," role category in *zaju*

*The glossary gives explanations of alphabetically listed technical terms mentioned in the text. Only the English terms in quotation marks are actual translations; many of the Chinese originals are not susceptible to sensible translation.

fumo, "jester," role category in *zaju*

geju, "sung drama," a form of modern Chinese opera, in which the orchestral accompaniment is mainly comprised of Western instruments

guzi ci, "drum lyrics," Song dynasty theater form

huadan, type of flirtatious *dan* character

huaju, "spoken drama"

huqin, generic term for bowed two-stringed Chinese fiddles

Jiaofang, "Imperial Academy of Music"

jing, male role category; clown in *zaju* or southern plays; "painted face" in Beijing opera

jingju or *jingxi,* "Beijing opera"

kai, type of costume for military officers

kunqu, literally, "the tunes of Kunshan"; a famous aristocratic style of drama

laodan, old *dan* character

laosheng, type of male character representing mature men of good standing

mang, type of costume, embroidered with pythons, for high-ranking officials; the yellow *mang* was for emperors only

mo, male role category; major role in Yuan *zaju,* secondary in southern plays or *chuanqi*

moni, "actor-director," role category in *zaju*

nanxi, "southern plays," theater form

pei, type of costume, less formal embroidered dress

pipa, Chinese "lute," four-stringed plucked musical instrument

qin, "zither," seven-stringed musical instrument

qingyi, type of virtuous *dan* character

qu, type of song

sanxian, type of three-stringed plucked instrument

sheng, musical instrument, a type of mouth organ

sheng, male role category, for example, a young scholar (in Yuan *zaju* and later forms)

shuhui, "writing society"

wudan, military *dan* character

wuju, "dance-drama," a modern theater form

wusheng, military *sheng* character

wushu, "the fighting arts"

xiandai xi, "contemporary plays," one of the three types of plays performed in traditional theater forms in the People's Republic

xiangsheng, a form of witty cross-talk

xiangzheng shoufa, "stylization"

xiaosheng, type of younger male character, scholar-lover

xiezi, type of costume, daily wear for men

xiju, broad term for theater of all types

xin biande lishi ju, "newly written historical plays," one of the three types of plays performed in traditional theater forms in the People's Republic

xipi, one of the two main styles that form the Beijing opera

xiqu, generic term for all traditional forms of Chinese theater

yan, the unaccented beats of the bar

yangge, a form of folk song and dance from Shaanxi province

yinxi, "playleader," role category in *zaju*

Yiyang qiang, a system of regional theater, originating in the Ming dynasty, called after its place of origin, Yiyang, Jiangxi province

yuanben, principal form of Jin dynasty theater

yueqin, circular, four-stringed plucked musical instrument

yueren, "music man" (Zhou period)

zaju, principal form of Yuan dynasty drama

zhugong diao, "various modes," theater form in the Song period

zonghe xing, "synthesis"

INDEX

Compiled by Lisa Ho, Colin Mackerras and Alyce Mackerras

Production Notes

This book was designed by Roger Eggers. Composition and
paging were done on the Quadex Composing System and
typesetting on the Compugraphic Unisetter by the design and
production staff of University of Hawaii Press.

The text and display typeface is Garamond No. 49.

Offset presswork and binding were done by Vail-Ballou Press,
Inc. Text paper is Old Forge Opaque Vellum, basis 55.

WESTMAR COLLEGE LIBRARY